The Celluloid Empire

The
CELLULOID
EMPIRE

A History of the American Movie Industry

by
Robert H. Stanley, Ph.D.

COMMUNICATION ARTS BOOKS

HASTINGS HOUSE, PUBLISHERS
New York 10016

For Lillian Florence Ruter

Copyright © 1978 by Robert H. Stanley

Library of Congress Cataloging in Publication Data

Stanley, Robert H.
  The celluloid empire.

  (Communication arts books)
  Bibliography: p.
  Includes index.
  1. Moving-picture industry—United States—History.
I. Title.
PN1993.5.U6S75   338.4′7′791430973   77–18269
ISBN 0–8038–1246–9
ISBN 0–8038–1247–7 pbk.

Published simultaneously in Canada by
Copp Clark, Ltd., Toronto

Printed in the United States of America

Contents

Preface

THE PURPOSE of this book is to provide the reader with an informational frame of reference that will permit the formation of sound critical judgments concerning America's movie industry. The potential of the motion picture medium to enlarge human thought, emotion and experience is almost without limit. But more than any other art form, the creation of motion pictures is rooted in the realism of dollars and cents. Few artists in other fields have to work under the exacting circumstances which prevail in the movie industry. Indeed, the exigencies of business too often take priority over the principles of cinematic expression.

This book chronicles the transition of motion picture production from the realm of individual endeavor into a major industry with enormous power, influence and appeal. The primary focus is on the development, the corporate structure, and the managerial control of the major companies that have dominated the movie industry almost from its inception. The basic character and direction of the industry turns upon the corporate structures and relationships of these companies—their procedural agreements with each other, their policies, personalities and products. Several pertinent questions are considered: How did the oligarchical structure of the American movie industry evolve? What struggles have been fought, and by whom, for control of America's vast movie-making apparatus? In what ways has the economic posture of the movie industry affected its products? What has been the nature and extent of government and self-regulatory controls over motion picture content? How will new modes of movie distribution and exhibition—e.g., pay television and video discs—affect the prevailing structure of the movie industry?

The sequence of the text is the result of the juxtaposition of literally thousands of bits of information. Very little material is presented which could be directly attributed to any one source. The author was faced with the choice of inserting very extensive footnotes or none at all. The latter course was chosen. However, names and other details are given in the text where ideas are not part of the broad consensus in the field. Most of the books, articles, doctoral dissertations, government documents and other materials consulted are listed at the end of the text to provide further readings. Corporate annual reports and other information filed with the Securities and Exchange Commission also proved to be helpful.

There are several people who provided valuable source material for this book. The author wishes to express his appreciation to Kenneth Clark of the Motion Picture Association of America; Charles Emma of Cinerama Inc.; Sherman Frankston of Corporate Annual Reports; Arthur Krim, Andy Albeck and Ron Perkins of United Artists; H. H. Martin and Jerry Evans of Universal; and James L. Stewart of Walt Disney Productions. Appreciation is due also to Ms. Sheryl Ford, who assisted the author in gathering research materials. The author is particularly grateful to his colleagues Samuel Fleishman, Ruth Ramsay and Charles Steinberg for reading parts of the manuscript and offering critical suggestions and comments. Above all, the author wishes to express his deep appreciation to his wife, Eija Ayravainen-Stanley, without whose encouragement and assistance this book would not have been completed.

New York   Robert H. Stanley
March, 1978

The Origins
of the Movie Industry

THE GENESIS OF the motion picture medium as it exists today occurred toward the end of the nineteenth century. There were, during that time, simultaneous efforts in France, Germany, England, and Russia to produce "pictures that moved." A Frenchman, Etienne-Jules Marey, had conceived the idea of a series of pictures on an advancing film strip, although he had not been able to determine the mechanism for keeping this advance regular. In America, the British-born photographer, Eadweard Muybridge, had been developing a rapid exposure camera. These two, among others, had been working for many years in an attempt to capture a permanent record of that which the eye can see—motion. Concern with picturing motion existed for varied reasons—for art's sake, for didactic purposes, as a medium of expression. Throughout history attempts have been made to give visual indications or depictions of motion, but by the waning years of the nineteenth century, almost all of the technical concepts were discovered, or about to be discovered, somewhere in the world. The man who synthesized this knowledge, and added an important technical

I

innovation—the perforation of the film strip at equi-distant intervals, thus controlling the speed of the film advance and, hence, the motion—was Thomas Alva Edison. His interest was the interest that has underlain the industry since its inception: commercial exploitation. The motion picture industry is precisely that—an industry, with profit as the imperative.

Nevertheless it was the conception and development of the basic technique by Thomas Alva Edison which stimulated the growth of the motion picture industry in the United States and throughout the world. Edison began his motion picture experimentation late in 1887 at his newly constructed laboratory in West Orange, New Jersey. He was assisted in this endeavor by a young Scotsman named William Dickson, who had come from London some years before to work under Edison. By the early 1890s, they had succeeded in perfecting a camera, called the "Kinetograph," that effectively photographed objects in motion. Since it weighed more than a ton, this bulky machine was necessarily stationary. They also devised a viewing mechanism to exhibit the positive prints made from the Kinetograph negatives. This, Edison named the "Kinetoscope." The device consisted of a large cabinet containing batteries and a motor which turned a strip of film on a spool bank and operated a light. Perforated holes along the margin of the film strip caused it to revolve on the sprocketed spools. For viewing, there was an eyepiece and a lens at the front of the cabinet through which one spectator at a time could peer at the film as it moved along the sprockets. (Since the viewer looked through a peep hole at the moving pictures, the name "peep-show" was soon adopted by the general public.) The film images were presented to the observer in rapid succession, thereby creating the illusion of movement.

Edison applied for United States patents on the Kinetograph and Kinetoscope in August, 1891, but, unaccountably, he neglected to spend the $150.00 necessary to secure foreign patent applications for his motion picture apparatus in England and Europe. This decision ultimately cost Edison millions of dollars. He committed another costly error by not mentioning the projection possibilities of the motion picture in his patent application. In a *caveat* filed with the Patent Office three years earlier, Edison referred to the possibility of using a projecting apparatus and a white screen. When his projection experiments proved unsatisfactory, however, he abandoned the idea. Edison's legal errors may be attributed partially to the fact that he considered movies as an unimportant plaything, hardly worthy of commercial exploitation. His view was confirmed when he was initially unable to interest investors in the promotion of his newest invention.

By 1893, however, Thomas Lombard, who promoted the sale of Edison's coin-machine phonographs, recognized the commercial possibilities of the Kinetoscope. Lombard and two wealthy associates, Frank Gammon and Norman C. Raff, contracted with Edison for the purchase of a large number of Kinetoscopes for $200 each. They formed the Kinetoscope Company to supply filmed material and coin-operated Kinetoscope machines to exhibition parlors. Edison agreed to manufacture the Kinetoscopes and produce motion pictures for the machine.

Early in 1893, construction was completed on a motion picture studio in West Orange, which was officially called the Kinetoscope Theatre. Its staff, however, referred to the studio as the "Black Maria" because of its resemblance to a police patrolwagon of the same name. The walls of the studio were covered with black tarpaper, and a stage at one end of the single room was draped in black. The roof opened in order to admit sunlight for shooting. The entire studio could be rotated to provide sufficient light from the sun throughout the day. To insure maximum contrasts, all Kinetograph subjects were filmed in the full glare of the sun against a black background.

The "Black Maria's" initial productions, which ran for little more than a minute, featured trained bears, cats, dogs, and monkeys. Within a short time, human subjects predomi-

MUSEUM OF MODERN ART/FILM STILLS ARCHIVE

Edison's "Black Maria" studio. This irregular oblong-shaped structure, costing less than $700 to construct, had both a sloping roof, hinged to permit utilization of natural light, and a pivot-mounted foundation—enabling the rotation of the building to follow the light of the sun.

nated. Among the early performers to achieve celluloid immortality were the popular pugilist Jim Corbett, the famous strong man Eugene Sandow, and such exotic attractions as Japanese dancers and French ballerinas.

In the spring of 1894, Edison's first shipment of Kinetoscopes was delivered to the eastern agents for the Kinetoscope Company, the Holland Brothers. On April 14, 1894, the first "Kinetoscope Parlor" was opened on lower Broadway in New York City. "The Wizard's latest invention," as the Kinetoscopes were billed, caused a sensation. Enthusiastic crowds waited all day and far into the night to see the "pictures that moved." A new industry—and a new mass medium of cultural communication—had arrived.

Among the many viewers at the newly opened Kinetoscope Parlor were two brothers, Grey and Otway Latham. Captivated by what they saw, the brothers soon joined forces with two friends, Samuel Tilden, Jr. and Enoch Rector, to form the Kinetoscope Exhibition Company. The new company contracted with Edison for the express purpose of exhibiting boxing matches on the Kinetoscope machines. In the summer of 1894, the interior of the "Black Maria" was temporarily converted into a boxing arena for a ten-round match between pugilists Michael Leonard and Jack Cushing. Nearly a thousand feet of film were used to record the fisticuffs which culminated in the knockout of Mr. Cushing.

The Kinetoscope Exhibition Company displayed the fight picture concurrently on six Kinetoscope cabinets in a parlor at 83 Nassau Street in New York to an enthusiastic public response. The Lathams and their associates, however, aspired to greater numbers. Their plan was to take the fight pictures out of the cabinets and project them on a screen so that a large audience could simultaneously watch the entire event without interruptions. Aided by their father, who was a chemist, the Lathams began experimentation with motion picture projection; the eventual result was the "Pantoptikon," a projecting version of the Kinetoscope. The technical quality of the Pantoptikon's pictures was poor, and the history of the projector was brief, indeed. The Lathams' camera, however, did employ certain innovations that would later prove important in patent litigation. The most important of these was a sprocket, devised by Enoch Rector, which provided sufficient slack in the film to prevent the stop-and-go-motion from tugging at the unwinding reel. This innovation, known as the "Latham Loop," permitted the use of greater lengths of film, making possible the development of more extensive presentations.

In the fall of 1895, another peep-show viewing machine came on the market called the "Mutoscope." This device contained postcard-size picture cards rather than strip films. The illusion of movement occurred as the viewer flipped the series of picture cards with a hand crank. The Mutoscope was marketed by the K.M.C.D. syndicate which was made up of E. B. Koopman, H. N. Marvin, Herman Casler and William Dickson, Edison's former employee. Dickson had left the Edison Company after the firm's financial manager, William Gilmore, had accused him of conspiring with the Lathams to develop a competitive movie projector. After a brief stint with the Lathams, Dickson became the "D" in K.M.C.D. syndicate.

The Lathams' initial attempts at motion picture projection, coupled with the commercial release of the Mutoscope, moved Norman Raff to urge Edison to perfect a projection machine. The inventor at first balked at the suggestion, apparently confident that the commercial value of motion pictures rested in the peep-show box. Edison, nevertheless, attempted to appease Raff by assigning one of his assistants, Charles Kayser, to work on the project. Edison's own efforts were directed toward the task of manufacturing a device he called the Kinetophone, which was a combination of his phonograph and peep-show machine.

While Edison's staff was cursorily pursuing the elusive goal of perfecting a projection machine, considerable progress was being achieved in other quarters. The Lumière brothers, Auguste and Louis, owners of a photographic factory in Lyons, France, substantially improved upon Edison's basic invention. They built a portable camera which could be used outdoors and made many other significant and enduring contributions, including the standardization of film width at 35mm, the movement of film at the speed of 16 frames per second, and the establishment of the concept that film movement must be intermittent to permit the projection of a clear sharp image on to a screen. Expanding on the work of Edison, the Lumière brothers developed a combined camera and projector in 1894, which they named the Cinématographe. Early in 1895 (the year the Mutoscope appeared in America), the Lumières shot their first film, *Workers Leaving the Lumière Factory.* By the end of the year, public presentations of projected films were given in the basement of a Paris cafe to paying audiences.

Significant advances in motion picture projection also were made in the United States by Thomas Armant who, working in conjunction with Francis Jenkins, developed a projector

The first films of August and Louis Lumière were truly literal in conception. The brothers merely turned on the camera to record the events that chanced to occur in front of the lens. *Workers Leaving the Lumière Factory* (above) was typical of their early work. Other Lumière films included *Boat Leaving the Harbor* and *Fish Market at Marseilles.*

which incorporated such now standard features as the intermittent movement of film, a sprocket which provided for a small loop before and after the film gate to relax film tension (somewhat parallel to the Latham loop for the camera), and a shutter device designed to give the screen long periods of illumination and relatively short periods of darkness.

When Raff and Gammon of the Kinetoscope Company learned of Armant's achievement, they offered to finance the manufacture and sale of his projector. Edison was invited to join this endeavor as the manufacturer of the projecting equipment. Since the Edison name had great commercial value, the projector would be promoted as the wizard Edison's newest invention. On April 23, 1896, only two years after the unveiling of the first Kinetoscope, the "Edison Vitascope" gave its first public exhibition at Koster and Bial's Music Hall, a leading vaudeville theatre in New York City. Armant remained discreetly in the background, but neither he nor Edison was happy with the arrangement. Consequently, a year or so later, when Edison devised his own projector, their agreement was terminated and Armant regained his patent rights.

Vaudeville houses soon adopted the motion picture as a standard element of their programs. Late in June of 1896, only some two months after the debut of the Edison Vitascope, B. F. Keith's Union Square Theatre exhibited a Lumière Cinématographe; and on October 12, 1896, the K.M.C.D. syndicate publicly exhibited its "American Biograph" projecting machine at Hammerstein's Opera House in New York.

The American Mutoscope and Biograph Company, called simply Biograph, was formed to promote the Mutoscope and Biograph commercially. Since Biograph's camera and projector, which were invented by William Dickson and Herman Casler, operated without sprockets and sprocket holes, they apparently did not infringe on Edison's patents. Moreover, the Biograph projector showed pictures which were larger and photographically superior to any other projector on the market. Following the success of these pioneers, other companies, sensing an opportunity, entered the motion picture field. Such movie-making firms as Vitagraph, Essanay, Kalem, Selig, Pathé, and Melies provided keen competition for the Edison Company. Beginning in 1897, Edison waged a major campaign in the courts against what he regarded as patent infringements.

Soon after the turn of the century, motion picture houses proliferated throughout the country, particularly in the densely-populated, immigrant, working-class neighborhoods. Empty cigar stores, restaurants, and pawn shops were converted into theatres which, for a very brief period, charged a nickel for admission, hence the term "nickelodeon." Within the walls of these small, uncomfortable makeshift theatres, immigrant slum dwellers would huddle together to live vicariously the adventures depicted on the flickering screen.

Early tentative efforts to reproduce reality were truly literal in conception. Audiences marvelled at the sight of onrushing locomotives, and crashing sea waves. As interest in such phenomena diminished, movie makers greatly expanded their repertoires of visual effects. Dickson's successor at West Orange, Alfred Clark, astonished theatre patrons with his production of *The Execution of Mary, Queen of Scots,* in which, by stopping the camera and replacing the actor (Mary was played by a man) with a dummy, he was able to give the illusion of Mary being decapitated.

The future of the motion picture medium as an art form of almost unlimited scope and range was foreshadowed, although obliquely, by the work of Edwin S. Porter. Porter joined the Edison company in 1899, after having toured throughout the Americas showing films in fair grounds and sundry other places. Edison soon put him in charge of his entire filmmaking operation. His first important film, conceived in the form of a dramatic sequence, was *The Life of an American Fireman* (1902), in which he employed the technique of dissolves to depict the rescue of a mother and child from a burning house. In his next effort, *The Great Train Robbery* (1903), Porter cinematically unfolded a Western tale of banditry and retribution which is now regarded as the classic prototype of the motion picture play. Audiences were captivated with the film's variety of scene and locale, its close-ups of the bandit firing at the camera, and its combination of suspense and movement.

As the movie industry expanded, the middleman emerged as liaison between the producer and exhibitor. He was called the "distributor" and worked out of a "film exchange," buying or leasing films from the producer and renting them to the exhibitor. The first such exchange was organized in San Francisco in 1902 by Harry and Herbert Miles, who purchased films from producers and rented them to exhibitors at one-fourth the purchase price. Within five years, more than 125 film exchanges were in operation, serving all areas of the country. Thus the tripartite structure of the film industry evolved—production-distribution-exhibition.

In this scene from *The Great Train Robbery*, bandits are about to force the engineer to uncouple the locomotive from the train. Released late in 1903, this film's popularity helped assure the success of the nickelodeons which soon began to appear across the country.

MOTION PICTURE PATENTS COMPANY

Within a remarkably few years, the movies were transformed from a small amusement business into a major industry affecting the values, dreams and aspirations of untold millions of human beings. By the end of 1907, movies were being shown in thousands of storefront theatres around the country. After years of patent disputes, the major movie companies realized it was to their mutual advantage to cooperate. Early in 1908, Essanay, Kalem, Lubin, Melies, Pathé Frères, Selig and Vitagraph became Edison licensees. The Biograph firm had successfully thwarted Edison's efforts in the courts to dominate the industry totally. Biograph, which had cross-licensing agreements with the Armant Moving Picture Company, refused initially to join forces with Edison, but the company's financial resources were rapidly becoming depleted. Toward the end of the year the Edison and Biograph factions agreed to negotiate a truce. A complex national monopoly over almost all phases of the nascent motion picture industry was organized in December 1908. It was called the Motion Picture Patents Company. Except for the qualifying shares held by its directors, stock in the Patents Company was wholly owned by Edison and Biograph. Some 16 patents were pooled: one for film, two for cameras, and 13 for projectors. The ownership of the various patents was held by four manufacturers: Armant, Biograph, Edison, and Vitagraph, each of whom received royalties for the assignment of their respective patents.

The formal signing of the licensee agreements took place at Edison's library in his laboratory at West Orange. The Patents Company's licensees were the American producers Biograph, Edison, Essanay, Kalem, Lubin, Selig, and Vitagraph, the French firm, Pathé Frères, and Kleine Optical, an importer of foreign films and equipment. A tenth producer, Gaston Melies, was licensed six months later. Six of the companies were based in New York City, three in Chicago and one in Philadelphia. Many of the companies, however, foreshadowing the eventual West Coast base of the industry, migrated to sunnier climates during the winter months. As early as 1907, director Francis Boggs of the Selig company of Chicago set up a production unit in Los Angeles to shoot some water scenes in *The Count of Monte Cristo* along the ocean front at Santa Monica.

The major financial beneficiaries from the trust agreement were the Biograph and Edison companies, both of which received several hundred thousand dollars annually in royalties. All of the licensed producers and importers, however, benefited from the exclusionary nature of the licensing agreement. For example, the Vitagraph Company, which was organized in 1897 by Albert Smith and J. Stuart Blackton with less than $1,000 in capital, had a gross income in 1912 of about $6 million.

Despite its liberal salaries to top executives, the company's net profits available for dividends were in excess of $1 million. Other licensees, by all indications, had done almost as well.

The Patents Company entered into an agreement with the Eastman Kodak Company, the country's sole manufacturer of raw film stock, whereby Eastman would supply film stock only to its licensees. (The threat of anti-trust prosecution, however, caused the Patents Company to abandon its exclusivity arrangement with Kodak in 1911.) The Patents Company attempted to control and manage all aspects of the expanding movie industry. In the weeks following its organization, the Patents Company granted licenses to over 100 film exchanges and exacted tribute from theatre owners for the use of movie equipment. Exhibitors wishing to continue in business were compelled to pay a weekly royalty fee of two dollars for the use of the patented projectors. The exchanges were given the task of collecting royalties from the exhibitors. In a concerted effort to prevent the intrusion of new competitors, the Patents Company threatened prosecution against any licensed exhibitor who showed films produced by outsiders.

The movement toward total monopolization of the motion picture industry in America accelerated in 1910 when the Patents Company organized its own rental exchange, the General Film Company. Each of the Patents Company licensees was allotted one-tenth of the stock in the new distributing agency and each was granted equal representation on its board of directors. By the end of the following year, General Film had bought up most of the major exchanges then in existence. Its nationwide system of exchanges distributed films exclusively for the manufacturers and importers of the Patents Company. Films were sold in standard lengths of 1,000-foot reels at rates based on theatre size rather than on the quality of the picture. Through its interlocking agreements, the Patents Company brought all aspects of the film industry within its sphere of influence.

THE OLD ORDER CHANGES

The Patents Company's control of the movie industry, however, was less than total. Of the 9,000 or so movie theatres in operation throughout the United States by the fall of 1910, only a little more than half were licensed. The theatres outside the Patents Company's orbit provided outlets for the so-called "independent" producers and distributors who sprang up in the ensuing months. In addition, General Film's policy of giving preferential treatment to exhibitors in more affluent neighborhoods and downtown areas, alienated many of the small storefront nickelodeon operators who were often left inadequately serviced. By the summer of 1912, the number of movie houses had increased to almost 13,000, a good percentage of whom were not Patent Company licensees.

Capitalizing on many exhibitors' discontent with, and resentment of, the General Film Company's oppressive policies, independent producers began turning out hundreds of films. Within a year after "the Trust," as the patents monopoly came to be called, was formed, a dozen new producing companies went into operation. Their film was obtained from Lumière, the French firm, who made its raw film stock available in the United States. To make their movies, many of the independents used the Patents Company's machines surreptitiously. The General Film Company initiated hundreds of lawsuits against the independents, charging patent infringement. Extralegal methods, such as sending thugs to wreck the equipment of the independents, were also employed. Nevertheless, the independents gradually gained in strength.

In the vanguard of those opposing the Trust was Carl Laemmle, a Chicago-based distributor. Born in the South German kingdom of Würtemberg in 1867, Laemmle arrived in the United States early in 1884. After working at various menial jobs, he achieved modest success in the haberdashery business. In 1906, at the age of 39, he embarked on a career in the growing film industry as a nickelodeon operator. Within three years, Laemmle developed one of the country's largest film distribution organizations, with exchanges in such major cities as Chicago, Minneapolis, Omaha, Salt Lake City and Portland, Oregon. Although Laemmle was licensed by the Trust, he was denied access to its inner circle and, in April 1909, he decided to become an independent. He launched a production company, the Independent Moving Picture Company, known as Imp, which, by the close of 1910, had produced over 100 films.

Carl Laemmle is generally credited with inaugurating the star system. The Patents Company licensees intentionally maintained the anonymity of their players in order to keep salary demands to a minimum. Movie patrons, however, quickly came to favor certain performers. Laemmle, in a daring raid on the Biograph Company, hired a popular player named Florence Lawrence, who was known to audiences only as "The Biograph Girl." He launched a spectacular publicity campaign to call the public's attention to the fact that Miss Lawrence would now be starring in pictures produced by Imp. To initiate the campaign, Imp representatives arranged for a St. Louis newspaper to carry the story that the former Biograph player, Florence Lawrence, had died in a streetcar accident. Laemmle lashed out at "the enemies" of Imp for circulating this false story. To prove that she was still alive, Laemmle arranged for Miss Lawrence to make a personal appearance in St. Louis, accompanied by Imp's leading male actor, King Baggot. This bold stroke was an enormous success, and one of the earliest "publicity buildups" by a film company. The Patents Company licensees were compelled to follow Laemmle's precedent and adopt the star system, competing with the independents for new performers.

Despite the efforts of Patents Company licensees to maintain supremacy, independent companies gradually gained dominance over all aspects of the movie industry. Early in 1909, Adam Kessel and Charles Bauman, owners of the Empire

Film Exchange, joined with the producer-director, Fred Balshofer, to form the Bison Motion Picture Company to produce films and the New York Motion Picture Company to distribute them. Another distributor, Patrick Powers, also started a production company, Powers Picture Players. The independents organized the Motion Picture Distributing and Sales Company in 1910 to provide an effective outlet for their films. Carl Laemmle was chosen to be president of the new company. The Sales Company, which soon represented most of the independent producers, gave various independent distributors the exclusive rights to market the independent producers' films in a specific state or territory, a practice known as "state's rights" distribution. Soon the independents were rivaling the Trust in total film production.

Two rival factions of independents developed when, in 1912, Harry E. Aitken, of Majestic (a new, independent, producing firm which released its films through the Sales Company), quarreled with Carl Laemmle. The dispute centered on Aitken's acquisition of several Imp players, including Mary Pickford. When Laemmle countered by increasing the percentage Majestic had to pay to the Sales Company, Aitken and his associates, with the backing of investment bankers Kuhn, Loeb and Company, organized the Mutual Film Corporation to distribute films nationally. Ten independent producers joined Mutual. Six other independents countered by forming the Universal Film Manufacturing Company to succeed the Sales Company. Carl Laemmle and Patrick Powers emerged as the central figures at Universal. The Universal offerings comprised one- and two-reel films. Licensed exhibitors began to defect. Gradually the Patents Company's entrenchment disintegrated. By 1914, internal dissension, inefficiency, and reluctance to change made the Patents Company almost wholly ineffectual. The General Film Company, the Patent Company's subsidiary branch, was dissolved by court order in 1915. Although the Patents Company had financial and organizational supremacy over the independents, many members of its hierarchy lacked sensitivity to the mercurially changing tastes of the audience. The crushing blow to the Patents Company came in 1917 when the U.S. Supreme Court declared that the purchaser of a patented projector could not be legally compelled to exhibit the manufacturer's films exclusively.

One of the most powerful of the independents was William Fox, who spent his early childhood in the tenements of Manhattan's Lower East Side. In 1904, he invested his $1,600 savings in a Brooklyn nickelodeon. This modest enterprise was ultimately to evolve into a corporate aggregation of staggering proportions. Fox's Brooklyn theatre developed into a chain of 15 houses. He then entered the film distribution field, forming the Greater New York Rental Company to buy and lease films for his and other theatres. Fox successfuly resisted the attempts of the General Film Company to buy him out and instituted a lawsuit against the Patents Company charging it with unlawful conspiracy in restraint of trade in violation of the 1890 Sherman Antitrust Act. It was this suit, which went to trial in 1913, that ultimately resulted in the dissolution of the Patents Company by the courts five years later. His battle with the Trust motivated Fox to buttress his position by creating a production company. He purchased the rights to Virginia Cross' novel *Life's Shop Window* for $100 and, filming in Staten Island, made it into a feature starring Claire Whitney and Stuart Holmes. Soon the production company was turning out a feature picture every week. In February 1915, Fox and his associates incorporated as the Fox Film Corporation. Stock in the new company was not offered to the public. William Fox took one-half and his associates, who invested $400,000 in the new company, took the other half.

The struggle for control of the immensely profitable and rapidly growing movie industry took a new turn when Adolph Zukor demonstrated successfully that movies would attract middle-class audiences. Zukor, like so many of his cinema contemporaries, came from humble origins. An impoverished immigrant from Hungary, his first job in the United States

Sarah Bernhardt, the most famous stage actress of the era, as she appeared in the title role of *Queen Elizabeth*. This 1912 film version of Elizabeth's love for Essex, was a huge success despite its plodding staginess.

was sweeping floors in a fur shop for $2 a week. He soon became a prosperous furrier and diversified his interests to include penny arcades, nickelodeons, and eventually, a chain of movie theatres. An early associate in his exhibition business was another wealthy furrier named Marcus Loew, founder of Loew's Inc., the parent company of MGM. Zukor initially worked in harmony with the Trust, but he broke away from its conservatism when, in 1912, he and his associates daringly invested $18,000 for the American rights to a four-reel French production titled *Queen Elizabeth*, starring the most famous actress of the period, Sarah Bernhardt. The film made its American debut at the Lyceum Theatre in New York City on July 12, 1912. The leading figures of the business and theatrical world, who did not ordinarily attend motion pictures, came in force to see the aging Miss Bernhardt. Despite the film's poor technical quality, audience response was very favorable. Zukor, with the assistance of film salesman, Al Lichtman, distributed the picture through state's rights exchanges, and made a handsome profit.

Acquisition of the rights to *Queen Elizabeth* encouraged Zukor, in partnership with Daniel Frohman, a well-known Broadway producer, to set up the Famous Players Film Company to produce movies starring well-known Broadway performers. Edwin S. Porter became production head of the new company. *The Prisoner of Zenda* with James K. Hackett, produced in 1913, was the new production company's first release, although Famous Players' first production, made late in 1912, was *The Count of Monte Cristo* starring James O'Neill (Eugene's father). Since another company had already produced a screen version of the Monte Cristo story, Famous Players decided to release its second production first. Famous Players' impressive list of players under contract soon included Minnie Maddern Fiske, Geraldine Farrar, and young John Barrymore. Since a national distribution network did not yet exist to handle feature films, Zukor continued to sell his films on a state's rights basis.

Adolph Zukor's success with *Queen Elizabeth* provided the incentive for others to import feature-length films from Europe, where economic considerations had not yet thwarted the desire for genuine experimentation. Early in 1913, George Kleine, a Patents Company licensee, bought the American rights to an eight-reel Italian-made spectacular, *Quo Vadis?* Since the General Film Company's distribution apparatus was geared for one- and two-reel films aimed at nickelodeon customers, it declined to modify its system to permit *Quo Vadis?* to be distributed separately from its regular program. Kleine, however, was not deterred. He joined forces with play producers, Sam Harris and George Cohan, in a scheme to show the film in large legitimate theatres on a percentage basis. *Quo*

Christian martyrs are about to be devoured by the wild beasts of the arena, in this scene from the feature-length Italian spectacular, *Quo Vadis?* Massive and ornate sets, enormous crowd scenes and impressive camera work all contributed to the film's appeal.

Vadis? had its American premiere on April 21, 1913 at the Astor Theatre in New York at an admission price of one dollar. The film played to capacity crowds for 22 weeks. By the middle of the summer, the Italian-made spectacle was attracting large audiences throughout the United States and Canada.

The overwhelming success of *Quo Vadis?* led inevitably to the importation of other feature-length films. *The Last Days of Pompeii, Anthony and Cleopatra* and *Les Miserables,* among other foreign imports, firmly established the appeal of feature films. In the United States, Carl Laemmle's Imp, which was prospering with one- and two-reel films, produced a six-reel feature, *Traffic in Souls,* for a modest $5,700. The Shuberts, prominent theatrical producers, bought a one-third interest in the film for $33,000 and agreed to feature it in their theatres. *Traffic in Souls* was advertised as a "$200,000 spectacle in

700 scenes with 800 players and showing the traps cunningly laid for young girls by vice agents." The profits from the film were enormous.

Scores of new producing companies emerged to take advantage of the growing audiences for feature films. Jesse L. Lasky, a vaudeville manager, went into partnership with his brother-in-law, Samuel Goldfish (later Goldwyn), a successful glove salesman; and with Arthur Friend, a lawyer, formed the Jesse L. Lasky Feature Play Company. The company's first movie was a six-reel feature titled *The Squaw Man* which starred stage actor Dustin Farnum. Cecil B. DeMille, a minor stage actor and playwright, directed the film with the assistance of Oscar Apfel. The novice filmmakers shot the picture with two cameras that had different frame lines, so when the positives were printed and projected, feet appeared above heads in many sequences. Fortunately for the fledgling company, Sigmund Lubin, a member of the Trust, recognized the problem and agreed to reperforate the film in return for the contract to make the prints. *The Squaw Man* was profitably sold to state's rights exchanges and successfully launched the Lasky Feature Play Company. By the end of 1914, the Lasky company had completed 21 features.

One consequence of the success of feature-length films was the rapid obsolescence of nickelodeons, which could not accomodate enough patrons at one showing to make the presentation of longer films profitable. Nickelodeons had prospered on the premise of presenting short programs with a quick audience turnover. In an effort to insure profits from feature-length presentations, larger theatres were built and admission prices were increased dramatically. Between 1914 and 1922 an estimated 4,000 new theatres opened. Many existing theatre were expanded and improved. Movie houses started to rival the sumptuousness, ostentation and admission scales of legitimate theatres.

In April 1914, the Strand, which had a seating capacity of 3,300, opened in New York City. The manager of the Strand,

Samuel Rothafel, nicknamed Roxy, soon went on to develop extraordinary movie palaces. He was responsible for creating the palatial atmosphere of such theatres as the Rialto, Rivoli, Capitol, Roxy, and that last survivor of the movie palace, Radio City Music Hall. Roxy's theatres supplemented the film presentation with symphony orchestras, a mélange of song and ballet, and live variety acts. Gargoyles, copies of Greek statutes, elaborate fountains, and thick carpets adorned his theatres. The ushers wore silk uniforms which matched the color pattern of the theatre.

On the West coast, Roxy was rivaled by Sidney Patrick Grauman who, in 1922, constructed Grauman's Egyptian Theatre on Hollywood Boulevard at the cost of $800,000. The theatre seated 1,760 people who were escorted by 28 usherettes attired in Egyptian-style costumes. Gilt sphinxes framed the proscenium. Five years later, Grauman opened his Chinese Theatre with the premiere showing of Cecil B. DeMille's *King of Kings.* The Chinese motif of his new theatre included objets d'art, draperies and statues imported from the Orient.

The feature film was dramatically affected through the emergence of one David Wark Griffith who joined Biograph as a director in the summer of 1908. The son of a Confederate colonel, Griffith left his rural Kentucky home and, for a brief period, worked for a Louisville newspaper. Subsequently he gravitated to movies, first as an actor, then—quite quickly— as a director. By the end of 1912, Griffith had made more than 400 films. He was, however, becoming increasingly dismayed by Biograph's adherence to a single-reel restriction. In the spring of 1911, he made a two-reel film, *Enoch Arden,* but Biograph released each reel separately. The following year he produced a four-reel biblical epic, *Judith of Bethulia.* When Biograph decided to shelve the film temporarily, he broke with the company to join Harry Aitken's Reliance-Majestic studios which distributed through Mutual. Griffith's disenchantment with Biograph had been accentuated by the company's refusal to give him stock options or a percentage of its profits. His contract with Aitken permitted Griffith to make two pictures a year independently.

Griffith soon embarked on an independent production of Thomas Dixon's novel glorifying the Klu Klux Klan, *The Clansman.* Mutual, through its president, Harry Aitken, invested $25,000 in the project. Directors of the company, however, objected to the costly expenditure, so Aitken and Griffith produced and distributed the film on their own. The Epoch Film Corporation was formed to exploit the film independently as a "roadshow," a technique through which the producer bypassed the distributor and dealt directly with exhibitors. *The Birth of a Nation,* the title given to the screen version of *The Clansman,* broke theatre records wherever it played. The picture was shown in the leading legitimate theatres in major cities on a reserved-seat basis with a top admission price of two dollars. After a spectacularly successful roadshow, *The Birth of a Nation* was sold to state's rights distributors.

Griffith's next major film following *The Birth of a Nation* was called *Intolerance.* In this latter film, Griffith intercut a modern story of class-hatred and the miscarriage of justice with three stories of intolerance from different historical periods: the overthrow of Belshazzar in Babylon, the Crucifixion of Christ in Judea, and the slaughter of the Huguenots in sixteenth-century France. All four stories progressed simultaneously with the climax building through the use of shorter and shorter cuts into a visual symphony of mounting suspense. The film cost a reported $1.9 million to make. The sets and the crowd scenes are overwhelming even today. The set for the Babylonian city was a mile wide and 300 feet high. The Wark Producing Corporation was created to finance and distribute *Intolerance.* Griffith invested most of his profits from *The Birth of a Nation* in that venture. Although *Intolerance* was not a commercial success, it remains a towering achievement and, above all, a motion picture from which innumerable directors have learned the art of film-making.

To capitalize on the expanding market for feature-length

Posters advertising the "roadshowing" of *The Birth of a Nation* at the Majestic Theatre in Peoria, Illinois. The dramatic power, eloquence and vigor of D. W. Griffith's 1915 classic constituted a significant milestone in the progress of the film medium towards recognition as an art form with a structure and aesthetic of its own. Griffith's artistry, however, is undeniably compromised by *The Birth of a Nation*'s promulgation of racist propaganda and its glorification of the hooded vigilante riders of the Klu Klux Klan.

films, a combine of five independent regional distributors was organized in 1914 under the leadership of William Wadsworth Hodkinson, who operated the Progressive film exchanges in San Francisco, Los Angeles and other areas in the Pacific region. The newly formed distributing agency was called the Paramount Pictures Corporation. Hodkinson was elected president of the new corporation. Stock in Paramount was divided equally among the five distributors. In return for exclusive distribution rights, Paramount advanced its contract producers $25,000 for each feature-length film they planned to make. The producing agent guaranteed Paramount 35 per cent of the gross rentals on each film. Paramount signed exclusive franchise agreements with Zukor's Famous Players, the Jesse L. Lasky Feature Play Company, and two smaller concerns, Pallas Pictures and Morosco Pictures. Hobart Bosworth, an actor and landscape painter who, with the financial backing of Los Angeles capitalist Frank Garbult, had produced *The Sea Wolf* for Hodkinson's Progressive exchanges, also became a Paramount producer. Paramount was soon releasing 104 features a year.

Hodkinson lost control of Paramount in 1916 and was succeeded as president by Hiram Abrams. Before that year was out Abrams was fired and Adolph Zukor, who had acquired substantial stock in Paramount, was in control of the company. Zukor and Lasky merged their production units with several smaller companies to form Famous Players-Lasky, with Zukor as president, Lasky as vice-president in charge of production, DeMille as director-general, and Samuel Goldfish as chairman of the board. Paramount became the distributing subsidiary of the new corporation. Paramount initiated the policy, known as "block booking," of insisting that an exhibitor who wanted any of its pictures would have to take all of them. The compulsory practice of block booking assured Zukor of a steady outlet for his products.

STAR POWER

Famous Players' biggest star was Mary Pickford, whom Adolph Zukor hired in 1913 for $20,000 a year. Miss Pickford's movie career had begun in 1909, when she was 16. D. W. Griffith hired her away from David Belasco's theatrical company to appear in films made at the Biograph studio where she initially earned $5 a day. The following year, Carl Laemmle enticed "Little Mary," as she came to be known, to his movie company with an offer of $175 dollars a week. Dissatisfied with Laemmle's low production standards, she left him for a brief stint with Harry Aitken's Majestic and then returned to Biograph in 1912. By the time she signed with Zukor, Miss Pickford was a major box-office attraction. With *Tess of the Storm Country* in 1914, she became the screen's premiere leading lady; in 1915, Zukor was paying her $2,000 a week. Miss Pickford's high salary was justified by her enormous box office appeal which was the prime reason that in its third year of movie-making, Famous Players cleared more than a million dollars. Miss Pickford's appeal was such that she became known as "America's Sweetheart," the woman whom every man would like to have—as a sister.

Mary Pickford's screen popularity was rivalled only by the incomparable Charlie Chaplin, who came to America in 1913 as part of Fred Karno's Pantomime Company. In December of 1913, Chaplin joined the Keystone studio in Glendale, California at a weekly salary of $150. Keystone was under the control of independent producers Adam Kessel and Charles Bauman, who ran the company from their New York office. The Keystone studio operation was dominated by Mack Sennett, who had been lured away from Biograph where he had worked under D. W. Griffith. Keystone's remarkable troupe of comedians included Ford Sterling, Roscoe "Fatty" Arbuckle, and Mabel Normand.

Chaplin's first film, *Making a Living* was only modestly successful. However, within a relatively short period, he was Keystone's biggest attraction. Beginning with his thirteenth film, *Caught in the Rain,* Chaplin wrote and directed all of his own pictures. During his year at Keystone, Chaplin made 35 films. In 1915, he signed with Essanay for $1,250 a week, almost ten times his previous salary. Among the 14 films Chaplin made during his year at Essanay was *The Tramp.* Essanay, which had earned well over $1 million from the Chaplin films, tried to retain its star performer with the offer of a profit-sharing contract which guaranteed him an annual minimum income of $500,000. Instead, Chaplin went over to Mutual in February 1916, where he was paid $10,000 a week plus $150,000 bonus, a total of $670,000 a year.

As producers competed with each other for star performers, salaries spiraled upward. The offer of increasingly inflated salaries became the mechanism by which companies secured the services of major box-office attractions. Control of talent became a key factor in the domination of the industry. Enormous sums of money were spent to publicize and advertise new players. The value of flamboyant publicity soon became apparent. The Fox Film Corporation, for example, catapulted several players to stardom through the use of sensational publicity campaigns. The company's most famous female star from 1915 to 1919 was the seductive and sinister Theda Bara (né Theodosia Goodman, the daughter of a Cincinnati tailor). Her screen name (an anagram of "Arab Death") and her exotic background were fabricated by Fox's publicity department, who presented her to the American public as the child of a French artist by his Arabian mistress, born on the desert sands in the shadow of the Sphinx. The alluring Theda received $75 a week for her first film, *A Fool There Was.* Four years and 40 pictures later she was earning $4,000 a week.

In a spectcular maneuver to capitalize on the popularity of star performers, Harry Aitken, having just been ousted as president of Mutual, combined his production units with those of Adam Kessel and Charles Bauman in July 1915, to form the Triangle Film Corporation. Triangle boasted the directorial talents of D. W. Griffith, Thomas Ince, and Mack Sennett. Each of the Triangle programs, which in large cities were presented in converted stage theatres at an admission price of two dollars, consisted of one feature film from Griffith, another from Ince, and a two-reel comedy from Sennett. The new company drew dozens of the top Broadway performers to appear in its pictures at enormous salaries. Most of the stage actors,

Theda Bara in a publicity still for her title role in the 1918 Fox studio production of *Cleopatra*. An assiduous use of publicity techniques contributed considerably to Miss Bara's screen success. She was moviedom's first wholly fabricated star personality.

however, proved to be unsuited to the unique demands of the screen. Audience interest in the Triangle features diminished quickly. Exhibitors soon began to cancel contracts; and Triangle was compelled to reduce the maximum admission price in its own theatres from two dollars to 25 cents.

One Broadway actor who made a successful transition to the screen was Douglas Fairbanks. He made his movie debut in Triangle's *The Lamb,* which opened as part of a "double-bill" at the Knickerbocker theatre in New York on September 23, 1915. Fairbanks made 13 pictures for the ill-fated Triangle Corporation before being coaxed away with a lucrative contract from Adolph Zukor.

Famous Players-Lasky's reservoir of talent soon included such popular performers as Gloria Swanson, William S. Hart, Roscoe "Fatty" Arbuckle, Mack Sennett, and D. W. Griffith, all of whom had been enticed away, along with Douglas Fairbanks, from the Triangle Film Corporation with handsome contracts. Under the guidance of Charlotte Pickford, Mary's mother, the Mary Pickford Picture Corporation was formed in 1916, in partnership with Adolph Zukor, to allow Miss Pickford to produce her films independently. Charlotte Pickford became treasurer of the new producing company with the authority to approve all expenditures. Mary Pickford received $10,000 a week, plus half the profits on her pictures which thereafter were sold individually through a separate distribution organization, Artcraft Pictures Corporation. Douglas Fairbanks, under the guidance of Adolph Zukor, also formed his own production unit, the Douglas Fairbanks Picture Corporation, to distribute through Artcraft.

CONSOLIDATION

In an emerging age of American hegemony, the rapid expansion of the movie industry developed world-wide ramifications. By the time the United States government declared war on Germany early in April 1917, Adolph Zukor had become a cinema potentate of unparalleled power. During the years of World War I, the American film industry grew without hindrance. As a result of the war, foreign competition, particularly from the French, virtually disappeared. By 1918, Paramount was distributing some 220 features a year to over 5,000 theatres.

In the years following World War I, Paramount, along with several other movie companies, began to assume the vertically integrated shape that dominated the industry for the next three decades. Consolidation of control was facilitated by interdependency of film production, distribution and exhibition. At one end of the spectrum, exhibitors were acquiring production and distribution organizations; producers and distributors, in turn, were moving into the field of exhibition; therefore, vertical integration proceeded simultaneously from both ends of the movie business. To combat Zukor's domination of the industry, 27 major exhibitors, controlling important theatres in key cities, combined in 1917, under the direction of Los Angeles-based exhibitor Thomas Tally, to form their own distribution channel, First National Exhibitors Circuit. In an effort to circumvent any association with Paramount, First National signed up such major stars as Charlie Chaplin and Mary Pickford.

Under his contract with the newly formed First National for eight pictures which were to be produced in his own studio, Charlie Chaplin received $1 million, plus a $15,000 bonus for signing. First National advanced $125,000 to make each negative (the amount included Chaplin's salary). If a picture ran longer than two reels, he was to receive $15,000 for each additional reel. First National was to defray costs of prints, advertising promotion, distribution costs, and various incidentals. In return, First National received 30 per cent of the total film rentals. After all expenses were recouped, Chaplin and First National shared the profits equally.

While at First National, Chaplin produced his first feature-length picture, *The Kid* (1921), which ran to six reels. Since, under his First National contract, the $15,000 he was to receive for each reel beyond the initial two would not have covered the production costs, Chaplin invested $300,000 of his own money to make the film. After the company's executives viewed the film, First National, with some reluctance, renegotiated Chaplin's contract and gave him $600,000. The film grossed over $2.5 million and launched the spectacularly successful career of young Jackie Coogan who appeared in the title role. Subsequent films like *Peck's Bad Boy, Trouble, Oliver Twist* and *Circus Days* made Coogan the most popular child star of the 1920s.

When Mary Pickford's contract with Artcraft expired in 1918, First National won her away from Zukor with an offer of $675,000 for three pictures, plus 50 per cent of the profits. Miss Pickford was further attracted by the assurance that she would have complete authority over her productions. The business acumen displayed in the signing of Pickford and Chaplin led to a development, by 1921, in which First National was linked to some 3,400 theatres throughout the country. The following year, First National built a huge production studio in Burbank, California, a venture financed by an issue of preferred shares floated by the brokerage firm of Hayden, Stone and Company.

This entry by First National into the production arena, severely jeopardized Zukor's bid for supremacy in the movie industry. Recognizing the importance of first-run outlets in key cities, Zukor moved with alacrity to compete with First National in theatre holdings. In 1919, he bought several large theatres in New York and Los Angeles. That same year, Kuhn, Loeb and Company, the investment banking firm, floated a $10 million issue of preferred stock for Famous Players-Lasky. Zukor acquired an enormous number of theatres, controlling some 600 in a span of less than three years. In 1926, he bought two-thirds of the powerful Balaban and Katz theatre circuit (First National's profitable outlets in and around Chicago)

Charlie Chaplin and Jackie Coogan are under the watchful eye of a policeman in this scene from *The Kid*. Released early in 1921, *The Kid* was a smash hit. Chaplin was reported to have made more than a million dollars from the film. The waif-like Coogan, with his bangs and floppy hat, became the most popular child star of the decade.

for $13 million. He organized his theatre holdings into a new corporation called Publix, with Sam Katz as its head. Zukor's absorption of the Katz-Balaban circuit greatly weakened the foundations of the First National enterprise. Only a Federal antitrust action prevented Zukor from absorbing the entire First National organization.

METRO-GOLDWYN-MAYER

As consolidation of control in the movie industry began to assume alarming proportions, Marcus Loew, an enterprising exhibitor, who by 1919 had forged a chain of more than 100 theatres, decided to safeguard his position by entering the production and distribution field. Beginning in 1920, his formidable production unit began to take shape. That year, he bought Metro Pictures Corporation, an impoverished producing and distributing company formed five years earlier by Richard Rowland and his associates. Metro had acquired the screen rights to Spanish writer Vincente Blasco-Ibanez's widely read romantic novel of World War I, *The Four Horsemen of the Apocalypse*. The novelist was given an advance of $20,000 against 10 per cent of the distributor's gross revenues from the film version of this popular book.

A little known Italian-born actor, Rudolph Valentino, was cast in the leading role of Julio Desnoyers, an Argentine playboy in Europe who goes to war to redeem his father's name and later dies a hero's death. The film, which was directed by Rex Ingram, was a phenomenal success. Valentino, who was paid $350 a week for his acting services, soared to stardom. Marcus Loew recouped much of his investment in the Metro company from the film's large profits. Blasco-Ibanez relinquished his financial interest in the picture for a flat payment of $170,000. By the end of 1925, *The Four Horsemen of the Apocalypse* had grossed an estimated $4 million.

Early in 1924, Marcus Loew acquired Goldwyn Pictures,

Rudolph Valentino as he appeared at the height of his popularity. Valentino's starring role in the 1921 Metro release *The Four Horsemen of the Apocalypse* catapulted the swarthy Italian actor to fame. When Metro refused to give him a $100 a week raise for his next assignment, Valentino went over to Famous Players where his first picture was *The Sheik*. The latter picture won him the devotion of seemingly half the females in the United States. His brief career as the screen's greatest lover ended on August 23, 1926, when he died of peritonitis. An estimated 125,000 people, mostly women, lined ten city blocks outside Frank Campbell's funeral parlor in New York City to look one last time at the screen idol.

MUSEUM OF MODERN ART/FILM STILLS ARCHIVE

a company founded in 1916 by Samuel Goldfish. Soon after the Lasky company merger with Famous Players, Goldfish had come into conflict with Adolph Zukor. As tension increased, Zukor gave the board of directors an ultimatum, either he or Goldfish would have to go. The board sided with Zukor and Goldfish was forced to resign. Goldfish sold his shares in the company for nearly a million dollars. Late in 1916, he joined forces with the Selwyn brothers, Broadway producers, to form Goldwyn Pictures, which took its name from the "Gold" in "Goldfish" and the "wyn" in "Selwyn." Samuel Goldfish apparently liked the euphonious sound of Goldwyn so much that he legally adopted it as his surname. The Goldwyn company, which was financed by the du Pont family of Delaware and the Chase National Bank among others, prospered for several years. When the company began to flounder in the early 1920s, however, the du Ponts became increasingly dismayed by Goldwyn's stewardship. Early in 1922, Goldwyn was dislodged from the organization in a power play by Frank Joseph Godsol, who was closely allied with the du Ponts.

The acquisition of Goldwyn Pictures by Loew's Inc. proved advantageous for the shareholders of both companies. The entire transaction was consummated through an exchange of stock. Metro and Goldwyn were merged, forming a new production company, Metro-Goldwyn Pictures, with Goldwyn shareholders receiving preferred stock in exchange for their shares, and Loew's Inc. receiving all of the common stock. Samuel Goldwyn received a cash settlement for the stock he still held in the company he founded. The new producing organization adopted the Goldwyn company's trademark of Leo the lion, with his head enhaloed by a scroll proclaiming the Latin *Ars Gratia Artis* (Art for Art's Sake).

Marcus Loew further advanced and consolidated his position by absorbing the physical assets and some of the personal contracts of Louis B. Mayer Pictures. The Mayer corporation was purchased outright by Metro-Goldwyn for $75,000. The asset which most interested Marcus Loew and his associates was Louis B. Mayer himself. Once a scrap metal merchant, Mayer became first a theatre manager and later helped to form Metro Pictures, where he held the title of secretary for a brief period. Mayer entered the production arena in the fall of 1917 with the incorporation of Anita Stewart Productions. The new-born firm's major asset was Miss Stewart, who had achieved stardom in the Vitagraph production, *A Million Bid.* Under his three-year contract with Miss Stewart, Mayer paid her some $2,000 a week to star in such vehicles as *Virtuous Wives* and *Her Kingdom of Dreams.* Mayer soon expanded his production activities, adding Mildred Harris Chaplin (estranged wife of the comedian), Kathleen MacDonald, and Barbara La-Marr, among others, to his roster of stars. Louis B. Mayer Pictures was formed to consolidate his expanding assets.

The most fortuitous addition to the Mayer company was young Irving Thalberg, who had entered the movie industry in 1918 as a secretary at Universal. Within two years, Thalberg, who at the time was only 20-years old, was managing the studio at Universal City at a weekly salary of $450. During Thalberg's tenure at Universal, the studio produced one of the most distinctive films of the period, *The Hunchback of Notre Dame,* starring Lon Chaney in a poignant portrayal of the suffering Quasimodo. The film was a major critical and box office triumph. Thalberg left Universal in February 1923 to join the Mayer company as vice president and production assistant at a salary of $600 a week.

During the negotiations for Loew's acquisition of the Mayer company, it was agreed that Louis B. Mayer would head the recently formed Metro-Goldwyn (Mayer was not added to the corporate title until later). However, Marcus Loew reportedly wanted his son Arthur to serve as chief of production. Mayer demurred, insisting that young Thalberg was better qualified than anyone to assume the production helm. When the contracts were drawn up, Louis B. Mayer was designated first vice president and head of the Metro-Goldwyn studio at a weekly salary of $1,500. Thalberg became second vice president in charge of production at $650 a week. J. Robert Rubin, the attorney who handled the merger negotiations, became secretary and New York representative of the studio at $600 weekly. In addition to their salaries, Mayer, Thalberg, and Rubin received a percentage of MGM's profits. Initially some 20 per cent of MGM's net profits were to be paid to Mayer who, in turn, agreed to divide this amount with his partners, keeping a little more than one half for himself and sharing the remainder between Thalberg and Rubin.

Immediately upon taking command of Metro-Goldwyn, Mayer and Thalberg were confronted with a production problem of incomparable dimensions. The Goldwyn company, under Frank Joseph Godsol, had started to produce a film version of Lew Wallace's famed novel, *Ben-Hur, A Tale of Christ,* in

Italy early in 1924, on a budget of $750,000. By the time the Goldwyn company was absorbed by Loew's, the production was more than a million dollars over budget and much of the completed footage lacked drama and excitement. Mayer, at Thalberg's urging, convinced the Loew's hierarchy that the director and the star, Charles Brabin and George Walsh respectively, should be replaced. Thalberg cast Mexican-born Ramon Novarro as the young aristocratic Jew, Judah Ben-Hur. Mayer company stalwart, Fred Niblo took over the directorial chores. Shooting resumed in Rome, but the new footage also proved unsatisfactory. In January 1925, the troupe was ordered back to California. Under Thalberg's supervision, the entire undertaking was reorganized and several scenes were shot anew. A replica of the Antioch Coliseum was constructed in Culver City at a cost of $300,000. Some 3,300 extras filled the seats in the huge coliseum set as 42 strategically placed cameras filmed the fierce, exciting chariot race which was to be the high spot of the picture. The total cost of the production fell just short of an unprecedented $4 million.

Although *Ben-Hur* earned more than $6 million, it was not a profitable film for the studio. The Goldwyn company had agreed to give one-half of all the money earned from its production of *Ben-Hur* to the Classical Cinematograph Corporation, the company that held the film rights. Speaking at the Harvard Business School in 1927 at the invitation of Joseph Kennedy, the unlettered Loew lamented, "It is a contract I do not want to claim credit for."

On Labor Day morning in 1927, Marcus Loew, whose resourcefulness and energy had brought him to the zenith of the movie industry, died at the age of 57. He was succeeded as head of the Loew empire by Nicholas Schenck, his close friend and business associate. Under Schenck's financial guidance, Loew's Inc., and its production subsidiary MGM, eventually emerged as the unquestioned leader of the movie industry. MGM's entertainment empire employed a greater array of star performers than any other studio in history.

UNITED ARTISTS

The apparently insatiable public appetite for screen celebrities was not lost on the stars themselves, who, realizing their strategic importance to the movie industry, demanded increasingly greater remuneration for their services. In 1919, four of the industry's leading personalities—Mary Pickford, Douglas Fairbanks, Charlie Chaplin, and D. W. Griffith—founded United Artists to provide the distribution machinery necessary to publicize and rent the independent productions of its owners. When the head of the Metro studio, Richard Rowland, learned of the new company, he quipped. "So the lunatics have taken charge of the asylum." But the "lunatics" proved to be remarkably adept at the business of movie-making. Why toil for others, they apparently reasoned, when the enormous profits from their films could be kept for themselves. The communal status of the UA producers was peculiar to the conventional structure of the movie industry. Each of the four artists retained control of his or her respective producing activities. United Artists *per se* had no actors under contract, did not produce any movies, and owned no studios. Some of the individual owners, however, maintained studios. For example, Douglas Fairbanks and Mary Pickford, who were married soon after UA was incorporated, bought a studio on Santa Monica Boulevard. Charlie Chaplin had a studio on a five-acre lot located at the corner of La Brea and Sunset Boulevard in Hollywood.

The details of the incorporation of United Artists were worked out by President Woodrow Wilson's Treasury Secretary, William Gibbs McAdoo, who for a brief period was UA's general counsel and an equal partner in the company. McAdoo had become acquainted with the four artists when they toured the country to sell War Bonds. When United Artists was formed, nine equal blocks of common stock were authorized, but only five were issued initially. The additional stock had been authorized to enable other well-known artists to join the venture. William S. Hart participated in the preliminary discus-

The founders of United Artists at the signing of the certificate of incorporation—(from left to right) D. W. Griffith, Mary Pickford, Albert Banzhof, Charlie Chaplin, Dennis O'Brien and Douglas Fairbanks. O'Brien was the counsel for Pickford and Fairbanks, while Albert Banzhof represented Griffith. Nathan Burkan (not shown) served as Chaplin's counsel. The three lawyers became members of UA's board of directors along with Mrs. Charlotte Pickford and Oscar Price.

sions to organize the company, but backed out before the papers were signed. An offer from Adolph Zukor for $200,000 per picture apparently persuaded the grim-visaged Western hero to forsake artistic autonomy for the lure of quick money.

Stock in UA could only be purchased in blocks, not individual shares. Control of the company rested with the common stockholders; all decisions required their consent. Anyone withdrawing from UA was morally obligated to sell his stock back to the company. Each of the four artists signed agreements which, upon completion of their respective contracts with other distributors, gave United Artists the exclusive right to distribute their films for five years. Since UA was viewed as a service organization for its owners, the domestic distribution fee was set at 20 per cent, an amount which fell far below that charged by other distributors. UA films were sold and promoted individually rather than in blocks. Initial financing of the UA operation came from the sale of preferred stock to its four producer-owners. Oscar Price, who had been the Treasury Department's chief publicist, became UA's first president at a salary of $18,000 a year plus a small percentage of the gross. McAdoo's relations with the four producer-owners deteriorated rapidly, when he refused to share fully in the company's liabilities. He sold his stock back to UA in 1920 for $25,000, and he and Price severed association with the company. Hiram Abrams, UA's general manager, succeeded Price as president. Abrams held that position until his death in 1926.

The burden of production for the new company fell initially upon Fairbanks, since Pickford, Griffith and Chaplin had contractual obligations to First National. The first film to be released under the UA banner was Douglas Fairbanks' *His Majesty, the American,* which premiered on October 24, 1919 in what was then the largest movie house in the world— the newly opened Capitol Theatre in New York City. D. W. Griffith's first United Artists release, *Broken Blossoms,* starring Lillian Gish and Richard Barthelmess, quickly followed. This film had actually been made for Famous Players-Lasky, but Zukor thought it too poetic for the average movie patron. UA advanced Griffith $250,000 to purchase the film in return for its distribution rights. In January 1920, Mary Pickford's *Pollyanna* was released. This picture inaugurated UA's policy of renting films on the basis of a percentage of a theatre's box office gross, as opposed to a flat fee. Abrams persuaded

Adolphe Menjou and Edna Purviance in a scene from Charlie Chaplin's first United Artists picture, *A Woman of Paris*. This film introduced to the screen a new natural and subtly simple style. Chaplin often made from 50 to 200 retakes to achieve the nuances of detail and action so characteristic of his work. The film cost some $800,000 to produce—a munificent amount for 1923.

many exhibitors to advance money for productions by Pickford and Fairbanks—without interest, against future rentals—since the drawing power of these stars was so strong. The artists nevertheless had to invest substantial amounts of their own money to cover production costs; the return on their investments, although regular, was slow. Within a short time, United Artists was distributing films throughout the United States. In 1923, Charlie Chaplin released a sophisticated, intimate drama called *A Woman of Paris,* which he wrote, produced, directed, and even appeared in briefly (and almost unrecognizably) in the role of a porter. Mary Pickford and Douglas Fairbanks each made eight pictures during the first five years of UA's operation, and Griffith produced nine.

Since the number of films supplied by the founding members of United Artists was insufficient to maintain the enormous overhead of operating the distribution agency, other independent producers were invited to release their films through the company. Near the close of 1924, Joseph Schenck, who at the time served on the Bank of America's board of directors, moved from First National to become a member-owner of United Artists and was elected chairman of its board of directors. He later succeeded Abrams as president. Schenck brought into the UA fold such silent screen immortals as Norma Talmadge (then his wife), Rudolph Valentino (who was making a comeback after a brief retirement from the screen), and Buster Keaton, all of whom were under contract to him personally or to the company he controlled, Art Cinema. D. W. Griffith, beset by financial reversals and dismayed by the way in which his films were being distributed, left United Artists in 1925 to produce three pictures for Paramount at $250,000 each, but retained his UA stock in escrow. All of his UA productions, with the exception of *Way Down East*, had lost money.

Gloria Swanson, Paramount's biggest box-office attraction at the time, joined UA as a producer-owner in 1925. Her production company, the Swanson Producing Corporation, released its first picture, *The Love of Sunya*, through UA in 1927. This film was only modestly successful. It was followed by the screen version of *Rain*, Somerset Maugham's play about sexual seduction in the South Seas, which was released under the title of *Sadie Thompson* with Miss Swanson in the title role. Although *Sadie Thompson* was a financial success, box-office returns came in slowly and Miss Swanson's company had difficulty raising capital to begin a third picture. Financier Joseph Kennedy assisted Miss Swanson in setting up a new production unit under the name of Gloria Productions, Inc. Art Cinema agreed to take over the debts of the old company in return for the rights to its two releases.

Although Kennedy was Miss Swanson's intimate companion as well as her banker and advisor, he financed her pictures at normal rates, and kept the negatives until the money was repaid. The first Swanson vehicle he backed was the ill-fated *Queen Kelly*, directed by Erich von Stroheim. Under von Stro-

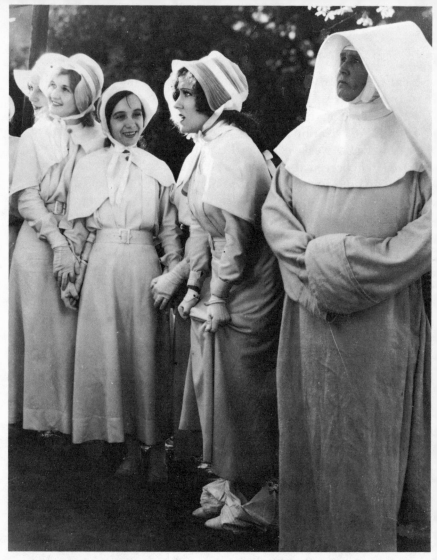

In this scene from *Queen Kelly,* Gloria Swanson (who was actually 30 at the time) plays a young convent orphan. When she is ridiculed for her somewhat embarrassing situation (depicted above) by a scoundrel prince, played by Walter Byron, she throws the undergarment in his face. He later carries her off to his palace apartment. Although *Queen Kelly* was never released in the United States, a brief excerpt from it was seen in the 1950 film, *Sunset Boulevard.* The latter film featured Miss Swanson as a faded movie queen reviewing her past triumphs.

heim's impulsive direction, the original script, which Kennedy had approved before leaving on a Palm Beach vacation, underwent radical changes. In the opening scene of the film, von Stroheim showed a priest administering the last sacrament to the dying madame of a bordello. Another scene vividly depicted the seduction of a convent girl. Miss Swanson, realizing the movie would never pass a censor's scrutiny, telephoned Kennedy in Palm Beach to alert him to what had happened. Kennedy hurried back to Hollywood to view the rushes. What he saw apparently astonished him. He fired von Stroheim and tried to salvage the movie by hiring another director, the talented but more predictable, Edmund Goulding. After investing some $800,000 in *Queen Kelly,* Kennedy released the film in Europe, but decided against showing it in the United States.

Samuel Goldwyn, releasing through First National, had gained a deserved reputation as a first-rate independent producer. Late in the summer of 1925, he signed a five-year distribution contract with United Artists. Goldwyn's roster of talent included Vilma Banky and Ronald Colman. During his first year with United Artists, Goldwyn released three films through the company: *Partners Again, Stella Dallas,* and *The Winning of Barbara Worth* (the latter film introduced Gary Cooper). In the fall of 1927, Goldwyn became a member-owner of United Artists.

HOLLYWOOD

The rapid expansion of the movie industry had provided the impetus for the move westward to Southern California where the clement weather and unique geographical advantages of ocean, deserts, mountains and forests provided the ideal setting for movie-making. Hollywood, with all its mythical glamour and glitter, eventually became the hub around which almost all production activity centered. Sunshine and seacoast, however, were not the only attractions of Southern California.

Los Angeles at the time was the nation's leading open-shop, nonunion city. Labor costs there ranged from 25 to 50 per cent below those in New York. Patents Company licensees as well as independents were drawn to the climate, geography and, above all, economy of the Los Angeles area. In November 1909, the Selig Company purchased land in the Edendale section of Los Angeles and within a few months constructed a studio on Alessandro Street which covered a city block. Late in 1909 the Bison Motion Picture Company, first of the independents to go to California, converted a former grocery and feed store down the block from Selig into a modest studio. D. W. Griffith initiated a policy, early in 1910, of taking Biograph players to Los Angeles for the winter months. His first feature-length production, *Judith of Bethulia,* was shot in the open, rocky terrain in the western part of the San Fernando Valley. In 1913, the Jesse L. Lasky Feature Play Company opened a studio on Selma Avenue in Hollywood. Many companies set up production facilities in outlying communities. Imposing new studios were erected on huge tracts of land. In March 1914, Carl Laemmle and his associates, who had wrested control of Universal from Patrick Powers, purchased 230 acres in the San Fernando Valley, ten miles out of Los Angeles near the Cahuenga Pass, for $165,000. The first ground was broken in October 1914 for the construction of Universal City, a new municipality founded for the sole purpose of producing motion pictures. Universal City had its own police force, railroad, post office and private reservoir.

Harry Culver, a wealthy real estate developer, conceived of a unique way of promoting the sale of a large area of desolate land five miles southwest of Hollywood, which he unabashedly called Culver City. As an inducement for people to settle there, Culver decided to create a movie colony. In 1915, he made a gift of 12 acres to Thomas Ince, who constructed five stages which were glass-enclosed to admit natural light for indoor shooting. This impressive production facility was taken over by the short-lived Triangle Film Corporation. When Triangle collapsed, Samuel Goldwyn bought the studio property and expanded it through the purchase of 23 adjacent acres. Goldwyn's 35-acre studio eventually became the home of MGM. William Fox, too, moved the production part of his enterprise to Southern California in 1916. Although most companies maintained their business offices in New York, close to the hub of finance, they centered their production activities in California.

SMALLER COMPANIES EMERGE

Hollywood, and its environs were home, not only to the studios of the major companies, but also to a number of shoe-string producers. Many of these were located in offices on a block along Beachwood Drive near Sunset Boulevard known as "Poverty Row." The most successful enterprise to emerge from this humble beginning was CBC Film Sales, a company formed in 1920 by three former Universal employees, Joe Brandt and Harry and Jack Cohn. Harry Cohn, who had served as Carl Laemmle's secretary at the studio in Universal City, established a base of operations at a tiny studio on Sunset Boulevard between Gower Street and Beachwood Drive while his partners ran the business from New York. A loan of $100,000 from banker A. H. Giannini had helped the new company get started. CBC's first film venture was a low-budget comedy series called *The Hall Room Boys,* which starred the vaudeville team of Edward Flanagan and Neely Edwards. In 1922, the fledgling company produced its first feature film, *More to Be Pitied Than Scorned,* at a total cost of $20,000. The film, which was sold to state's rights exchanges, realized sales of some $130,000. A series of modestly successful features followed. CBC used the profits from each completed picture to help finance its next venture. On January 10, 1924 CBC assumed a new corporate identity, Columbia Pictures.

Harry Cohn perfected the technique of shooting scenes

out of sequence to achieve maximum economy. This is common practice today. Indeed, in making pictures, art and economics are inseparable. A major feature film is rarely photographed in continuity. Fifty or so master scenes are each broken down into six or seven camera scenes, making more than 300 scenes in all. Each individual scene is designed to lend variety to the action. The plot is then temporarily transformed into dramatic chaos. Cost efficiency compels a director to shoot the scenes out of sequence. The action, for example, must follow the expensively constructed sets (instead of the reverse, as occurs in the final editing). Expensively-salaried actors who may appear only in scenes 5, 8, 27, 34, and 50, when kept idle represent undue expense, so scenes in which such stars appear are shot in close sequence. Extras and support actors, who are hired by the day, must shoot their scenes with minimum delay. Many of the scenes involving contract players, who are paid regardless of whether or not they work are, for economy, filmed last. The chief expense in film production is time. The cost of a motion picture corresponds directly to the time it takes to film.

Operating under rigid cost controls, Columbia advanced steadily. In 1926, Harry Cohn induced his associates to attempt to shed Columbia's "Poverty Row" image by purchasing a small Gower Street lot that had two stages and a small office building. The company also began to acquire exchanges of its own. Within three years Columbia was able to consolidate its studio and exchanges into a national producing-distributing organization of the first rank.

Another company to rise from rather unpromising beginnings to a position of prominence in the movie industry was Warner Brothers Pictures, a family enterprise which was incorporated in 1923. The four Warner brothers—Samuel, Harry, Albert, and Jack—experienced their first major success in 1917 when they secured the film rights to Ambassador James W. Gerard's famous book, *My Four Years in Germany*. Using a rented studio, they adapted the book into a highly successful film that grossed nearly $800,000. Their next important feature was *Open Your Eyes,* a semi-documentary about the dangers of syphilis. It was filmed under the supervision of the U.S. Public Health Service. Jack Warner, the youngest brother, appeared in the movie as a young soldier. In the early 1920s, the Warners presented a series of dramas which examined various social themes. One of these, *School Days,* a study about a small town boy who is corrupted in the big city, cost $50,000 to produce and grossed more than half a million dollars.

The Warners acquired the histrionic talents of the eminent stage actor, John Barrymore, for their 1924 release, *Beau Brummel.* Seventeen-year-old Mary Astor, on loan from Paramount, also appeared in the film. In Barrymore's second Warners' feature, *The Sea Beast,* he portrayed Captain Ahab in a free-screen adaptation of Herman Melville's classic novel, *Moby Dick.* In addition to Barrymore, the mainstay of Warners' financial structure was a German shepherd dog named Rin Tin Tin. The Warner films starring the talented canine were among some of the biggest box-office attractions of the American silent screen.

The second year after incorporation in 1923, Warner Brothers Pictures cleared $1 million. The company's methods of obtaining capital for film production, however, precluded the possibility of even bigger profits. In return for financing and distribution, Warners gave a percentage of the income from its films to various state's rights distributors. In addition, Warners often borrowed money at interest rates of as much as 40 per cent. To free themselves from the money lenders and exchange operators the brothers sought expert assistance. Early in 1925, they joined forces with Waddill Catchings of the brokerage firm of Goldman, Sachs and Company. Catchings was a prominent figure in financial circles. As head of Goldman, Sachs' investment division from 1919 on, he had guided the expansion of small regional businesses like Woolworths and Sears-Roebuck into major national corporations. In order to establish permanent financing for Warners' pro-

ductions, Catchings, after much effort, secured revolving credit
with National Bank of Commerce and the Colony Trust Company, among others, at the standard 5 per cent interest rate.

The Warner brothers, meanwhile, had already begun to
enlarge their operation. They purchased the ailing Vitagraph
Company (sole survivor of the ill-fated Patents Company)
which had a nationwide system of exchanges, two well-
equipped studios—one in Flatbush, Brooklyn and the other
in Hollywood—a large laboratory, and an 18-year back-log
of films. Warners also acquired two affiliated companies operating foreign exchanges. Under the guidance of Catchings, who
became a member of Warners' board of directors and chairman
of its finance committee, the Warner brothers continued to
expand their holdings. They bought first-run theatres in several
major cities and leased exhibition outlets in other key locations.
In the summer of 1925, they purchased the 1,500-seat Picadilly
Theatre at Fifty-Second and Broadway for some $800,000,
and renamed it the Warners' Theatre.

THE ADVENT OF SOUND

Soon thereafter, during the late 1920s, Warner Brothers,
along with the rest of the movie industry, underwent a dramatic
metamorphosis, brought about by the advent of sound movies.
Sound, of course, did not make itself heard on the movie scene
overnight; it was the result of a long prelude of technical
achievements and entrepreneurial endeavors. As early as 1894,
Edison had attempted to market a combination of his Kinetoscope and phonograph called the Kinetophone. The system
lacked adequate amplification and was soon withdrawn from
the market. In March 1909, the Motion Picture Patents Company licensed the Gaumont firm to manufacture and lease
"talking motion pictures." Gaumont's system, called Cronophone, employed two phonographs combined with a motion
picture projector. The Cronophone was a failure, both techni-

cally and financially. In the ensuing years, a number of unsuccessful phonograph-linked sound systems appeared on the market. In October 1912, Edison, in conjunction with the Keith-Albee vaudeville theatre chain, launched the American Talking Picture Company in another attempt to exploit an improved version of the Kinetophone commercially. Several Keith-Albee vaudeville theatres in New York were equipped with Edison's sound apparatus, but public response to the harsh, metallic sounds coming from the phonograph was not favorable. After a fire in the Edison laboratories, in December 1914, destroyed the motion picture department, the Kinetophone venture was abandoned altogether. Lee De Forest, a pioneer in the early development of radio, also began experimenting with sound movies. He developed a method of photographing sound directly on the film itself. In April 1923, De Forest demonstrated his sound-on-film system, called Phonofilm, at the Rivoli Theatre in New York City. Various attempts to market the Phonofilm system met with failure, and the addition of sound was to be accomplished later by those with more business acumen.

The eventual adoption of sound by the movie industry required the investment of vast amounts of capital which even the big studio aristocracy were unable to supply from their own resources. All aspects of the movie industry, from studio production to presentation in the theatre, were radically altered. The hierarchy of Hollywood was understandably disquieted by the unprecedented amalgamation of power that resulted from the conversion to sound motion pictures.

The Hierarchy
of the Movie Industry

SOUND CAME TO motion pictures only months before the great
Depression enveloped America. The concentration of capital
necessary for the conversion to sound, coupled with the ruinous
financial crisis which prevailed throughout the nation, eventually debilitated the giant movie companies. During this period
of economic infirmity the major companies were forced to
turn to the eastern banking firms, particularly the Morgan
and Rockefeller financial groups. In this manner, the banks
expanded their holdings and greatly increased their influence
in the motion picture industry. All of the major movie companies underwent extensive financial readjustment and reorganization, which eventually led to domination of the major studios
by their sources of financing.

The ultimate product of this reorganization was a hierarchy of eight major companies. The "Big Five"—those that
were vertically organized, i.e., the companies which controlled
all three facets: production, distribution, and exhibition—were
Warner Brothers, RKO, Twentieth Century-Fox, Paramount,
and MGM. The "Little Three" were Universal, Columbia,

and United Artists. Of these, Universal and Columbia were producer-distributors while United Artists was solely a distributor. Together the eight controlled 95 per cent of the films shown during this period in the United States. The subsequent history of the industry turns upon the corporate structures and relationships of these companies—their procedural agreements with each other, their policies, personalities and products. Out of the chaos of the Depression and the technological impact of sound movies evolved the economic structure that prevailed in the industry for almost three decades.

SOUND MOVIES

The pyramiding of control in the movie industry into fewer and larger entities was greatly accelerated with the advent of sound movies. The big electrical companies, particularly AT&T, a mammoth corporation almost entirely controlled by the J. P. Morgan banking interests, were determined to reap the rich financial harvest that would inevitably result from the movie industry's conversion to sound movies. Research engineers at Western Electric, the manufacturing subsidiary of AT&T, had experimented with both sound-on-film and sound-on-disc recording and reproducing systems for almost a decade. By the fall of 1924, they had developed a workable sound-on-disc system that synchronized the sound recorded on phonograph records with the movements on the screen. When sound movies became a technical reality, the lure of large profits attracted the attention of entrepreneurs, speculators, investors, and wheeler-dealers. Few organizations, however, had AT&T's technical expertise, financial resources or manufacturing facilities. Most importantly, AT&T had the basic sound patents necessary to forestall legal challenges and complications. Nevertheless, the reigning powers of the movie industry were not immediately convinced of the wisdom of converting to sound. Since the major companies were making big profits under the prevailing silent system and were reluctant to invest the many thousands of dollars required for the installation and utilization of sound equipment, Western Electric's initial efforts to promote its sound-on-disc system met with failure.

The fierce internecine warfare which prevailed in the movie industry, however, eventually made Warner Brothers Pictures responsive to Western Electric's overtures. Warners had been experiencing increasing difficulty in securing exhibition outlets for its films with the larger movie circuits, particularly the Paramount and First National chains, and was looking for a competitive edge. As part of its general expansion program, early in 1925 Warners had purchased the equipment of a bankrupt radio station and, with the assistance of Western Electric, had set up KFWB, Los Angeles. This acquisition brought the Warners into association with Nathan Levinson, Western Electric's representative for the Los Angeles area. Levinson induced Sam Warner to attend a demonstration of sound film at the recently created Bell Laboratories. Impressed by what he had experienced, Sam soon convinced his brothers not only of the sound system's merits, but also of its economic potential. Harry Warner, at first, had been particularly skeptical about the advisability of investing in talking pictures; all previous efforts to introduce sound to movies had met with failure. However, when he witnessed a filmed presentation of a five-piece muscial group, he too saw the value of the system. Immediately, he envisaged the potential of using the sound apparatus for musical accompaniment to Warners' pictures. Harry Warner and Waddill Catchings moved at once to secure the rights to the system. Their undertaking, however, was complicated by one Walter J. Rich, a manufacturer of automobile speedometers. Rich previously had obtained exclusive rights from Western Electric for the commercial development of its sound-film apparatus. Eventually, unable to interest any of the big movie companies in talking pictures, Rich agreed reluctantly to a partnership with the Warners.

In the fall of 1925, Western Electric installed sound reproducing and recording equipment in the old Vitagraph studio
in Flatbush, Brooklyn. The entire facility was converted for
sound. By the spring of the following year, short test films
using the sound system were being produced regularly. The
Western Electric system used by Warners was the same synchronized sound-disc system that had initially impressed Sam
Warner.

The Vitaphone Corporation was formed in April, 1926
for commercial exploitation of Western Electric's sound apparatus. The Warner brothers, who agreed to finance the entire
venture, owned 70 per cent of the stock in the new company.
Among the company's officers were Sam and Albert Warner;
Waddill Catchings was on the board of directors. The remaining 30 per cent of the stock belonged to Walter Rich, who
became Vitaphone's first president, at a weekly salary of $500.
The Warner brothers had a three-year option to buy his stock
in Vitaphone for $2 million. Under its contractual arrangement
with Western Electric, Vitaphone agreed to sublicense other
motion picture producers. The proceeds from the sublicenses
were to be shared equally between the two companies. Vitaphone was to pay Western Electric a minimum annual royalty
of $40,000 in 1927, increasing the sum to $175,000 in 1931.
The Vitaphone Company also agreed to purchase a total of
2400 complete theatre sound units over a period of five years.

The acquisition of Vitagraph, coupled with theatre purchases and sound movie experiments, left Warners heavily
in debt. To many observers the company seemed to teeter
on the brink of bankruptcy. In actuality, Warners' short-term
indebtedness was carefully planned and well-financed. Nevertheless the future of the studio depended upon its success in
effectively promoting the Vitaphone sound system. In late 1925,
Warner Brothers had completed a silent film entitled *Don Juan,*
starring John Barrymore. The company decided to delay its
release so that a musical score played by the New York Philhar-
monic could be synchronized with the film. Warners also

prepared a supporting program of short musical films that included the talents of Metropolitan Opera tenor Giovanni Martinelli, and master violinist Efrem Zimbalist. *Don Juan* and the accompanying short films premiered at the Warners' Theatre in New York City on August 6, 1926. The program was preceded by a film presentation of Will Hays, the president of the Motion Picture Producers and Distributors Association, extolling the wonders of sound movies. Audience response to the Vitaphone presentation was very favorable. Adolph Zukor, William Fox, and Nicholas Schenck were among the enthusiastic industry leaders who attended this opening night.

Despite the positive response to its Vitaphone demonstration, Warners experienced difficulty in selling the sound apparatus. Most of the major movie firms apparently were reluctant to deal with a sound company owned by a competitor. Early in 1927, several of the major companies signed an agreement to postpone any decision regarding the use of sound for their pictures for one year. The industry leaders also decided that uniform adoption of one system was to their mutual advantage. The eventual conversion to sound at this point now seemed clearly inevitable, but the companies wanted time to determine the best system to adopt. A committee, headed by Sidney Kent of Paramount, was set up to investigate the merits of the various sound systems. Each of the movie companies agreed to abide by a majority vote of their respective representatives on the committee, after adequate data had been accumulated. The general introduction of sound movies was thereby postponed until 1928.

As a result of this collusion on the part of the major companies, Vitaphone was forced to negotiate a new contract with Electrical Research Products Inc. (ERPI), a wholly-owned subsidiary of Western Electric, formed at the end of 1926 for the development of patents outside the telephone field. In return for release from its original purchasing commitments, Vitaphone, in May 1927, relinquished its exclusive rights to the sound apparatus. The new agreements called for Vitaphone to receive 37.5 per cent of all royalties received by ERPI from new licensees. As part of the transaction, Warners purchased Walter Rich's 30 per cent interest in Vitaphone. Under the new pact, Vitaphone became a non-exclusive licensee of ERPI.

In the interim, Warner Brothers had premiered a second Vitaphone program of short sound films and a synchronized feature presentation. The feature, *The Better Ole* starring Sydney Chaplin, opened in October, 1926 at the Colony Theatre in New York. Al Jolson appeared in one of the accompanying short films entitled *Al Jolson in Plantation Act.* In another short, George Jessel delivered a comic monologue. The audience response was again enthusiastic. A third Vitaphone program premiered in February 1927. The synchronized feature presentation, entitled *When a Man Loves,* starred John Barrymore. Yet again, audiences responded most favorably. Other Vitaphone programs were presented during the ensuing months. *Old San Francisco,* starring Warner Oland, dramatically demonstrated Vitaphone's ability to combine sensational sound effects, e.g., screams and thunderous crashes, with a synchronized musical score.

The future of sound movies and the fate of Warner Brothers Pictures was presaged by *The Jazz Singer,* starring Al Jolson, which was produced on Warners' newly constructed sound stage at Sunset and Bronson in Hollywood. The film premiered on October 6, 1927, at the Warners' Theatre on Broadway and 52nd Street in New York City. (Unfortunately, none of the Warner brothers were in the audience. Harry, Albert and Jack were in California where Sam had died the night before.) This was the first feature film with seemingly spontaneous dialogue and ad-libbing. After singing his first song, "Dirty Hands, Dirty Face," Jolson uttered the prophetic words, "Wait a minute. Wait a minute. You ain't heard nothin' yet!" He continued to speak, introducing his next song, "Toot, Toot, Tootsie." Midway through the picture Jolson engaged in a synchronized dialogue with his screen mother, played by Eugenie Besserer. The dialogue in the natural speaking voices of the performers

A poster from Warners 1927 release, *The Jazz Singer.* The landmark film about a cantor's son who enters show business was based on Samson Raphaelson's highly successful Broadway play. George Jessel, the star of the Broadway production, was originally scheduled to play the title role in the screen version. When Jessel demanded too much money, Warners replaced him with Al Jolson.

COURTESY OF UNITED ARTISTS

created a sensation. The film broke box office records almost everywhere it played. A new epoch in motion pictures had begun.

The phenomenal success of *The Jazz Singer* persuaded Warners to include talking sequences in three pictures that were in production: *Glorious Betsy, Tenderloin,* and *Lion and the Mouse.* In February 1928, Warners' release of its first all-talking movie, a prohibition-era melodrama entitled *Lights of New York,* dispelled any lingering doubts among industry leaders about the public's willingness to pay for sound movies. The film, which was directed by Bryan Foy, grossed $75,000 in a single week at the Strand Theatre in New York City. In the autumn of 1928, Warners released another Al Jolson talkie, *The Singing Fool.* In its premiere engagement at New York's Winter Garden, the film grossed $40,000 a week for several months.

WARNERS: A SOUND SUCCESS

The daring venture into sound film carried Warner Brothers Pictures from the status of rank outsider to the forefront of the motion picture industry. To solidify this position, the company expanded its holdings of theatres and studio facilities. Warners acquired the Stanley Company of America which controlled some 250 theatres and owned one-third of First National Pictures. Warners purchased additional stock in First National Pictures from various stockholders for $4.4 million and, in November 1928, it acquired the final third from William Fox for $10 million. Following this acquisition, Warners purchased Skouras Brothers Enterprises, which owned most of the first-run theatres in St. Louis. Within a short period, Warners controlled a coast-to-coast theatre chain of more than 700 houses. Spyros Skouras became the head of Warners' new theatre chain at a salary of $150,000 per year. Warners invaded the field of music publishing in 1929 by purchasing three already established firms: M. Witmark and Sons, Harms, Inc., and Remick Music Corporation. Between 1925 and 1929, the value of Warners' assets had increased from $5 million to more than $160 million. The company's net profit for 1929 exceeded $17 million, a record high for the movie industry.

In addition to the sagacious advice of Catchings, the rapid expansion of Warner Brothers Pictures could also be attributed to the unique financial arrangement of the four Warner brothers. When the company was incorporated in 1923, the brothers, in payment for their partnership assets, received 300,000 of the 350,000 shares issued. They put their stock in a family holding corporation called Renraw (the family name written backwards), which was administered by the frugal Harry Warner. Whenever cash was needed to finance sound experiments or to expand the company, Renraw sold some of its stock and then loaned the resultant money to Warner Brothers Pictures without security at current banking rates or less. By 1928, Renraw, which had advanced the company some $5 million, was down to its last 60,000 shares. Renraw had also endorsed some $5.6 million of Warners' other borrowings. The common stock in Warner Brothers Pictures had gone from $39 to $139 a share during the summer of 1928. After the Stanley deal, Warner Brothers received $16 million from a public issue of stock, which permitted Renraw to regain its stock position. By the beginning of 1930, Renraw again controlled some 300,000 shares in Warner Brothers Pictures, although its proportion of the total was now much smaller since the number of shares had increased substantially. When, however, Catchings resigned from Goldman, Sachs, the Wall Street investment house that had guided Warners' financial fortunes, that firm, in turn, refused to float a new stock issue. Warners was then unable to pay the $16 million in bank loans that were due, but once again Renraw came to the rescue. In the first six months of 1930, it sold $16.5 million in stock to cover Warners' debts. Hayden, Stone and Company then entered the scene and floated a $15 million issue of new stock in Warners', making it possible to pay the bank loans without Renraw's assistance. Since the Depression had caused the market to decline sharply, Renraw was able to buy back 325,000 shares of Warner stock for $7.5 million, and hence it ended the year with more stock than it had started with, at a cost of $9 million less. Renraw also bought most of Warners' preferred stock, which had stopped paying dividends in 1932. Renraw, as the majority holder of preferred stock, elected most of the company's directors.

The momentum gained in pioneering sound movies carried Warner Brothers Pictures through 1930, a year after the stock market crash. But in the fiscal years 1931 through 1934, despite the release of many highly successful melodramas and musicals, Warners' losses totalled almost $31 million. To reduce the company's funded debt, which at its high point in 1931 exceeded $100 million, Warners sold or abandoned its unprofitable theatre holdings. To further cut its costs, Warners, along with all the other major studios, reduced the salaries of its highest paid workers for an eight-week period in 1933.

Harry M. Warner, president of the company, commuted between New York and Hollywood, and concerned himself primarily with financial matters. Albert M. Warner headed the New York office. The company's 135-acre studio in Burbank was under the control of the youngest brother, Jack L. Warner, who was a steadfast adherent to the assembly-line method of making pictures. Warner Brothers Pictures released few, if any films—regardless of the fame and prestige of the producer or director—without the final identification, "Jack L. Warner, Executive Producer." Next in charge at the studio was Darryl Zanuck, who approved scripts, assigned budgets and generally supervised the entire production schedule. Zanuck, born in Wahoo, Nebraska in 1902, started his meteoric rise in the movie industry as a script writer for William Fox in 1923. A year later, he wrote scripts for Warners. He first gained prominence as a screen writer for the incredibly successful Rin Tin Tin series. Within three years, he headed his own production unit at Warners, with a share of the profits. He helped to guide Warners through the difficult transition to sound and, by 1931, he was in charge of all Warner Brothers productions. The films produced by Warner Brothers Pictures during the 1930s were, for the most part, fast-moving, superficial and action-oriented. More than any other major studio, Warners employed assembly-line, factory-like methods for making movies. The studio turned out some 60 pictures a year on a budget of about $25 million. Discipline and order took priority over temperament and talent. Costly retakes were generally avoided and production schedules were adhered to rigidly.

Darryl Zanuck's style of hastily-made, fast paced, action-filled, topical melodrama helped to sustain Warners through the early years of the Depression. His 1930 production of *Little Caesar,* which was directed by Mervyn LeRoy under the First National imprint, made Edward G. Robinson a major star. The film began a new genre of utterly non-sentimental portrayals of crime. The following year, in *The Public Enemy,* directed by William Wellman, James Cagney achieved stardom as a ruthless, though not always unsympathetic hoodlum. Although most of the crime films produced by the Warner studio lacked subtlety or depth, and the characters were more caricatured than real, they were attractively cast and surged with a definite vigor and excitement. By far the best film in Warners' early crime cycle was Mervyn LeRoy's *I Am a Fugitive From a*

THE COLD-BLOODED HOT-HEAD WHOSE GUNS ROARED ACROSS THE 'DECADE OF DEATH'!

"PUBLIC ENEMY"

JAMES CAGNEY

JEAN HARLOW JOAN BLONDELL WILLIAM A. WELLMAN

COURTESY OF UNITED ARTISTS

The Public Enemy, a 1931 Warners release, was produced in about 16 days for $151,000. At the time James Cagney appeared in the title role of this film, he was earning $450 a week as a Warners contract player.

Platinum blonde chorines in hoop skirts swirl around the stage to "The Shadow Waltz" while playing illuminated white violins in this Busby Berkeley production number from *Gold Diggers of 1933*. Berkeley's intricate and complex designs reportedly cost about $10,000 for each minute of screen time.

Chain Gang, starring Paul Muni as an unemployed war veteran who is unjustly sentenced to hard labor on a chain gang in an unnamed Southern state. The film's harrowing view of the brutal, dehumanizing treatment of prisoners caused a public outcry that resulted in somewhat improved prison conditions in the state of Georgia.

In addition to its crime melodramas, Warner Brothers released a cornucopia of musical extravaganzas. *Forty-second Street, Gold Diggers of 1933, Dames, Footlight Parade,* and a host of other similar films used to full advantage the singing and dancing of such able young performers as Ruby Keeler, Ginger Rogers, and Dick Powell. The musicals were enhanced greatly by Busby Berkley's lavish, and, for that period, daring and lascivious, kaleidoscopic production numbers. But even in its musical fare Warners presented the stark, often bleak surface realities of American existence. Backstage life was depicted as being far from glamorous.

Despite the various attempts to wrest control from them, the Warner brothers survived the Depression retaining both managerial and financial control. Hal Wallis succeeded Darryl Zanuck as Warners' production head in 1933, with a competent staff of producers working under him. Sam Bischoff produced an average of 12 to 14 high-budgeted pictures a year. Many of the more ambitious, artistic assignments fell to Henry Blanke. Lew Edelman specialized in low-budgeted military and topical pictures. Bryan Foy turned out about 26 low-budget films a year.

Throughout the latter half of the 1930s, Warner Brothers continued to emphasize fast-moving, action stories with hard-surfaced characters. The studio's female stars also had a certain calculated hardness. Bette Davis, for example, often portrayed willful, sometimes unscrupulous heroines in many Warner features. Warners' gangster cycle continued on its profitable, predictable course. Humphrey Bogart joined the studio's roster of tough-guys in 1936, with his chilling portrayal of Duke Mantee in the screen version of Robert E. Sherwood's *The Petrified Forest.* Bogart quickly became typecast and during the next three years he appeared in some 30 gangster-type roles. Paul Muni, on the other hand, soon graduated from gangster roles. A master of elaborate makeup, he starred in several biographical costume dramas: *The Story of Louis Pasteur* (1936), *The Life of Emile Zola* (1937), and *Juarez* (1939). Warners also initiated a series of romantic adventure films in 1935 with the release of *Captain Blood,* starring Errol Flynn as the swashbuckling, dashing Peter Blood. Flynn went on to play essentially the same role in several highly successful Warner films, the most notable of which is *The Adventures of Robin Hood* (1938). For a generation of children, Flynn remained the only possible Robin Hood, and Warner Brothers meant sound, action, entertainment.

THE
ADVENTURES
OF
Robin
Hood

THE SPLENDOR
OF IT ALL IS ALL
IN COLOR BY
TECHNICOLOR

STARRING
ERROL
FLYNN
OLIVIA
de HAVILLAND
WITH
BASIL
RATHBONE
AND
CLAUDE
RAINS
ALAN HALE
EUGENE PALLETTE

DAZZLING TO THE EYE...STIRRING TO THE HEART—A GREAT ENTERTAINMENT FROM **WARNER BROS.**

DIRECTED BY
MICHAEL CURTIZ and WILLIAM KEIGHLEY   Original Screen Play by Norman Reilly Raine and Seton I. Miller
Based upon Ancient Robin Hood Legends · Music by Eric Wolfgang Korngold

Warner Brothers spared little expense in its Technicolor production of *The Adventures of Robin Hood.* A woodland area in Chico, California, nearly 600 miles north of Hollywood was temporarily transformed into Sherwood Forest. Most of the film's principals and 300 extra players, members of the crew, wardrobe, hairdressing, make-up and technical personnel were on location in Chico for six weeks. At the Burbank studio, the setting for a banquet in Nottingham Castle was carefully reconstructed, complete with roasted oxen, sides of venison, gas flares, musical pipes and hooded falcons. The entire picture took some four months to shoot, at a cost in excess of $2 million.

SOUND INVESTMENTS

The financial success of Warners' talking pictures provided the incentive for the other major companies to convert to sound. By the middle of 1928, Paramount, First National, Loew's-MGM, United Artists and Universal had become ERPI licensees. Several smaller companies subsequently fell into line. At the close of 1929, some 90 per cent of all the sound pictures produced in the United States were made by ERPI licensees, and over 37 per cent of the sound-equipped theatres in the country had Western Electric installations. AT&T attempted to monopolize the control of sound in the film through the imposition of restrictive contracts. For example, an "interchangeability" clause appeared in ERPI's initial contract agreements which stated that a producer's pictures could be played only on sound equipment which had quality equal to that obtainable on Western Electric reproducing apparatus. This clause had the effect of preventing a licensee from renting films to exhibitors using a competitive reproduction system. Exhibitors licensed by ERPI were, in turn, permitted to show only those sound motion pictures which were recorded on Western Electric equipment. In addition, a "double royalty" provision required ERPI licensees to pay a fee for films they wished to distribute which were not made with Western Electric equipment. A producer holding a license from a competing sound equipment manufacturer would have to pay one royalty to the company to which he was licensed and another to ERPI if he wished to have his film distributed by any of the major companies.

The royalty agreement between Vitaphone and ERPI had called for licensees to pay 8 per cent of that part of their gross traceable to the use of sound equipment. In order to sign up the major companies, who were unalterably opposed to paying a fixed percentage of gross receipts, ERPI, without Vitaphone's consent, changed the licensee royalties to a more acceptable flat fee of $500 a reel. This action, coupled with other charges and counter-charges of contractual infractions, resulted in Warner Brothers and ERPI entering into protracted arbitration. The dispute was not settled until June 1934, more than six years later, when ERPI agreed to pay Warners $5 million in back royalties. In turn, Warner Brothers consented to waive any demand for future royalties because, although ERPI's aggregate profits between 1927 and 1935 exceeded $28 million, its profit rate fell dramatically after 1930 when the industry had nearly completed its conversion to sound. ERPI realized a profit of more than $10.1 million in 1927, but by 1933 its profits had plummeted to $94,424. Although ERPI was also involved in the licensing and merchandising of submarine cables and public address systems, some 90 per cent of its business was in the motion picture industry.

The Radio Corporation of America which, under cross licensing agreements effected in 1919–20, had equal rights to the same patents as AT&T and its subsidiaries, appeared initially to be disenfranchised from the burgeoning business of sound movies. RCA had been formed in conjunction with the U.S. Navy in October 1919 by Owen Young, the general counsel for the Morgan-controlled General Electric Company, to take over the operating organization and assets of the old American Marconi Company, a firm which held key patents for radio communication. General Electric, which had purchased Guglielmo Marconi's stock in the old firm, became the principal stockholder in the new company. Individual stockholders in the Marconi Company received comparable shares in RCA. Almost all of the American Marconi employees stayed on to work for RCA, including David Sarnoff, who was made commercial manager. Within a few months, AT&T, which controlled the patents for an amplification system developed by Lee DeForest, established cross-licensing agreements with GE and RCA. Westinghouse, which managed to get a foothold in radio by acquiring some important patents, also was invited to join the RCA consortium.

During the early 1920s, a research team headed by Charles

A. Hoxie and C. W. Hewlett of the General Electric Laboratories in Schenectady, New York, developed a sound-on-film device. GE used patents which were cross-licensed with those of AT&T's manufacturing subsidiary, Western Electric. For the next few years GE worked to perfect its sound-on-film "Pallophotophone" system. In the fall of 1926, David Sarnoff, who was now RCA's general manager, was given the task of commercially exploiting GE's sound system. Sarnoff's overtures to major movie companies met initially with some success, but negotiations eventually broke off when RCA failed to produce a marketable system in time to compete with ERPI. Moreover, RCA's sound-on-film system had suffered frequent breakdowns, resulting in costly delays and repair bills. When it became apparent that the big movie firms were going to prefer the Western Electric–ERPI system, Owen Young and David Sarnoff took swift action. In the spring of 1928, they formed a new corporation, RCA Photophone, Inc., with Sarnoff as its president. RCA, GE, and Westinghouse held 50, 30 and 20 per cent of the stock, respectively. To provide an initial market for the Photophone sound-on-film system, Sarnoff sought to combine a film-producing company with a chain of theatres.

RCA Photophone's entry into the sound film market was orchestrated by the same Joseph Kennedy who had guided Gloria Swanson's abortive venture as an independent producer. Kennedy had begun modestly in the movie business with an investment in a chain of 31 small theatres in New England. The chain soon acquired a regional franchise from Universal Pictures. Early in 1926, a syndicate headed by Kennedy, aided by financial backing from the Wall Street firm of Hayden, Stone and Company, took control of the British-owned Robertson-Cole production company and its distribution affiliate. Kennedy reorganized these holdings as Film Booking Offices of America (FBO), installing himself as president and chairman of the board. FBO, which had studios in California and 35 exchanges throughout the United States, specialized in low-budget features aimed primarily at rural audiences. The company, using assembly-line methods, turned out a feature almost every week, each costing about $30,000 to produce. FBO's biggest box-office attraction was a graduate of Princeton Theological Seminary, Western star Fred Thomson. Thomson's movies were so popular that FBO paid him $15,000 weekly, a munificent fee for 1927. Others who starred in FBO's melodramas were Richard Talmadge, Evelyn Brent, and ex-gridiron hero Harold (Red) Grange.

Late in 1927, Kennedy sold a substantial block of FBO's stock to RCA for nearly half a million dollars. His grand design now rapidly began to take form. The following February, Kennedy joined the Keith-Albee-Orpheum (KAO) theatre circuit at a weekly salary of $2,000, as a special advisor to Pathé Exchange Inc., the overall name for the vaudeville chain's recently acquired motion picture interests. Kennedy's next move, with the backing of a Wall Street syndicate, was to purchase a controlling interest in Keith-Albee-Orpheum and Pathé. FBO and Pathé became Photophone licensees in April 1928. The following October, FBO and Keith-Albee-Orpheum were merged with RCA Photophone to create Radio-Keith-Orpheum (RKO), a new holding company with assets in excess of $80 million. David Sarnoff was elected president of the new corporation. FBO, now a subsidiary of RKO, was renamed RKO Radio Pictures in May 1929. Joseph Schnitzer initially headed the new corporate studio outgrowth. Hiram Brown later succeeded Schnitzer as president. Joseph Kennedy, some $5 million richer for his efforts, left for broader fields to conquer. (This search eventually led to a diplomatic post in the Roosevelt administration, an honor which paled only in comparison to the election of his son to the Presidency of the United States in 1960.) Kennedy remained associated with Pathé (which was left out of the initial merger) until December 1930, when it was purchased by RCA. Pathé provided RKO with additional production and distribution facilities, as well as the acting talents of Constance Bennett and Helen Twelvetrees, among others.

RKO: A FITFUL GIANT

During the first few years of its operation, RKO had been modestly successful. The company realized a profit of $1.7 million in 1929 and some $3.4 million in 1930. The following year, however, as box office receipts diminished, the company showed a deficit of $5.6 million. In October 1931, David Sarnoff hired David Selznick to serve as RKO's production head. Selznick had first gained experience as a producer in 1926 at MGM where he made Tim McCoy Westerns. From MGM he moved to Paramount for a three-year stint under Benjamin Schulberg. In his new post at RKO Selznick reorganized the production budget to produce fewer, but more expensive films; he combined the production operations of RKO Radio and RKO Pathé under one staff; he enforced rigid cost controls; and he instituted the principle of unit production whereby independent producers were contracted to make a specific number of films without studio interference or supervision. Selznick assembled an impressive production staff which he drew primarily from his associates at Paramount. Merian Cooper, an explorer and soldier of fortune who had worked with Selznick at Paramount on *The Four Feathers,* became his executive assistant at RKO. Cooper had first gained attention in the movie industry with a critically acclaimed feature-length documentary called *Grass* which he co-produced with Ernest Schoedsach. The film, which was released by Paramount in 1925, examined the migration habits of the Bakhtiari tribe of northeast Persia.

Although Selznick only remained at RKO for little more than a year, he was responsible for some of the studio's most notable films. Among the films made at the RKO studio under

Selznick was *A Bill of Divorcement,* starring John Barrymore, Billie Burke and an angular young screen novice with a distinctive articulation, one Katharine Hepburn. Selznick initially had been reluctant to sign Miss Hepburn because of her unconventional appearance and manner. He agreed to cast her in the film only after being persuaded by director George Cukor, who had been impressed with Miss Hepburn's performance on Broadway in *The Warrior's Husband.* Other RKO films made during Selznick's brief tenure included *What Price Hollywood,* with Constance Bennett and Lowell Sherman, *Bird of Paradise,* with Joel McCrea and Dolores Del Rio, and *Animal Kingdom,* a comedy with Leslie Howard, Ann Harding and Myrna Loy. The last named film opened a whole new career for Miss Loy who had heretofore been limited to playing Oriental sirens.

Undoubtedly, the most-remembered film made at RKO under the Selznick regime was *King Kong,* which starred Fay Wray, Robert Armstrong and Bruce Cabot. James Creelman and Ruth Rose wrote the script based on a story outline by Merian Cooper and English mystery writer Edgar Wallace. The film was co-directed by Merian Cooper and Ernest Schoedsach. *King Kong* took 55 weeks to produce at a cost of $650,000. Some measure of the film's popularity can be seen from the fact that *King Kong* was shown simultaneously to capacity crowds at the Roxy Theatre and the Radio City Music Hall in New York City, then the two biggest theatres in the world. An estimated 40,000 people saw the film on the first day of its New York City premiere on March 2, 1933.

The high level of technical proficiency achieved in the movie industry by the early 1930s, was evidenced in Willis O'Brien's special effects for *King Kong.* A pioneer in the field of animation, O'Brien had first used animated three-dimensional models to represent prehistoric life in the 1915 production of *The Dinosaur and the Missing Link.* That film had a running time of about 5 minutes and took almost two months to complete. The "missing link" was an ape-like creature who proved

RKO RADIO PICTURES

A massive preopening publicity campaign helped to excite interest in RKO's production of *King Kong*. It was one of the first films to be promoted on the rival medium of radio. Over their radios, listeners heard, "King Kong is coming! A monster! All powerful! Beating down all weapons, smashing all barriers! You won't believe your eyes! Here he comes . . . listen!" A tremendous roar followed. The campaign apparently worked. The film grossed $89,931 in the first four days of its New York City showing.

to be the precursor of O'Brien's most famous creation, King Kong.

The animated miniature figures used in animation for *King Kong* were all constructed by Marcel Delgado, who had worked with O'Brien at First National on one of the first full-length features to use animated models, *The Lost World* (1925). To construct King Kong, who stood 18 inches high and weighed almost ten pounds, Delgado used a metal skeleton which he covered with cotton padding. He then applied liquid latex rubber to the model and covered it with rabbit fur. Some of the models of the prehistoric animals were fitted with rubber bladders to give them a realistic-looking breathing effect. Appropriately scaled models of the human performers were also made. A full-sized foot, hand, and bust of Kong were built for close-up shots. Kong's bust had a face six and a half feet wide, ears a foot long, and a 36-foot chest. Six men huddled inside the bust to operate the 86 motors powering the facial and head movements.

The animation of Kong and the other models was achieved through the use of stop-motion photography. After each slight movement, the model was photographed, the camera stopped, and the model was reset. Live actors were combined with the animated models through the use of rear screen projection. There is, for example, a scene in the film in which Kong removes some of Miss Wray's clothing. To achieve this effect, Miss Wray was filmed by herself while invisible wires pulled away her clothes. This footage was then projected on a rear screen, and the movements of Kong in front of the screen were animated to correspond with the disrobing. This sequence alone is said to have taken 23 hours to film. Ironically, although RKO's *Kong* produced under Selznick's aegis made film history, Selznick and RKO parted company when his contract expired early in 1933.

The departure of Selznick was attributed in part to the policies of one Merlin Aylesworth, who succeeded Hiram Brown as head of the company. At the time Aylesworth assumed the presidency of RKO, he was president of the National Broadcasting Company, a post he continued to hold. At RKO Aylesworth had insisted on final approval of every script and budget, a situation Selznick found quite unpalatable. Selznick joined MGM as a vice-president in charge of his own production unit at a weekly salary of $4,000. Merian Cooper succeeded him as RKO's studio head.

Despite the release of a number of successful films by its feature producing subsidiary, RKO finished 1932 with a loss of $10.6 million. In January 1933, the Radio-Keith-Orpheum Corporation, with assets of about $133 million, was placed in equity receivership by Federal Judge William Bondy. The Irving Trust Company was appointed receiver. The movie company was not reorganized in the federal courts until seven years later. Although RKO was solvent, its large investments in theatres deprived it of the liquid assets with which to meet future obligations. The receivership of Radio-Keith-Orpheum did not include RKO Radio Pictures, RKO Distributing Corporation, RKO Studio Inc., Pathé News, the Keith, Procter and Mid-West theatre groups, or the corporation operating the two new theatres in Radio City. All of these companies continued to operate with their management in full control. The Orpheum Circuit Inc., a $23 million operating company with theatres in 27 cities, entered a voluntary bankruptcy, as did two other theatre subsidiaries, RKO Western and RKO Southern.

Although *King Kong* had been an enormous financial success, RKO ended 1933 with a net loss of more than $4.3 million. Of the 35 pictures released by the studio in the last half of 1933, only four *(Little Women, Flying Down to Rio, Wild Cargo, Morning Glory)* were money-making hits. The following year, the financial fortunes of RKO began to show a marked improvement. The 1934–35 production schedule included three Katharine Hepburn vehicles: *Joan of Arc, The Forsyte Saga,* and *The Little Minister.* Other films in the schedule included Edith Wharton's *The Age of Innocence,* with Irene Dunne and John Boles, *The Fountain,* with Brian Aherne and Ann Harding, and *The Three Musketeers,* with Francis Lederer and Walter Abel. By the end of 1934, RKO had reduced its net losses to $310,575.

A poster from *Flying Down to Rio,* the first RKO movie to feature the combined dancing talents of Fred Astaire and Ginger Rogers. This film was the Christmas attraction at Radio City Music Hall in 1933. The talented dance team soon received top billing in such popular RKO releases as *The Gay Divorcee* (1934), *Top Hat* (1935), *Swing Time* (1936) and *Shall We Dance* (1937). In all, there were nine RKO films featuring Astaire and Rogers. These films ranked among the industry's top box-office hits during the 1930s.

RKO RADIO PICTURES

In the fall of 1935, Floyd Odlum's Atlas Corporation in conjunction with Lehman Brothers (the Wall Street banking firm), bought part of RCA's controlling interest in RKO for $11 million. In an effort to revitalize the bankrupt film company, Leo Spitz, a Chicago-based lawyer specializing in theatre finances, was brought in to assume RKO's presidency. Merlin Aylesworth moved up to chairman of the board, replacing David Sarnoff who had resigned. The Rockefeller minority interest in RKO continued, however, through direct holdings in the movie company's stock by Rockefeller Center Inc. Late in 1938, George Schaefer, formerly vice-president in charge of distribution for United Artists, was brought in to succeed Leo Spitz as RKO's president at the urging of Nelson Rockefeller in an effort to resuscitate the company's ailing financial condition. During Schaefer's tenure at RKO, the studio produced a number of distinguished, but not especially profitable, features including *Gunga Din, The Hunchback of Notre Dame* and *Citizen Kane.* The latter film eventually proved to be Schaefer's undoing at the studio.

Citizen Kane was produced and directed by Orson Welles, who also appeared in the title role. The script for *Citizen Kane,* which was written by Welles and Herman Mankiewicz, loosely paralleled the career of one of America's most powerful and enigmatic publishing figures, William Randolph Hearst. An iconoclast of the conventional wisdom, Welles employed extreme up-angle shots, stark contrasts of light and dark, and vast in-depth perspectives in the presentation of his brilliant psychological and biographical study.

Fearing assaults from Hearst's newspapers, many theatres refused to show *Citizen Kane.* Even the Rockefeller-controlled Radio City Music Hall, where most of RKO's major features premiered, declined to present the picture. Louella Parsons, Hearst's syndicated movie columnist, reportedly had threatened Nelson Rockefeller with a family exposé in the Hearst papers if the film appeared at the Music Hall. Louis B. Mayer, on behalf of several industry leaders, even offered to pay George Schaefer in excess of $800,000 to destroy the negative and all the prints.

Despite growing pressure to scuttle the film, Schaefer in an uncharacteristic display of resoluteness for a movie executive, determined to release *Citizen Kane* nationwide. Only after he threatened the major theatre chains with a suit charging conspiracy, was Schaefer able to secure adequate bookings, Hearst was so outraged over the film that for a while he banned publicity for all RKO features in his newspapers. *Citizen Kane,* although it has become a film classic, was a disappointment at the box office and, by mid-1942, Schaefer was finished at RKO.

In this famous scene from *Citizen Kane,* Orson Welles, in the title role, campaigns for governor. Some critics contend that the unconventional film techniques employed by Welles detract from the human drama. The public apparently agreed, since the movie was a failure at the box-office.

COMPROMISE

The Radio Corporation of America, RKO's progenitor, eventually acquired an assured place in the sound film equipment field. This came about because of ERPI's restrictive practices, which by the middle 1930s had resulted in suits totalling more than $175 million. Although very little in damages was actually collected, AT&T was compelled to yield its dominant position and, in the face of much widespread criticism, ERPI entered into reciprocal agreement with RCA whereby exhibitors were permitted to show films of either firm free of the payment of royalties. In June of the following year, Warner Brothers and Columbia, among others, installed supplementary RCA sound equipment, a definite financial advantage. In the interim, General Electric and Westinghouse, as a result of antitrust suits in 1930 and 1932, had relinquished their holdings in RCA. RCA's ties to the Morgan group were thereby loosened, while at the same time the Rockefeller interests entered RCA's directorate. The Rockefellers, through the Chase National Bank, soon gained the largest single financial interest in the motion picture industry, and the Morgan-controlled Telephone Company was second only to the Chase Bank and the Rockefellers. In this way, every aspect of motion picture activity came under the influence of these industrial giants.

WILLIAM FOX

The concentration and consolidation of power in the movie industry that occurred during the innovation of sound film production culminated with the incredible activities of William Fox. Up until 1925, the Fox Film Corporation had experienced gradual, but unbroken progress. In that year, Fox recapitalized his film corporation and offered shares to the public. In November 1925, Fox Theatre Corporation was established. The new company's theatre holdings grew into a formidable chain, including the Roxy circuit with its "cathedral of motion pictures," the 6,214-seat Roxy Theatre (demolished in 1960); the Poli Chain of 20 theatres in New England; and some 313 theatres in New York, New Jersey and Ohio. Fox's film company, in addition to turning out a feature every week, also began to acquire theatres. In August 1925, the Fox Film Corporation acquired about one-third of the common stock of West Coast Theatres, Inc., with theatres in California and the western states. The purchase, by Fox, in March 1928 of all the common stock of the Wesco Corporation, a holding company which controlled 216 theatres located primarily in the West, gave the Fox Film Corporation one-third interest in First National Pictures.

In the summer of 1926, William Fox bought the patent rights to the sound-on-film system of Theodore Case and Earl Sponable. The Fox-Case Corporation was formed to develop and promote the sound system under the name "Movietone." The major drawback in the recording and reproducing apparatus developed by Case and Sponable was that in order to be marketable it needed an amplification system. The basic patents for amplification were controlled by the members of the RCA consortium who had access to each other's patents under their cross-licensing agreements which were renegotiated in 1926 and again in 1932. Fox-Case first approached General Electric for a license, but negotiations were terminated when the giant electric company decided to undertake commercial exploitation of its own system. Late in December of 1926, the Fox-Case Corporation secured a license from the Vitaphone Corporation. This immediately solved the amplification problems for Movietone. An addendum to the licensing agreement provided for the cross-licensing of patents between Fox-Case and Western Electric. A potentially competitive sound-on-film system, Tri-Ergon, had been developed by three Swiss-German inventors, Joseph Engl, Joseph Massolle, and Hans Vogt. In an effort to safeguard his own Movietone sound-on-film system, William Fox purchased, in his own name, the American rights to this

Tri-Ergon system which used a flywheel mechanism to prevent variations in speed as the film moved through the sound reproduction equipment. This device later proved to be a key element in patent litigation.

Beginning early in 1927, Movietone equipment was installed in several of Fox's theatres. The Movietone system made its public debut in February 1927 at the Sam Harris Theatre in New York. The program consisted of Movietone shorts of a musical number, a comedy routine, and several songs of a Spanish performer, Raquel Meller. The program of shorts served as the prelude to the feature *What Price Glory,* starring Edmund Lowe and Victor McLaglen.

The first Movietone films to be released on a regular basis were newsreels. In May 1927, Fox Movietone News (the name given to the Fox newsreels) filmed Charles Lindbergh's take-off at Roosevelt Field, Long Island, for his historic trans-Atlantic flight. The Lindbergh newsreel was an enormous financial success, providing an important impetus toward industry-wide adoption of sound movies. By the end of 1927, a new Movietone newsreel package was being released weekly. In the fall of the following year on a 96-acre lot outside Beverly Hills, Fox Film Corporation opened its new $10 million sound studio complex called Movietone City.

To finance the expansion of his film companies, William Fox secured the services of Harold Stuart, president of the investment banking firm of Halsey, Stuart and Company. John Otterson, of Electric Research Products, Inc. also gave Fox financial assistance. With the support and encouragement of Stuart and Otterson, William Fox attempted to execute one of the most incredible amalgamations of movie companies in the history of the industry—the takeover of Loew's Inc., a holding company which controlled a chain of some 200 theatres, and a prosperous producing subsidiary, Metro-Goldwyn-Mayer. In February 1929, Fox Theatre Corporation bought 433,000 shares of Loew's Inc. from the Loew family for $50 million. The deal was made through Nicholas Schenck, who had assumed control of the company after the death of Marcus Loew in 1927. This block of Loew's stock constituted slightly less than a one-third interest in the company. To ensure his control, Fox formed a syndicate of family and friends, and acting through several brokers, bought an additional 227,000 shares of Loew stock on the open market for about $20 million. This strategy gave him majority power.

To obtain the funding necesary to consummate these mammoth transrctions, Fox put his companies heavily in debt. From ERPI alone, he borrowed $15 million on a one year note. Halsey, Stuart and Company, lent Fox $10 million, again for one year, and aided him in raising the remaining $25 million for the initial purchase of stock in Loew's Inc. To acquire additional Loew's stock, Fox stripped his companies of virtually all their cash. The Fox-Loew combination was the biggest entertainment complex in the United States. Fox now expanded his empire internationally with the purchase, for $20 million, of Gaumont British Pictures Corporation, a British company operating about 300 theatres in the British Isles; $14 million was paid in cash and $6 million was in notes due in six months. This purchase proved to be very advantageous for ERPI, since it opened the British market to ERPI sound equipment.

In his craving for power, William Fox had failed to see the portents of disaster. His investments now totalled some $90 million. The Fox companies, whose cash reserves had been depleted, could not possibly pay their enormous debts out of earnings. Their only salvation was through the issuance of new stock. Inexplicably, Fox delayed taking this action. The precarious financial state of his companies was jeopardized further when in July 1929, Fox was physically incapacitated as the result of a serious automobile accident. To aggravate matters still more, Fox put a strain on his relationship with ERPI by failing to make his Tri-Ergon patents available to the company to help it bolster its competitive position in the European market. With the first tremors of the October 1929 stock market crash, the Fox pyramid began to crumble. His short term debts came due. In desperation he sold Fox Film's interest in First National Pictures to Warner Brothers for $10 million. In November 1929 another blow fell when the Justice Department filed suit in Federal District Court in New York to dissolve Fox's ownership of Loew's Inc. Creditors instituted receivership action against the Fox companies. To secure additional money, Fox turned to Stuart and Otterson for assistance. In order to avert bankruptcy, Fox, on counsel of the famed Charles Evans Hughes, acceded to a trusteeship agreement which established three trustees as guardians of the Fox companies: Harold Stuart, John Otterson, and Fox himself.

Ostensibly, the purpose of the trusteeship was to alleviate the immediate monetary difficulties of the Fox companies and, most important, develop a plan for long-range financing. In actuality, Stuart and Otterson, two of the three trustees, had total control over the Fox empire. Although he had abdicated authority, Fox seemingly thought he could continue his reign. He soon became aware of the invidious implications of his minority position on the trustee board. Amid allegations of trickery and fraud, he attempted to abrogate the trust agreement. After several months of acrimonious struggle and litigation, Fox, finding himself in an untenable position, reluctantly sold his controlling stock in Fox Film and Fox Theatre to General Theatre Equipment Inc., a company closely allied with Halsey, Stuart and Co., Inc. He resigned the presidency of the film companies and the administration was assumed by Harley L. Clarke, president of General Theatres Equipment, who was also president of Utilities Power and Light Corporation, a company which operated many electric and gas utilities in the Mid-West.

William Fox was hardly left destitute; he received $18 million for his shares, and was retained as a special advisor at $500,000 per year for the succeeding five years. Fox, however, was determined to reclaim his crown. He subsequently expended millions of dollars in an unsuccessful bid to regain supremacy in the American movie industry through his control of the American rights to the Tri-Ergon sound patents. Fox's American Tri-Ergon Company was ultimately defeated in its court fight for back royalties and damages which Fox contended were due because subsidiaries of AT&T and RCA had pirated his "flywheel" device. In March 1935, the U.S. Supreme Court ruled in favor of the giant corporations, reversing a lower court decision. If Fox's suit had been sustained by the High Court his company would have collected immense sums in damages and license fees. After suffering defeat in the courts, Fox began a slow, grueling descent into oblivion. In October 1936, William Fox, whose personal fortune six years earlier had exceeded $100 million, declared bankruptcy, listing his total assets as valued at $100. Five years later, he was convicted of bribing the judge in his bankruptcy case and served almost six months of a one year sentence in the Northeastern Penitentiary in Lewisburg, Pennsylvania.

TWENTIETH CENTURY-FOX

In the fall of 1931, the Fox companies were forced into reorganization as a result of financial collapse. Harley Clarke's reign over the Fox empire had lasted only 18 months. He was succeeded as president by Edward Tinker, former chairman of the Rockefeller-controlled Chase National Bank. The Fox board of directors was comprised of such industry tycoons as General Cornelius Vanderbilt and Winthrop Aldrich, head of the Chase National Bank. The General Theatre take-over of the Fox companies had been financed largely by Chase. In the reorganization of the Fox companies, control passed from General Theatres to the Chase interests. Sidney Kent, formerly sales vice-president at Paramount, was selected by the Chase management to succeed Tinker as president of Fox Film early in 1932. The Wesco Corporation, the holding company acquired in 1928, went into receivership in 1933, but in the following year it readjusted its capital structure and the

Chase National Bank acquired 58 per cent of its stock. Fox's controlling stock in Loew's Inc. had also reverted to the Chase Bank and other creditors, and was gradually disposed of in the open market. During the upheavals at Fox Films, Winfield Sheehan had remained at the production helm. However, his profligate ways and penchant for expensive "epic" type films, dismayed the new management. He maintained his stature in the company through occasional box office successes like *Cavalcade,* the 1933 smash hit starring a predominantly British cast led by Clive Brook and Diana Wynyard.

In 1935, Fox Film merged with Chase-controlled Twentieth Century Pictures. Joseph Schenck (Nicholas' brother), William Goetz (then Louis B. Mayer's son-in-law and a producer at RKO), and Darryl Zanuck had formed Twentieth Century Pictures in 1933 to produce films for United Artists. Joseph Schenck, who had served for 11 years as chief executive at United Artists, became chairman of the newly amalgamated Twentieth Century-Fox. Sidney Kent assumed the presidency and Darryl Zanuck became vice-president and chief of production. Winfield Sheehan, who had 18 months remaining on his Fox contract, was induced, for a sizeable cash settlement, to relinquish his production post.

The most consistently profitable films at Fox were the "B" pictures (inexpensive formula films designed to fill out double bills) produced under the supervision of veteran Sol Wurtzel, a specialist in program pictures that were always competent, and sometimes very good. Among the most profitable films of this genre, were the saccharine sagas starring child-star Shirley Temple. During her years of pre-adolescence, Miss Temple is reported to have earned over $20 million for the studio. The low-budget bucolic comedies of crackerbarrel philosopher, Will Rogers (who died in a plane crash in 1935), and the popular "Charlie Chan" series, starring Swedish-born Warner Oland as the redoubtable Oriental sleuth, also helped to fill the company's coffers. Oland made 17 Chan films before

Shirley Temple began her motion picture career in 1932, appearing in a series of one-reel comedies called *Baby Burlesk.* Two years later, she was signed by Fox Film to a seven year contract at $150 a week. After presenting her in the 1934 Fox musical *Stand Up and Cheer,* the Fox studio loaned its talented moppet to Paramount for the title role in *Little Miss Marker* as well as for a feature part in *Now and Forever,* both of which were released in 1934. Her contract was soon renegotiated, elevating her salary to $1,000 a week. By 1937, Miss Temple's yearly income of over $307,000 made her the seventh highest paid person in the United States.

MUSEUM OF MODERN ART/FILM STILLS ARCHIVE

his death in 1938. Sidney Toler, a Missourian of Scottish-descent, succeeded Oland in the role of Chan and made 11 more films in the series for the Fox studio.

Under the banner of Twentieth Century-Fox, Darryl Zanuck, an advocate of efficient production, turned out films that, with rare exception, had formula plots, stereotyped characters, surface conflicts, and predictable denouements. During the mid-1930s, Fox's production budget was about $20 million for 53 features, an average of about $375,000 each. Some 29 of the pictures were produced under Zanuck, for about $500,000 each, at the Fox Movietone City studio. The other 24 were made under the supervision of Sol Wurtzel at an aggregate cost of about $5 million, some $200,000 for each feature. Wurtzel's program pictures were produced on the original eight-acre Fox lot on Western Avenue.

Twentieth Century-Fox's leading male performer was Tyrone Power, whose first important screen appearance was in the 1936 production, *Lloyds of London*. This film made Power, who was at the time only 23, a major star. During the next several years, he played opposite most of the studio's female stars, including, among others, Alice Faye, Sonja Henie, Linda Darnell and Betty Grable. Don Ameche often appeared in the same films.

Near the close of the decade, Twentieth Century-Fox produced one of the most poignant and beautiful pictures to come out of Hollywood—the film version of John Steinbeck's novel about the social injustices endured by America's migrant workers, *The Grapes of Wrath*. Nunnally Johnson's screenplay, Gregg Toland's photography, Alfred Newman's music and the performances of Henry Fonda and Jane Darwell combined to make the movie a masterpiece, and a high point in Twentieth Century-Fox's history.

PARAMOUNT IN TROUBLE

The economic vicissitudes during the 1930s affected the entire movie industry. The large theatre holding companies, in particular, were trapped in the whirlpool of economic depression. The problem of dwindling theatre receipts was further exacerbated in June 1932, when a federal tax of 10 per cent was imposed on all admissions over 40 cents. In an effort to attract more patrons, theatre operators in the New England area had started offering two features for the price of one. This practice, known as the "double feature" or "double bill," soon spread to other parts of the country. Games, cash prizes, and other inducements were also added by exhibitors to the regular movie program in an attempt to prop up sagging box office receipts. In most cases, resulting increase in attendance did not defray the cost of these incentives. By the end of 1932, the third year of the Depression, theatre admissions had dropped by more than 30 per cent. The sharp fall in movie attendance, which had begun in 1931, caught the industry by surprise.

Even Adolph Zukor's industrial domain, which comprised some 1500 theatres, a major international distribution network and impressive production facilities, had reached the nadir of its economic fortunes by the end of 1932. To buttress his expanding empire against potential encroachment from the newly burgeoning field of radio, Zukor, in the fall of 1929, had established a corporate link with Columbia Broadcasting System, a radio network formed two years earlier to compete with RCA's powerful broadcasting subsidiary, the National Broadcasting Company. Zukor exchanged 58,823 shares of Paramount-Publix stock for a half-interest in CBS. The agreement called for Zukor to buy back the Paramount shares from CBS's president, William Paley and his associates for $5 million by March 1, 1932, provided that CBS earned $2 million within the ensuing two years. Zukor's stronghold seemed impenetrable. In 1930, Publix theatres grossed $130 million. That same year, Paramount's film exchanges, under the direction of Sidney Kent, took in $69 million.

During 1931, however, the economic depression had begun to take its toll on the movie industry. Paramount's record high profit of $18 million the previous year dropped precipitously to $6 million. As the Depression deepened, Adolph Zukor lost his capacity to deal with the company's financial problems. To protect its investment, Kuhn, Loeb & Co. had induced John D. Hertz, a retired Chicago taxicab magnate, to serve as chairman of Paramount's finance committee. Hertz, who assumed this post in November 1931, drastically cut expenses, but he was unable to reverse the company's tumbling gross receipts. The funded debt, bank loans, and the contingent liabilities incurred as a consequence of Zukor's theatre expansion—coupled with the enormous outlay in converting studios and theatres to sound—had drained the company of its working capital. Many of Publix's theatres, for example, had been acquired through an exchange of stock with a guarantee to repurchase at $80 a share. When the repurchase agreements fell due, the company's stock was below $50 and cash was not obtainable easily.

The novelty of sound had helped bolster movie attendance during the first harsh years of the Depression, but poverty-stricken Americans soon turned to cheaper forms of entertainment. Network radio broadcasting, in particular, assumed an increasingly more important role in people's lives. Under the guidance of William Paley, the Columbia Broadcasting System had greatly strengthened its position in the radio industry. Those individuals who gained substantial stock in CBS included Herbert Bayard Swope (brother of the president of General Electric) and representatives of the firm of Lehman Brothers. In an extraordinary turn of events, Paley and his associates bought back the half-interest in CBS from Paramount. The movie company was given back the 48,000 Paramount shares which the Paley group still held, plus an additional $1.2 million. Paramount had little alternative but to accept this arrangement, since under the earnings clause of its original contract with the Paley group, it would have had to purchase CBS's Paramount stock, which by 1932 had greatly depreciated in value, for a staggering $85 a share. The CBS deal did little to offset Paramount's losses. In 1932, the movie company suffered a loss of $21 million. Although Paramount had enormous physical assets, it could not muster enough hard cash to meet its overhead and mortgage commitments. The company's theatre gross dropped by $25 million. Correspondingly, as debts accrued, common stock values plummeted. On January 26, 1933, Paramount, with assets totalling $160 million, filed bankruptcy proceedings in Federal District Court in New York and was placed in equity receivership. Six weeks later, the company took another downward step into voluntary bankruptcy.

When Paramount emerged unsteadily from receivership in July 1935, corporate control of the company passed from Kuhn, Loeb & Co. to Lehman Brothers and Floyd Odlum's Atlas Corporation, an investment trust firmly within the Morgan sphere of influence. With a new corporate structure to subsume its old assets, the company assumed a new identity, Paramount Pictures Inc. (The company had gone through several name changes: In 1927, it was called Paramount-Famous Lasky; three years later its name was changed to Paramount Publix.) John Otterson, who had served as head of ERPI, became Paramount's president. Adolph Zukor, his power reduced substantially, assumed the nominal post of chairman of the board.

Late in April 1936, Joseph Kennedy joined Paramount as a special advisor to investigate the company's financial difficulties. Kennedy and his staff spent several weeks scrutinizing every aspect of Paramount's operation. During his lengthy visit to the West Coast studio, Kennedy found gross mismanagement and inefficiency at all levels. Shooting schedules were being ignored; expensive scenarios were being discarded; costly stars were being alienated; negative costs were exceeding their budgets by $7 million annually; and the planning of the 1936–37 program was in seemingly hopeless disarray. Much of the fault for the studio's wasteful practices, said Kennedy in his 54-page, 15,000-word report, lay with Paramount's incompetent New York City headquarters. To avert another receivership, Kennedy recommended removal of the businessmen who were managing the company. Paramount's board acted swiftly. Otterson, in office only a year, was replaced as president by Barney Balaban. In the next several months, 10 changes occurred on Paramount's board of directors. Balaban, who with his four brothers and brother-in-law Sam Katz, had built a powerful theatre circuit in Illinois, quickly launched a recovery program based on Kennedy's recommendations. Adolph Zukor, who remained as board chairman, was put in charge of production. His primary function was to handle the delicate diplomacy of contract negotiations and establish the lines along which the studio's pictures were made. William Le Baron supervised the daily activities of the studio's 60-odd departments. A loose federation of powerful producers controlled the actual production.

During the latter half of the 1930s, Paramount's 12 producers, 65 writers, 15 directors, and 80 contract players turned out some 52 pictures annually, about half of which were low-budget "B" pictures. Harold Hurley produced the "B" pictures for an average cost of approximately $200,000 each. Independent producers provided another 19 or so pictures a year for Paramount release. Paramount, for example, financed and distributed the independent productions of Manny Cohen on a profit-sharing basis. The studio's roster of contract players included Claudette Colbert, Marlene Dietrich, Bing Crosby, W. C. Fields, Carole Lombard, Fred McMurray, and George Raft. Next to its stars, the studio's greatest asset was its imposing array of producer-directors: Cecil B. DeMille, Leo McCarey, Ernst Lubitsch, King Vidor, and Henry Hathaway.

MGM REMAINS SOLVENT

During the Depression, not all of the major movie firms suffered the same degree of earnings decline and corporate upheaval. The company which managed to weather the Depression with the least amount of corporate turmoil was Loew's Inc. and its production subsidiary, Metro-Goldwyn-Mayer (MGM). Throughout the 1930s Loew's continued to pay dividends to its stockholders, the only movie company to do so. Since Marcus Loew and Nicholas Schenck had been cautious in financing their modest theatre expansion during the 1920s, the company was able to maintain its solvency in the worst throes of the Depression. Even so, its net earnings plummeted from $15 million in 1930 to $4 million in 1933.

The major force in shaping MGM's film output during the studio's formative years was Irving Thalberg, a small, fragile man who had been stricken with rheumatic fever as a teenager. Few films left the studio without his personal imprint. Indeed, much of MGM's early prosperity can be attributed directly to Thalberg's stewardship. He was especially adept at supervising the editing of a film, probably the most essential ingredient in making a successful movie. The final pace, tone and character of a film are determined largely in the editing room. In making the average feature, about 200,000 feet of film was shot. Generally, this footage was cut down to less than 8–10,000 feet. Using his considerable skill at editing pictures, Thalberg was responsible for making many otherwise mediocre films good and, occasionally, he made a good film great.

Under the aegis of Thalberg, MGM lavished vast amounts of money on its productions. The studio's weekly payroll averaged $250,000. The writing staff alone, which included at various times Frances Marion, William Faulkner, Moss Hart, Anita Loos, and Charles MacArthur, cost $40,000 a week. Sometimes as many as a dozen writers would work on the same script simultaneously. MGM's screenplays generally eschewed controversy. Epics and drawing room comedies were preferred over dramas and social commentary. Lavish settings, stylish attire, and escapist romanticism became the MGM trademark.

One of MGM's more costly films was *Rasputin and the Empress,* starring the Barrymores—Ethel, Lionel, and John. The story was loosely based on the life of Gregori Efimovich Rasputin, the diabolical Russian monk who wielded so much power in the court of Czar Nicholas II through his influence over the Czarina. The film took four months to complete at a cost of a million dollars. The combined salaries of the actors alone totaled $150,000, but additional costs were incurred which were extraneous to the production itself. Most of the characters in the movie version of the story were identified by their actual historical names. However, Prince Felix Yousopov, one of the Russian nobles thought to have participated in the death of Rasputin (who was assassinated in December of 1916), was called Paul Chegodieff and his fictional fiancee was named Princess Natasha. In the film, Natasha is violated by the lecherous monk. The real Prince Yousopov's wife, Princess Irina, sued MGM in England (where the film was released under the title *Rasputin, the Mad Monk*), claiming that she had been defamed. The British court that heard the case awarded the princess damages of 25,000 pounds or $125,000 at the rate of exchange in 1934. Similar verdicts in other countries netted the princess another $250,000.

Another costly "princess" at MGM was Marion Davies whose $6,000 a week salary was rarely justified by the box office returns on her films. The conventional legerdemain of profit and loss, however, did not fully explain the value of Miss Davies to MGM. Miss Davies was the favored star of Cosmopolitan Pictures, a company owned by publishing magnate William Randolph Hearst. At the height of his power, Hearst controlled 29 daily newspapers in 18 large cities, a substantial publicity outlet. Hearst's association with MGM proved to be a most felicitous one for the studio. Louella Parsons, the star Hollywood reporter of the Hearst publishing empire (her flagship paper was the Los Angeles *Examiner*), lavished extravagant praise on all MGM releases, especially the pictures of Marion Davies about which she wrote in rapturous terms. In 1934, when Irving Thalberg refused to cast the gamin-like Miss Davies as Elizabeth Barrett in his MGM screen version of *The Barretts of Wimpole Street,* Hearst indignantly moved his favored film star to Warner Brothers. The role of Miss Barrett went to Thalberg's wife, Norma Shearer. Reportedly, Hearst instructed the editors of his newspapers never again to mention Miss Shearer's name in print.

Irving Thalberg, although always in delicate health, expended enormous energy in overseeing all phases of the 40 or 50 films produced by the studio each year. In most production decisions, Louis B. Mayer deferred to Thalberg. However, the complexities of sound production soon made the studio structure established by Thalberg increasingly unwieldy. Thalberg would end each work day in a state of exhaustion. Finally, one night late in December 1932, Thalberg collapsed from what was diagnosed as a mild coronary thrombosis. He took an extended vacation in Europe to recuperate.

In the spring of 1933, Mayer, with the support of Nicholas Schenck, reorganized the studio into separate, autonomous production units. Under the new system, the supervisors who had worked under Thalberg were formally designated as full-fledged producers, with responsibility for their own productions. One of the new units was headed by David Selznick, who, it will be recalled, joined MGM early in 1933 as a vice-president on a two-year contract at $4,000 a week. During the next two years, Selznick produced several of MGM's most successful films including, *Manhattan Melodrama, David Copperfield* and *A Tale of Two Cities.*

After an absence of almost nine months, Thalberg returned to MGM, his authority clearly eroded by the unit system that had been created while he was away. Instead of supervising the studio's entire product, Thalberg was given his own autonomous unit with the understanding that he would concentrate on a relatively few select film projects a year. Although Thalberg's immense salary and profit participation were not affected by the new arrangement, the balance of power had perceptibly shifted away from him. For the remainder of his short life (he died in September 1936 of heart failure), Thalberg reportedly harbored feelings of bitterness against Louis B. Mayer.

A noticeably strengthening feature of Loew's Inc.'s financial standing during the early 1930s, was the sliding-scale policy for MGM film rentals. Under that plan which was put into effect in 1931 by Felix Feist, the company's head of distribution, the top seven films produced by the studio each year rented for 35 per cent of what they grossed in the theatres, the next seven rented for 30 per cent, and the remaining inventory commanded no less than 25 per cent. Each film's market potential was determined by the amount of time, talent, money and effort that went into its making. The Feist plan soon became standard practice in the industry, although movie makers were quick to realize that there is no accurate yardstick to predict whether or not a film will appeal to the public. A few years later, Al Lichtman, who had joined MGM in 1935, modified the company's distribution format to garner even greater returns on high quality films. Under Lichtman's scheme, the percentage terms for rentals were determined by how well a film did in its initial run in 30 key theatres. Popular films earned a top rental fee of 50 per cent of the gross. The MGM release which commanded one of the most spectacular rentals in the company's history was *Gone With the Wind,* for which theatre owners paid 70 per cent of their gross. Interestingly, this film was not produced by MGM, but rather Selznick-International Pictures.

Selznick-International was an independent company set up by David Selznick to develop technicolor productions after he left the MGM studio in 1935. Investors in Selznick's company included Dr. A. H. Giannini of the Bank of America, Wall Street financier Robert Lehman, and Cornelius Vanderbilt Whitney, all of whom were directors of the company. Selznick was president and John Hay Whitney served as chairman of the board. Selznick-International originally distributed through United Artists under a three-year contract. While producing for United Artists, Selznick bought the screen rights to Margaret Mitchell's Civil War epic, *Gone With the Wind.* He delayed in filming the story, however, until after his UA contract had expired. Selznick wanted Clark Gable, who was under contract to MGM, for the role of Rhett Butler. Louis B. Mayer agreed to lend his prize star only on the condition that MGM be given the distribution rights to the film and half the profits.

In addition to Gable, MGM put up half of the estimated production cost of $2.5 million. Although the actual cost of the film exceeded $4 million, MGM provided no additional funds.

Gone With the Wind became the biggest box office success in history, selling more movie tickets than any other film ever made. When Selznick-International was liquidated in 1942, David Selznick, in a financial transaction that later proved to be a costly error, sold his interest in the picture to John Hay Whitney. Two years later Whitney sold his rights to the film to MGM for a huge profit. *Gone With the Wind* continued to make money for the studio for the next three decades. The picture was technically renovated in 1967 for large-screen, 70 mm projection, with enhanced color and stereophonic sound. NBC-TV paid a reported $5 million for its November 1976 two-part presentation of *Gone With the Wind*

UNIVERSAL AFTER LAEMMLE

The prolonged economic collapse during the 1930s resulted in dramatic shifts of corporate and managerial control within the movie industry. Burdened suddenly with fixed debts and dwindling receipts, Universal also plunged into a receivership in 1933 which lasted two years. During this period, Universal sold the 66 theatres it had acquired during the middle 1920s.

Despite its poor earnings record, Universal produced several films during the early 1930s which are now regarded as classics by many film buffs. In 1931, Carl Laemmle Jr., who had been put in charge of the studio operation by his father as a twenty-first birthday present, produced one of the greatest anti-war films of all time, *All Quiet on the Western Front.* Young Laemmle also started a new trend of horror films beginning in 1931 with *Frankenstein* and *Dracula.* Other Universal films in the horror genre included *Freaks, The Mummy, Murders in the Rue Morgue, Old Dark House* and *The Invisible Man.* Most of these features, however, were not large enough

The film version of Erich Maria Remarque's anti-war novel, *All Quiet on the Western Front,* cost some $1.4 million to produce. Universal recruited a private army of 2,000 ex-soldiers from the forces of the United States, Great Britain, France, Germany, Italy and Belgium for the battle scenes. More than 20,000 pounds of black powder and six tons of dynamite were used to give the effect of shell fire and mine explosions. A French village, covering ten acres, was especially constructed and then blown to pieces during the bombardment scenes. Director Lewis Milestone, who had no military experience and knew nothing of actual war, managed to capture much of the brooding horror of Remarque's book.

commercial successes to compensate for the box-office failures of such big-budgeted movies (also under Laemmle, Jr.'s aegis) as the $2 million production of *The King of Jazz.* Eventually, the elder Laemmle, with much reluctance, removed his son from the production helm.

Plagued by mismanagement and inefficiency, Carl Laemmle, Sr., one of the last of the pioneer film moguls to maintain control of his company, sold his stock in the ailing Universal concern in 1936 to an investment group headed by John Cheever Cowdin, a British financier, and financed in part by Electrical Research Products, Inc., Eastman Kodak, and J. Arthur Rank, heir to a chain of British flour mills. ERPI, seeking to preserve a source of royalties on sound equipment, invested some $2 million in the struggling movie company. High finance had captured another movie bastion. (Three years later, at the age of 72, Laemmle died.) Carl Rogers, who had produced program pictures at RKO and Paramount, became the new studio head. It was during Rogers' tenure that Universal released the most famous of its many chapter-plays, the *Flash Gordon* serial.

Universal's major asset in the latter half of the 1930s was a teenager named Deanna Durbin. The 14-year old movie novice's first starring vehicle, *Three Smart Girls,* was produced by Joe Pasternak for about $400,000, and grossed over $1.6 million. Universal spent $725,000 on Miss Durbin's next picture *100 Men and a Girl,* and released it in September 1937 to 225 theatres simultaneously. Miss Durbin's original contract with Universal, which paid her $150 a week, was renegotiated and her salary was increased to $1,250 a week, plus a $10,000 bonus on the completion of each picture. She quickly became the studio's most important star. Universal signed her to a five-year contract in June 1938, calling for $1,750 a week plus a $50,000 bonus after the completion of each picture. The contract also provided for raises of $250 a week each year until 1943. Miss Durbin's salary was more than justified since her films were consistently profitable.

Although the Durbin films were commercially successful, the studio, still recovering from the inefficiency of the old Laemmle regime, frequently operated at a loss. A new management team took over Universal in January 1938 headed by a former exhibitor, Nate Blumberg, and his four associates, Matthew Fox, Clifford Work, William Scully and Joseph Seidel-

A poster from *100 Men and a Girl,* the film that firmly established Deanna Durbin as a major star. Miss Durbin's early films were developed under the aegis of two arrivals from Universal's defunct European division, producer Joe Pasternak and director Henry Koster. The Durbin pictures were the mainstay of Universal's financial structure during the latter half of the 1930s.

COURTESY OF UNIVERSAL

man. Under their leadership, Universal reduced overhead, expanded its entire production schedule, and increased sales. They attracted major stars to the studio by giving them a percentage of the profits from their films. Bing Crosby, W. C. Fields, Jimmy Stewart and Marlene Dietrich, among others, made movies under the Universal imprint. Such classics as *Frankenstein* and *Dracula,* were resurrected from the studio's vaults and reissued to raise money for new productions. By the close of 1940, Universal had made an impressive economic recovery.

COLUMBIA GAINS IN STRENGTH

There was an extremely high mortality rate among the smaller studios. Second-level movie companies like Tiffany, Sono Art-World Wide, Invincible and Mayfair Pictures among others, were casualties of the economic austerity and sagging movie attendance which prevailed during the early 1930s. A few of the smaller operations, however, not only survived but prospered during this troubled time. For example, Columbia Pictures, which unlike the majors was not encumbered by the weight of empty theatres, accelerated its ascent to the upper stratum of producer-distributors. In 1929, the studio produced its first all-talking feature, *The Donovan Affair,* a murder mystery starring Jack Holt. The story, based on a play by Owen Davis, was ideal for the early sound era since nearly all of the action took place in one house. During the infancy of sound shooting, cameras had to be encased in stationary sound-proof booths to exclude extraneous mechanical equipment noises from the filming. Despite the lack of flexibility in shooting, *The Donovan Affair,* which was directed by Columbia's greatest asset, Frank Capra, was received with favor by both the critics and the public.

The internecine warfare at Columbia was fierce, Harry and Jack Cohn fought incessantly. In an unsuccessful *coup d'etat,* Jack Cohn and Joe Brandt tried to force Harry Cohn to relinquish his control of the studio operation. A. H. Giannini of the Bank of America, who, in addition to his support of Selznick was also a major investor in Columbia Pictures, sided with Harry Cohn and, consequently, the *coup* failed. Joe Brandt retired, selling his interest in the company for $500,000. He was succeeded as president in 1932 by Harry Cohn. Jack Cohn continued as vice-president and treasurer at the company's New York office, but it was a fragile alliance since the sibling conflict persisted without abatement. After assuming Columbia's presidency Harry Cohn continued in his post as production chief, the only movie magnate to hold both positions simultaneously. Since he was also a principal stockholder in the company, Harry Cohn wielded enormous power at Columbia Pictures. Under Cohn's leadership the company grew rapidly. In 1935, Columbia expanded its physical assets by purchasing a 40-acre tract of land (later expanded to 80 acres) in Burbank, California. By major studio standards, however, Columbia's was a relatively small operation. The company's gross receipts had doubled to $20 million in the first five years of Harry Cohn's presidency. Columbia's peak year of the decade was 1935, when profits exceeded $1.8 million.

Columbia Pictures specialized in low-budget features designed to fill out double bills. Among the studio's staples were the Westerns of Buck Jones and Tim McCoy. The studio had a scant list of contract players. Columbia's legitimate claim to artistic prestige was Frank Capra's *It Happened One Night,* starring Clark Gable and Claudette Colbert. Miss Colbert exercised an option in her Paramount contract that permitted her to make one outside picture a year. Cohn was able to secure the acting services of Gable by offering Louis B. Mayer the directorial talents of Frank Capra for a one picture exchange. More commonly, the practice in the industry was to rent the stars of one studio to another. The lending studio generally received about 75 per cent more than the star's actual salary to compensate for its temporary loss. The borrowing studio enjoyed the advantage of the star's services without incurring the cost of a long-term contract.

Filmed in four weeks at a cost under $300,000, *It Happened One Night* was the smash hit of 1934. The film, which broke records for long-run engagements at many theatres, resulted in Academy Awards for Gable, Colbert, Capra, and screenwriter Robert Riskin. In the triumphant aftermath of the film's success, Harry Cohn signed Frank Capra to six-picture contract at $100,000 a picture plus 25 per cent of profits.

During the latter half of the 1930s Frank Capra made several highly successful social-minded, but somewhat saccharine, films. Capra filled Columbia's coffers with the receipts from such pictures as *Mr. Deeds Goes to Town, Lost Horizon, You Can't Take It With You* and *Mr. Smith Goes to Washington.* Most of Capra's pictures reflected a *Saturday Evening Post* middle-class ethic. In Capra's view of the universe, the gullible and the naive ultimately triumphed over the cunning and the powerful. Screenwriter Robert Riskin and cameraman Joseph Walker contributed significantly to the distinctive Capra style.

In addition to the high-budget Capra films (*Lost Horizon* cost $2 million to produce), Columbia also churned out a large number of "B" pictures. The studio had several series of feature films which flourished during the late 1930s and 1940s. Among the most successful series were *Blondie,* starring Penny Singleton and Arthur Lake, *Boston Blackie,* starring Chester Morris, and *Lone Wolf,* with Warren William portraying the gentleman thief created by Louis Joseph Vance. Some 70 per cent of the 50 or 60 features produced by Columbia each year fell into the low-budget second feature category.

UNITED ARTISTS: UNEVEN FORTUNES

During the Depression years, most of the founding members of United Artists fared badly in their production activities. Mary Pickford, whose popularity as an actress had waned as she outgrew ingenue roles, retired from the screen after appearing in a 1933 production, *Secrets.* Douglas Fairbanks' acting career also declined precipitously during the early 1930s. His final screen performance was in the title role of the 1934 production *The Private Life of Don Juan.*

D. W. Griffith returned to United Artists in 1927 as an employee of Art Cinema for which he directed four pictures: *Drums of Love* (1928), *The Battle of the Sexes* (1928), *Lady of the Pavement* (1929), and *Abraham Lincoln* (1930). The last named was his first all talking-picture. For the most part these pictures were disappointing, both financially and artistically. Griffith exercised an option in his contract with Schenck which permitted him to produce his fifth picture independently. His independent venture, entitled *The Struggle* (1932), was a failure in every respect. In order to pay his debts, Griffith sold his UA stock back to the company for a reported $200,000.

Gloria Swanson, who had joined United Artists at the height of her career, also fared badly in her association with the company. After the *Queen Kelly* debacle, which was filmed in the twilight of the silent era, Joseph Kennedy financed Miss Swanson's first talking-picture, *The Trespasser*. Miss Swanson, unlike many of her silent screen contemporaries, was able, at least initially, to make a successful transition to sound, *The Trespasser,* which was written and directed by Edmund Goulding, was a big hit. But Miss Swanson's success was short-lived. Kennedy backed her second talking-picture, the less successful *What A Widow!,* before abruptly ending the brief partnership. "I questioned his judgment," Miss Swanson told Kennedy's biographer, Richard J. Whalen. "He did not like to be questioned." Miss Swanson then starred in two pictures for Art Cinema, *Indiscreet* and *Tonight or Never,* for which she received a straight salary. To help finance her next independent production, *Perfect Understanding,* Miss Swanson sold her stock in UA back to the company. The film, which opened in New York City in February 1933, was a box-office disaster. Gloria Swanson's career as a producer came to an end.

The enigmatic Howard Hughes had helped to augment United Artists' profits considerably in 1927 with his production of the highly successful *Two Arabian Nights,* a comedy starring William Boyd and Lewis Wolheim, with additional cast members Mary Astor and Boris Karloff. Three years later, Hughes contributed *Hell's Angels,* an aerial spectacular about the heroic flyers of World War I. Every foot of the film bore Hughes' personal imprint. To shoot the movie, he purchased some 80 old airplanes and hired over a hundred stunt pilots. During the filming of the aerial sequences, there were engine failures, mid-air collisions, and a host of other mishaps. Hughes himself, who had learned to fly in preparation for making the movie, was seriously injured when the vintage World War I plane he was piloting crashed. The protracted shooting of *Hell's Angels* took from October 1927 to late 1929—and cost $3 million to produce even though it was shot as a silent picture. During this period the advent of "talkies" had caused a dramatic metamorphosis in the movie industry. Hughes invested another million dollars and remade the film with a sound track. The addition of sound was complicated by the fact that the film's female lead, Scandinavian actress Greta Nissen, spoke little English. Hughes decided to replace her and reshoot the scenes in which she appeared. After testing several actresses he selected an unknown movie extra named Jean Harlow, who had been appearing in Hal Roach's Laurel and Hardy comedies. *Hell's Angels* was a smash hit and Miss Harlow enjoyed a meteoric rise to stardom.

Howard Hughes followed *Hell's Angels* with the release of *The Front Page* (1931), a movie based on the play that Charles MacArthur and Ben Hecht had written about Chicago's politics and newspaper activity. The movie starred veteran actor Adolphe Menjou as city editor, Walter Burns, and newcomer Pat O'Brien as the star reporter, Hildy Johnson. Mary Brian, Edward Everett Horton, and Slim Summerville were also in the cast. *The Front Page,* which was directed by Lewis Milestone, was an artistic and a financial success. The reviewer for the *New York Times* called it "a distinct tribute to the talking film." However, the next three films Howard Hughes released through United Artists *(Age for Love, Cock of the Air,* and *Sky Devils)* were all box office failures.

Hughes ended the first phase of his movie career with the 1932 release, *Scarface,* starring a relatively little known stage actor named Paul Muni in the title role. Another unknown, George Raft, played a key supporting role. Howard Hawks directed *Scarface,* from a screenplay written by Ben Hecht. *Scarface* brought Hughes into his first major confrontation with the censors. The film contained what was, for those times, unprecedented violence. When Hughes' company, Caddo Productions (the name was changed July 1940 to Hughes Productions), submitted the film for approval to the self-regulatory agency of the movie industry, then called the Hays Office, dozens of cuts were demanded. Without the Hays Office's seal of approval most theatres around the country would not show the film. In a rare conciliatory gesture Hughes conceded to most of the dictates of the Hays Office and the film was approved. But despite the Hays Office seal, censorship boards in New York, Pennsylvania, Ohio and other places objected to the violence in the film and refused to allow it to be shown. Hughes brought legal action against the censors, and in most cases he was victorious. *Scarface* filled theatres to capacity throughout the United States and launched Paul Muni and George Raft on phenomenally successful movie careers.

Another able and enterprising independent producer, who released his works under the UA banner, was Walt Disney. He began to distribute his animated cartoons through United Artists in 1932. Disney had first come to Hollywood from Kansas City nine years earlier. He and his brother Roy set up an animation studio together in the rear of a real estate office. One of their early assignments was a cartoon series for Winkler Productions, who distributed through Universal. It was called *Oswald, the Lucky Rabbit.* Around the time that sound films were beginning to revolutionize the movie industry, Walt Disney introduced a rodent-like cartoon character called Mickey Mouse. Disney signed an agreement with the Powers Cinephone Corporation to use the company's recording device exclusively, in return for the financing necessary to produce a series of Mickey Mouse cartoons with sound. Synchronizing music to the frantic pace of a cartoon proved to be a difficult task, but, at length, Disney was successful. On November 18, 1928, Mickey Mouse made his public debut in *Steamboat Willie* at the Colony Theatre in New York City. The musical cartoon was an immediate hit. Soon after the success of Mickey Mouse,

Disney created the first of his Silly Symphony cartoons, a charmingly grotesque mosaic of motion and sound depicting a nighttime outing of skeletons in a graveyard which he called *The Skeleton Dance.* In 1929, Columbia bought Disney's contract from Powers Cinephone for a reported $100,000. For the next three years, Disney distributed his cartoons through Columbia, but he became increasingly dissatisfied with the low production advances he received and he objected particularly to Columbia's practice of block-booking his works with what he regarded as inferior cartoons.

During his years with United Artists, Disney released about 20 cartoons annually—half featuring Mickey and the other half in the Silly Symphony series. The latter included all short films without the mouse. Each cartoon required some 10,000 separate drawings and cost about $27,500 to produce. Prints (Disney for two years had the exclusive rights to Technicolor's three color process for cartoon production), advertising, shipping and various other items added an additional $22,500 to the cost of each cartoon. Under his contract with United Artists, Disney received about 60 per cent (he was paid on a sliding scale) of the rentals paid by the theatres throughout the world that exhibited his cartoons. His gross annual income from these rentals was about $1.4 million. He also received royalties from the 80 or so manufacturers who used the Disney characters to help sell their products. The upbeat theme song, "Who's Afraid of the Big Bad Wolf?," from his 1933 short, *Three Little Pigs,* became a nationwide hit, and added to his profits. When Walt Disney's contract with UA expired in 1937, he switched to RKO where he produced his first feature-length cartoon, the phenomenally successful *Snow White and the Seven Dwarfs.* The primary reason for the prescient Disney's departure from UA, was Samuel Goldwyn's refusal to allow him to keep the television rights to his cartoons.

Several other distinguished independent film producers released their pictures through United Artists at various times during the 1930s and early 1940s, including David O. Selznick,

A scene from *The Skeleton Dance* (top), first of the Silly Symphonies—a series of cartoons based on musical themes, rather than some central character. Throughout the ten year life of the Silly Symphonies series, from 1929 to 1939, seven of the cartoons won Academy Awards. The series ended sometime after Disney's *Snow White and the Seven Dwarfs* (bottom) established that expanded cartoons of the same type had great audience appeal. *Snow White,* a 1937 RKO release, was shown at Radio City Music Hall for five weeks, exceeding by two weeks the run of any film up to that time.

Walter Wanger and Hal Roach. Alexander Korda, the prominent British producer, brought his production unit, London Films, under the UA banner in 1933. His first United Artists' release was *The Private Life of Henry VIII*, starring Charles Laughton in a memorable performance as the much-married monarch. The picture had its world premiere at the Radio City Music Hall in October, 1933 to an enthusiastic public response. Korda's initial contract with United Artists called for two pictures. After the success of Korda's second film, *Catherine the Great*, Schenck signed him to a 16-picture contract. In 1935, Korda became an equal partner in United Artists through the purchase of a block of stock for $640,000. When his subsequent pictures failed to do well at the box office, Korda's relationship with United Artists gradually deteriorated.

In the meantime, United Artists was undergoing changes in its managerial control. Early in 1933, Joseph Schenck decided to dismantle Art Cinema (its production activities had been curtailed because of severe financial losses), and join forces with Darryl Zanuck to form Twentieth Century Pictures (Zanuck had recently left his $5,000 a week job at Warner Brothers after a dispute with Harry Warner). In its first year of operation, the new company produced 12 pictures for United Artists, among which were such big money-makers as *The Bowery* with Wallace Beery, George Raft and Jackie Cooper, *Bulldog Drummond Strikes Back* starring Ronald Colman as the debonair sleuth, and *The House of Rothschild* featuring George Arliss. After various plans to make Twentieth Century a UA partner had failed, Schenck resigned from United Artists and sold his stock back to the company. In the spring of 1935, as noted earlier, Twentieth Century merged with the Fox Film Corporation. Before its merger, Twentieth Century Pictures had produced a total of 18 films for UA release.

Al Lichtman, who had operated United Artists' high-powered distribution system, succeeded Joseph Schenck as president. However, Samuel Goldwyn, by virtue of his prodigious output of profitable films, emerged as the dominant force in United Artists' power constellation. After several heated confrontations with Goldwyn, Lichtman, in office only three months, beat an ignominious retreat. Mary Pickford, United Artists' first vice-president, assumed control of the company temporarily. Relations between Goldwyn and the other United Artists' principals became increasingly strained. By mutual agreement in mid-1936, Dr. A. H. Giannini of the Bank of America, which financed many United Artists' productions, was elected to serve as president and chairman of the board of United Artists under a five-year contract. As a concession to Goldwyn, the UA owners agreed to formalize the understanding that all major decisions in the company would be made by unanimous vote. Management, in essence, was divested of its power. Frustrated in his efforts to keep the feisty Goldwyn in check, Dr. Giannini resigned in the spring of 1938. He received a reported settlement of $168,000 from the company.

Murray Silverstone, formerly head of United Artists' European sales division, was subsequently given the administrative reins at United Artists. He implemented several changes to give greater rewards to United Artists' more active producers. Among the financial incentives he introduced was a reduction in the distribution charges that UA levied against its producers' earnings. But Goldwyn was growing more and more resentful over the failure of the original founders to carry their share of the production load. He is reported to have described Pickford, Fairbanks, and Chaplin as "parasites" and to have said they were "drinking his blood." At the annual meeting of the UA directors in 1939, Goldwyn, through his lawyer Richard Dwight, accused his partners of mismanagement and demanded a sole voting trusteeship. Goldwyn's disenchantment with the other members of the UA hierarchy resulted in a bitter court fight, and in 1941, he sold his stock in United Artists for a reported $300,000.

The profitable productions of the prolific Samuel Goldwyn

Charlie Chaplin in a scene from *The Great Dictator*. In this October 1940 release, Chaplin played a dual role, appearing both as a timid Jewish barber and as Adenoid Hynkel, the ranting, posturing dictator of Tomania. The film alternates between incidents in the life of the little barber and episodes in the career of the hysterical dictator. Their lives come together at the end of the film, when the barber, mistaken for Hynkel, takes the dictator's place before the microphones and delivers a fiery, impassioned, albeit cliché ridden plea for peace and understanding. The picture was banned in several European countries and in Argentina.

had helped considerably to pay the overhead for UA's domestic and international distributing organization. The taste he brought to his productions and his attention to detail became known in the film industry as "the Goldwyn touch." In his 14 years with United Artists, Goldwyn had produced some 50 pictures, 13 more than the combined output of Pickford, Fairbanks, and Chaplin. By 1940 only Charlie Chaplin and Mary Pickford remained of the original founders (Douglas Fairbanks died in 1939), and only Mr. Chaplin was actively making movies. His 1940 release, *The Great Dictator,* a brilliant serio-comic representation of the Hitler mythology, caused a sensation, but his production pace was exceedingly slow. In the years between *A Woman of Paris* (1923) and *The Great Dictator* (1940), Chaplin had made just four films: *The Gold Rush* (1925), *The Circus* (1928), *City Lights* (1931), and *Modern Times* (1936). In its first 21 years of operation, United Artists released over 300 pictures and had a deserved reputation as the "Tiffany" of the movie industry. However, as the company entered the decade of the 1940s, the quality and quantity of its film releases began to decline steadily.

IN UNION THERE IS STRENGTH

The severe economic crisis of the 1930s had given rise to unionism in the movie industry, as it did in other industries. Throughout the era of the silent film, most of the movie industry's creative talent had remained outside the labor movement. The studio craftsmen—carpenters, painters, plumbers and others whose skills were not confined to the movie industry—became the first motion picture employees who attempted to organize and bargain collectively with the studios. In July of 1918, some 500 craftworkers went on strike to achieve a wage increase. The strike, which lasted until September, had forced several studios to close down. Although the craftworkers reached a compromise with the studios on the wage dispute, the producers continued to maintain an open shop. Another strike by the craftworkers in 1923 again failed to gain recognition for their unions. The International Alliance of Theatrical Stage Employees and Moving Picture Machine Operators (IATSE), which had organized projectionists in 1908, had also attempted to unite the various studio crafts and to achieve studio recognition as the representative organization of the craftsman. The result of this action was a jurisdictional dispute between the IATSE and the individual craft unions which aided the producers in maintaining open shop studios.

In 1924, the major studios joined together to form the Association of Motion Picture Producers (AMPP) primarily in an effort to develop a united policy toward labor. Two years later, the leading producing companies and the five unions representing stagehands, carpenters, electricians, painters and musicians signed a trade agreement, called the Studio Basic Agreement, designed to ensure higher wages and better working conditions. A union-management joint committee was set up under the agreement to handle all grievances and disputes; nevertheless, film-making remained an open-shop industry.

Creative and interpretive personnel in the movie industry were much slower to unionize than craftworkers. The Actors' Equity Association, which represented legitimate stage actors, had tried unsuccessfully on several occasions, to gain a foothold in Hollywood. After the studio craftworkers and the musicians had secured recognition of their unions under the Basic Studio Agreement, Equity renewed its drive to organize screen actors. To promote industrial harmony in Hollywood, industry leaders, in May of 1927, established the Academy of Motion Picture Arts and Sciences. It had five branches representing the major divisions of movie production—producers, writers, directors, actors, and technicians—and was open to membership by invitation only. The Academy in effect functioned as a company union, representing creative talent in their labor negotiations with the studios. When the introduction of sound brought an influx of Broadway players to Hollywood, Equity's position in the movie industry was strengthened. The association launched a campaign in 1929 to have 80 per cent Equity representation in every movie cast. Strife and dissension within its ranks, however, soon weakened Equity's bargaining power and the studios were able to stave off its demands. For a time at least, most screen actors seemed content to have the Academy handle their labor problems.

In the harsh economic realities of the early 1930s, however, it was inevitable that the Academy's policies would come under attack. In order to reduce costs and avert wholesale dismissals, industry leaders, working through the Academy, devised a plan to cut salaries for an eight-week period beginning in March of 1933. Salary reductions began at 25 per cent and went up to 50 per cent. Studio workers earning above $100 a week were cut by 50 per cent, providing their total salary did not drop below $75 per week. Those in the $75 to $100 per week bracket lost 25 per cent of their salary, taking home a minimum of $65 per week. An employee earning less than $50 per week lost no income. Full salaries were to be restored at the end of the eight-week period. Although the plan received general endorsement, it was far from popular. When some studios, including Warners and Goldwyn, refused to restore full salaries at the end of the salary-waiver period, many members of the Academy felt betrayed.

Organized labor's time had come in the movie industry. Screen writers were the first to defect from the Academy's ranks. In April 1933, the Screen Writers' Guild (SWG), which had been first formed 13 years earlier, was revived. July brought word that 18 actors, led by Alan Mowbray, had incorporated the Screen Actors Guild (SAG). The deathblow to the Academy as a bargaining agent for creative talent came early in October of 1933 when many of the movie industry's biggest stars, among them James Cagney, Gary Cooper, Ann Harding, Jeanette MacDonald, Robert Montgomery and Paul Muni, joined the Screen Actors Guild.

The mass exodus of star-players from the Academy was precipitated by the publication of the National Recovery Administration's (NRA) final draft of the *Motion Picture Code* in September of 1933. Earlier in the year, President Roosevelt, in an effort to revive the economy, had signed into law the National Industrial Recovery Act (NIRA). Businessmen were called upon to write voluntary "codes of fair competition" under the auspices of the newly formed National Recovery Administration. What the NIRA did in effect was to set aside the antitrust laws and permit industry leaders to devise and codify their own trade practices. As a concession to labor, the NIRA's historic section 7 (a) legitimized collective bargaining.

The final draft of the NRA's film code contained certain provisions which actors and writers found to be particularly objectionable. These provisions concerned fines for producers who used "excessive compensation" to raid a competitor's artists, time periods during which negotiations might be breached with talent under contract to other studios, and permissible activities for agents to engage in their clients' behalf. All of these provisions were designed to curtail the amount of financial maneuvering open to artists and creative workers. The Screen Writers' Guild joined with the Screen Actors Guild to forestall adoption of these protested provisions. SAG president, Eddie Cantor met with President Roosevelt in Warm Springs, Georgia to discuss the guilds' objections to the provisions. A short time later, the provisions were suspended by executive order. Talent guilds eventually became firmly entrenched in the movie industry. In 1936, 40 directors, most of them members of the Academy, struck out on their own to form the Screen Directors' Guild. King Vidor, Lewis Milestone and John Ford were among the new guild's officers. The following year, the Academy amended its by-laws, withdrawing from all matters which concerned labor-management relations. It has since concentrated on technical research and film awards.

In May 1935, the National Industrial Recovery Act was declared unconstitutional by the U.S. Supreme Court. The right of workers to bargain collectively with management through unions, however, was firmly established less than two months later when President Roosevelt signed into law the National Labor Relations Act. (Its constitutionality was upheld by the Supreme Court in April 1937.) Government legislation guaranteeing workers the right to organize and bargain through unions of their choice served to intensify the jurisdictional disputes among unions competing for the support of the movie industry's craftsmen. The IATSE, under the leadership of William B. Browne and William Bioff, who counted among their associates some of Chicago's most infamous gangsters, eventually forced the major producers to recognize it as the sole bargaining agent for studio technicians. To demonstrate its hold over the movie industry, IATSE had instigated a projectionists' strike against the Paramount chain in Chicago, darkening hundreds of theatres. The studio chieftains quickly got the message and decided to negotiate with the union. Early in 1936, IATSE won a closed shop agreement with the leading producing companies. Membership in IATSE became a first condition for employment in any of the classifications within the union's jurisdiction. Overnight IATSE's ranks swelled from 100 to 12,000 members.

The disreputable backgrounds and the gangland tactics of IATSE's hierarchy, however, did not go unnoticed. Newspaper columnist Westbrook Pegler launched a vigorous campaign against Browne and Bioff. In the course of his investigation, Pegler discovered that the two union leaders had a long history of criminal activity. Bioff had been arrested and questioned in connection with at least two murders in Chicago involving trade unionists. Further investigation revealed that Bioff had failed to serve a six-month prison sentence stemming from a 1922 pandering conviction in Chicago.

Browne and Bioff were eventually indicted and tried in federal district court for extortion. The major studios, under threat of strike action, had apparently paid large sums of money to the two union leaders. Executives from Warners, Fox, Loew and Paramount testified that they had made cash payments to Bioff since 1936 totaling $776,000. Nicholas Schenck, head of Loew's, told the court that he had not reported the alleged extortion because he was fearful of a strike. Harry Warner's reasons for acceding to the demands of the union racketeers were more personal. He testified, "I was afraid of bodily harm." Browne and Bioff were convicted and sentenced to long terms in federal prison.

Not all of the studio archons had escaped from the shoddy affair unscathed. Joseph Schenck, chairman of Twentieth Century-Fox and head of the AMPP, was convicted of income-tax evasion in connection with his testimony concerning a $100,000 payment to Bioff. He was sentenced to three years at Danbury prison and fined $20,000. When the government brought suit against Browne and Bioff, Schenck testified against the two labor leaders. In appreciation he was allowed to plead guilty to a charge of perjury and his sentence was reduced. He was paroled after serving four months of a one-year sentence.

RESTRAINT OF TRADE: ROUND ONE

To further compound the economic woes of the eight major movie companies, the Justice Department in 1938, after five years of intensive investigation, filed an antitrust suit against them charging monopolistic trade practices. The eight defendants were Paramount Pictures, Loew's (including Metro-Goldwyn-Mayer), Twentieth Century-Fox, Warner Brothers, Radio-Keith-Orpeum, Universal Pictures, Columbia Pictures, and United Artists. The first five companies, each of which had completely integrated structures of production, distribution, and exhibition, owned the controlling interest in 70 per cent of the first-run theatres in cities with populations exceeding 100,000. They also controlled nearly 60 per cent of the first-run theatres in cities with populations between 25,000 and 100,000.

A delegation of attorneys lead by Will Hays, head of the Motion Picture Producers and Distributors Association, met with President Roosevelt in an attempt to quash the suit, but the architect of the New Deal was unsympathetic to their cause. He referred the entire matter to his Attorney General where the action had originated. On November 14, 1940, the government filed an amended and supplemental complaint which charged the five vertically integrated companies with combining and conspiring to restrain trade unreasonably and with monopolizing the production, distribution and exhibition of motion pictures. Universal, Columbia and United Artists, in their turn, were charged with illegally conspiring with the "Big Five" to restrain trade and to curtail competition. The remedies sought in the government's petition included the elimination of block booking and blind selling, the abolition of unfair clearance, and the elimination of many other producer-distributor trade practices. Most significantly, the government asked for the divorcement of production and distribution from exhibition.

Three days after the case went to trial in the Southern District Court of New York, negotiations for a settlement were undertaken. On November 20, 1940, the government and the five vertically integrated companies became parties to a consent decree. The suit against Columbia, Universal, and United Artists was delayed since they did not own any theatres. Under the consent decree, the five majors, without admitting their guilt, agreed to modify or eliminate certain trade practices. Block booking was limited to five pictures; blind selling was curtailed by requiring trade shows; the forced rental of short films as a condition of obtaining features was abolished; and the use of unreasonable clearance was proscribed. In addition the five majors agreed not to acquire additional theatres during a specified period of time. The American Arbitration Association was selected to resolve any alleged infractions of the selling methods outlined in the decree. The right to initiate arbitration was vested only in the exhibitors. The government, apparently reluctant to disrupt a major industry at a time of international military crisis, did not demand the separation of production and distribution from exhibition. However, the Justice Department did reserve the right at the end of a three-year period to seek further relief if it felt that the decree had not proved effective. The major companies had managed to steal away with only minor concessions, but the wind of antitrust was rising which would eventually shake the economic foundations of the movie industry.

The War and Postwar Transition Years

DURING the Depression years, the diversionary film fare of the major studios had helped to mitigate the wholesale poverty and despair that inflicted the nation. With the dawn of the 1940s, the movies assumed a new significance and influence. As the ominous shadow of war began to envelop all of Asia and Europe in its darkness, Hollywood marshaled its talents and physical resources to combat the enemy on the psychological front. The normally bland fare that was Hollywood's prewar production style had not been offensive to any market—at home or abroad. With the diminishing of the foreign market, due to Hitler's advances and the fortunes of the war, the industry hierarchy allowed their anti-Nazi sentiments to come to the fore. These sentiments were well-expressed by some of the directors and writers who had fled to America, carrying with them the awareness of the extent of the military-political threat that was sweeping Europe. Despite the general isolationist sentiment which still prevailed throughout the country, the studio aristocracy turned to film themes that encouraged American involvement in the developing world war. The huge investments, production capacities and outputs of the major movie companies became an integral part of the nation's propaganda arsenal.

HOLLYWOOD GOES TO WAR

The first major studio to produce a war propaganda feature of any significance was Warner Brothers Pictures. Its explosive 1939 release, *Confessions of a Nazi Spy,* examined the subversive activities of the German-American Bund. Based on a true episode of the exposure of a German spy ring operating in New York, the film starred Edward G. Robinson and Francis Lederer, with Britisher George Sanders as the German head of the spy ring. The film's release caused an uproar from isolationists and pacifists. The German Consulate filed an official complaint, charging that the film was part of an American conspiracy. Fritz Kuhn, head of the American Bund, threatened Warner Brothers with a $5 million libel suit. The film's principal players reportedly received threats on their lives. The ballyhoo surrounding the film—both real and manufactured—served to inflate box-office receipts. During the first week of its premiere at Manhattan's Strand, the film's gross exceeded $45,000. The film was banned, however, in Norway, Denmark, the Netherlands, Sweden, Hungary, Switzerland, Argentina, Brazil, Java, Santo Domingo, San Salvador, Guatemala, Costa Rica, Peru, Ecuador, South Africa and Iraq—all non-aligned or occupied countries.

As the pace of war activity in the United States quickened, other studios joined in the propaganda effort. In the two years prior to American entry into the war, some 50 films with an anti-isolationist viewpoint were released. Early in 1940, Alfred Hitchcock made *Foreign Correspondent* for Walter Wanger. Released through United Artists, the film featured Joel McCrea as a naive American journalist who eventually uncovers an insidious web of Nazi espionage. At the film's conclusion, the

THE PICTURE THAT WILL OPEN THE EYES OF 130,000,000 AMERICANS!

Over there, they wouldn't allow you to see this picture. But this, thank Heaven, is America – where pictures like this can be made and seen and cheered – where a swastika can be called a swastika so that all the world may hear!

Trapped! CONFESSIONS OF A NAZI SPY

SENSATIONAL TRUTH ABOUT NAZI ACTIVITY IN AMERICA!

EDWARD G. ROBINSON

with FRANCIS LEDERER · GEORGE SANDERS · PAUL LUKAS · HENRY O'NEILL
An ANATOLE LITVAK Production

Presented by WARNER BROS.

COURTESY OF UNITED ARTISTS

Confessions of a Nazi Spy, a cinematic exposé of the espionage activities of pro-Nazi groups in the United States, was based on actual evidence presented at the trial of 18 accused spies, four of whom were convicted. The German diplomatic forces worked openly for suppression of the film in the United States as well as abroad. The film was banned unconditionally in 18 Latin American and European nations. American isolationists accused Warners of "war-mongering," a charge that led to Senate investigations in 1941.

reporter fervently enjoined America to arm herself against totalitarianism. United Artists again contributed to the anti-Nazi furor with its October 1940 release of Chaplin's *The Great Dictator,* a satirical examination of fascism in which the comedian, as Hynkel the dictator, brilliantly mimicked the splenetic rantings of Hitler. In MGM's *Escape* (1940), the plight of Nazi victims was dramatized. Another MGM release, *The Mortal Storm* (1940), based on the best selling novel by Phyllis Bottome, chronicled the vicissitudes of a German middle-class family in a small university town at the time of Hitler's rise to power. In Twentieth Century-Fox's 1941 release, *Man Hunt,* a tense melodrama directed by Fritz Lang, Walter Pidgeon portrayed a British big-game hunter who has Hitler in his sights but fails to shoot since he had deliberately neglected to load his rifle.

Series characters also participated in the propaganda campaign. In Fox's *Charlie Chan in Panama,* the famed Oriental sleuth prevented a saboteur from bombing the Canal. Universal updated Sir Arthur Conan Doyle's "The Adventure of the Dancing Men" to pit Sherlock Holmes against the Nazis in *Sherlock Holmes and the Secret Weapon.* Holmes had also battled the Nazis in *Sherlock Holmes and the Voice of Terror.* In *Blondie for the Defense,* a Columbia release, Penny Singleton organized her neighbors into Housewives for America, replete with uniforms and civil defense apparatus. Columbia's Ellery Queen faced a formidable spy group in *Enemy Agents Meet Ellery Queen.* Inevitably a certain uninspired sameness prevailed throughout most of these efforts. Under the guise of entertainment, Hollywood masked an intensive propaganda campaign against the Axis powers. Reaching into their well-worn bag of stereotypes, the studios took the villainous character actors of earlier years and dressed them in the military uniform of the enemy. Films portrayed a simple and stark contrast between good and evil. The threat of confinement in a concentration camp became standard fare. Every film had a seemingly obligatory Gestapo interrogation scene. The more complex underlying causes of the war were, for the most part, ignored. All problems stemmed solely from the evil of the enemy.

In addition to identifying the bestiality of our enemies, American films also served to bring us closer to our Allies. People in Allied countries were depicted as peace loving—although not always egalitarian—foes of tyranny and fascism. The fortitude and courage of the British were presented in such films as *A Yank in the R.A.F.* (1941), *Mrs. Miniver* (1942), and *The White Cliffs of Dover* (1943). In Warner Brothers'

The casting of Nigel Bruce (left) and Basil Rathbone (right) as Dr. Watson and Sherlock Holmes, respectively, was truly inspired. They are shown here in a scene from *Sherlock Holmes and the Voice of Terror,* a 1942 Universal release. This wartime film concerned Nazi sabotage and terror tactics. The film ended with a stirring ode by Holmes to England's plight: "There's an east wind coming, . . . such a wind as never blew on England yet. It will be cold and bitter, Watson, and a good many of us may wither before its blast. But it's God's own wind, none the less, and a cleaner, better, stronger land will lie in the sunshine when the storm has cleared." (The lines were taken from the final passage of Sir Arthur Conan Doyle's "His Last Bow.")

Mission to Moscow, a semi-documentary starring Walter Huston as ambassador John Davies, the tenacity and intelligence of the Soviet leaders was depicted—an ironic twist in view of the subsequent "cold war."

The movie industry's release of war-related films initially met with criticism from many quarters. Senator Burton K. Wheeler, isolationist head of the Interstate Commerce Committee, assailed Hollywood for its "war-mongering propaganda." In September of 1941, Wheeler's committee launched an investigation into the activities of the major studios. Criticism of the movie-makers, however, diminished rapidly after the Japanese attacked Pearl Harbor on December 7, 1941. After Pearl Harbor, the fragile facade of American neutrality collapsed and the country mobilized for war. Movie stars became an essential commodity in the war effort. The fanfare which followed the enlistment of a James Stewart or a Robert Montgomery proved a boon for military recruiters. Bing Crosby, Frank Sinatra, Rita Hayworth, and Marlene Dietrich, among many others, volunteered their talents to the United Service Organization (USO), which provided entertainment and diversion for American servicemen in 3,000 clubs in the United States and nearly 100 clubs in 35 foreign countries.

Major film directors also participated in the war effort. Frank Capra, who became a lieutenant colonel in the U.S. Signal Corps, produced a series of documentary films for the government under the rubric, "Why We Fight." These 50-minute films were intended to indoctrinate new recruits with information about the enemy, their allies, and the reasons for their being sent into battle. The first installment in the series, *Prelude to War,* proved to be such a potent propaganda vehicle that it was shown to civilian audiences throughout the United States. In all, seven films in the "Why We Fight" series were produced. In addition to being shown to American military personnel, the films were presented to civilian audiences in Allied countries.

The creative talent of Walt Disney's studio also contributed significantly to the nation's propaganda arsenal. Disney's studio produced hundreds of thousands of feet of film for the government on a diversity of topics. Subjects ranging from the topography of enemy-held islands to the surveillance of

Donald Duck is forced to carry a heavy bass drum in this scene from Walt Disney's propaganda cartoon *Der Fuehrer's Face*. The cartoon was originally titled *Donald Duck in Nutzi Land*. *Der Fuehrer's Face* was the name of a novelty song written for the film short by Oliver Wallace, a Disney studio composer. When Spike Jones' RCA Victor recording of *Der Fuehrer's Face* became a nationwide sensation, Walt Disney decided to change the title of the picture to that of the song. The lyrical affront to the Nazis began: "Ven der Fuehrer says: 'Ve iss der Master Race,' Ve Heil! Heil! Right in der Fuehrer's face." Every mock "Heil!" in the song was followed by a raucous razzberry (Bronx cheer).

enemy aircraft, were presented using the whimsical cartoon caricatures or other graphic skills of the Disney organization. For example, in *The New Spirit,* Donald Duck amusingly and convincingly explained the new wartime income tax laws, adding considerable numbers of new taxpayers to the rolls and increasing the government's income for the war effort. Some 1,100 prints of the film short were ordered by the Treasury Department for dissemination to theatres throughout the country. *The New Spirit* was seen by an estimated 26 million people, 37 per cent of whom reported in a Gallup poll that the film had a direct effect on their willingness to pay taxes. Disney's most popular propaganda film was *Der Fuehrer's Face,* a cartoon short in which the goose-stepping regimentation of Nazism is depicted when the irascible Donald Duck dreams that he is working in a German munitions factory. He awakens from this nightmare clutching a miniature Statue of Liberty.

In mid-1940, the leaders of the motion picture industry had formed the Motion Picture Committee Cooperating for National Defense. The purpose was to distribute, transport and exhibit government-made films dealing with national defense. The major studios assisted the government in producing a diversity of shorts. After the attack on Pearl Harbor, the Committee changed its name to War Activities Committee-Motion Picture Industry and expanded its membership to include exhibitors and theatre owners. Some 16,000 movie houses were committed to the exhibition of government propaganda shorts which were released every other week. On alternating weeks, the major studios provided a series of short subjects on various war themes under the heading *America Speaks.* Among the more effective films in this series was MGM's two-reel production *Mr. Blabbermouth,* which stressed the danger of careless talk in wartime. The studios produced the *America Speaks* series without any charge to the government. At the height of the war, some 50 per cent of the screen time available for shorts went to the government war effort. The War Activities Committee also promoted the sale of war bonds and netted close to $37 million from motion picture audiences.

To deal with the problem of propaganda and censorship, President Roosevelt, on June 13, 1942, established the Office of War Information (OWI). The agency was headed by Elmer Davis who, prior to his appointment, had been a news analyst and commentator for the Columbia Broadcasting System. The OWI included, under the direction of Lowell Mellett, a former Scripps-Howard editor, a Motion Pictures Bureau whose primary function was to serve as a liaison between the movie industry and the government. Among other services, the Bureau supplied motion picture makers with the special information necessary for the production of various war films. Although the Bureau's functions were purely advisory, the government had the power to invoke sanctions against recalcitrant movie makers through the War Production Board, a federal agency formed in January 1942 to set priorities for the nation's industrial and economic resources. The War Production Board held the power of life and death over Hollywood through control of raw film supply. Few means of coercion are as effective as those which threaten an industry's income and profits. Such potent instruments of control, however, rarely had to be invoked since the implicit threat was sufficient to compel compliance. The shortage of materials, nevertheless, took its toll on the movie industry. Lumber was a particularly scarce commodity. Paints, shellacs, lacquers, and thinners were also in short supply. As a result, costs for set construction on any one picture were limited to $5,000. In the pre-war years, the sets for a major production often exceeded $50,000.

Compounding the difficulties of the film industry due to economic stringencies were a series of political vicissitudes. Harry S. Truman, then Senator from Missouri, took up the Congressional cudgels against the movie industry in 1943. His Special Committee Investigating the National Defense Program, commonly known as the Truman Committee, wanted to know, among other things, how so many movie personnel had managed to wangle officers' commissions. Most important, the committee was concerned with the fact that a small number of studios seemed to dominate government contracts for film making. The allocation of government film projects was coordinated by the Research Council of the Academy of Motion Picture Arts and Sciences, which was chaired by Darryl F. Zanuck. During a 20-month period, beginning in January 1941, more than 70 per cent of the government's film business went to four studios—Paramount, Twentieth Century-

Fox, RKO, and MGM. Pressure from the Truman Committee resulted in the war department terminating its arrangement with the Research Council.

Although burdened by labor and material shortages, and forced to suffer an occasional outburst of Congressional scorn, the major studios, nevertheless prospered during the war. Indeed, the war provided an economic windfall for the entire movie industry. Throughout the war years, Hollywood's production of new features was only slightly below the peacetime level and the public attended movies with increased enthusiasm. Some estimates put the number of tickets being sold each week at 100 million, a figure much larger than the film industry was willing to admit. A more conservative estimate showed average weekly attendance at a stable 85 million.

REPUBLIC AND MONOGRAM

The box-office boom during the war years also provided a financial boost for several of the smaller companies that primarily turned out low-budget features, so-called "B" pictures, to fill the lower half of double bills in small-town and neighborhood theatres. The two most successful studios in this category were Republic and Monogram.

The Republic studio was the creation of a former tobacco executive named Herbert J. Yates, who operated a film-processing laboratory called Consolidated Film Laboratories. Early in 1935, Yates foreclosed on two of his customers, the Monogram and Mascot studios, and merged them with other small producing units to form a new company, Republic Pictures. One of the most successful film genres nurtured at Republic was the musical Western, which was launched in 1935 with *Tumbling Tumbleweeds*, starring Gene Autry. During his years with Republic, Autry made some 58 musical Western features. When Autry joined the military service in 1942, Roy Rogers replaced him in the saddle at Republic as the studio's number one musical Western star. The Autry and Rogers features were big box-office successes. Serials were another Republic staple. The studio ground out dozens of low-budget chapter-plays under such titles as *The Phantom Rider* and *Secret Service in Darkest Africa*. Republic's most important female star was Vera Hruba Ralston, a former skating champion from Czechoslovakia who, in the 1940s, became Queen of the studio after she married Yates. Her films, however, showed almost consistently poor returns at the box-office.

The Monogram imprint was resurrected in 1937 after the studio's founder, W. Ray Johnston, had decided to break with Republic and reorganize his own production company. By the end of 1937, the new Monogram had some 20 films in release. The studio's series pictures constituted staple production at Monogram. These featured cut-to-pattern characters who had gained audience acceptance. The box-office success of Boris Karloff as an urbane, oriental sleuth in the 1938 production *Mr. Wong, Detective,* for example, prompted the release of *The Mystery of Mr. Wong* and *Mr. Wong in Chinatown* the following year and two more *Wong*-Karloff features in 1940, *The Fatal Hour* and *Doomed to Die*. One of the most profitable series for Monogram featured several of the "Dead End Kids" from Samuel Goldwyn's 1937 production, *Dead End*. At Monogram the youthful actors became known as the "East Side Kids" in such vehicles as *Boys of the City, That Gang of Mine* and *Pride of the Bowery*. Bobby Jordan and Leo Gorcey were the first of the "Kids" to join the Monogram fold, followed by Huntz Hall and Gabriel Dell. The cheaply made Monogram films featuring the East Side Kids later became a staple of Saturday morning television. Other Monogram series included the *Cisco Kid, Charlie Chan* and *Bomba the Jungle Boy* films. (The latter series was produced by Walter Mirisch who, with his two brothers, later founded a spectacularly successful independent production company that made such critically acclaimed films as *The Magnificent Seven, West Side Story* and *In the Heat of the Night.*)

During World War II, both Republic and Monogram contributed their light artillery to the nation's propaganda weaponry. Republic's wartime releases included *London Blackout Murders,* in which all the victims are members of a Nazi spy ring, and *Secrets of Scotland Yard,* an improbable tale about a spy in the code room of the British Admiralty. Monogram's *Women in Bondage* dealt with the humiliation and shame suffered by women in Nazi Germany. The studio's other wartime releases included *Enemy of Women,* which featured Paul Andor as the infamous Dr. Paul Joseph Goebbels. Although both Republic and Monogram fared well during the war years, their profit margins were small, since most exhibitors would only show a B-picture on a flat-rental basis regardless of the film's box-office appeal. This practice, while often beneficial to the theatre owner, imposed an artificial ceiling on the potential profits of the production studio.

THE EMERGENCE OF TELEVISION

The major movie companies survived the war years with their powers and prerogatives intact. Industry leaders looked to the future with seemly justified optimism. Official estimates put average weekly movie attendance in 1946 at an all-time high of 90 million. Profits soared to a record $120 million. During the next few years, however, the production capacity of the movie industry began to exceed the public's willingness to consume its product. The reasons for the decline were numerous. A diversity of activities competed with motion pictures for the public's recreational and leisure time. Bowling and miniature golf became the rage. Automobiles, in scarce supply during the war, became readily available. Many families reverted to single-income budgets as soldiers resumed civilian jobs. The studio leaders were briefly confounded, but they recovered their composure quickly. Production schedules were slashed and long-term contracts with producers, directors, writers, actors and technicians were allowed to lapse. In the fall of 1947, MGM's Louis B. Mayer cut his studio staff by 25 per cent. Other studios soon adopted similar cost-cutting measures. Employment in the various craft unions fell from 22,100 in 1946 to 13,500 in 1949. An atmosphere of disquiet and anxiety pervaded the movie colony as the big studios went through retrenchment and reorganization. The most foreboding factor was the specter of television, which loomed ominously large on the horizon.

Television had been a technical reality since the late 1930s, but the intervention of war had impeded its commercial progress. After the war, television emerged as a medium of unparalleled power and reach. By 1948, television sets were being sold at the rate of 200,000 a month. In that year, the number of television stations in the nation increased from 17 to 41. In some areas, however, movie theatres had a brief respite from the onslaught of television. In the fall of 1948, the Federal Communications Commission (FCC), the regulatory agency for the broadcast industry, instituted a "freeze" on the allocation of new television channels so that it could study interference problems. At the time of the freeze there were 108 television stations authorized to go on the air. During the freeze period 11 cities across the country were without any television service. Major cities like Houston, Kansas City, Milwaukee, Pittsburgh and St. Louis had only one station each. New York and Los Angeles, however, each enjoyed seven television stations and although the FCC's freeze on new allocations lasted nearly four years, it did not forestall television's ascent into the entertainment industry's power constellation. Television's presence was quickly felt in many quarters. In many cities, restaurant and night club attendance fell off, taxicab receipts dropped, and radio listening declined sharply. Movie exhibitors, however, were hit hardest. All across the country theatre marquees darkened, permanently. Despite a sharp rise in the population of the United States in the decade following World War II—from 141 million people to 167 million—the estimated average weekly movie attendance fell from 90 million in 1946 to less than 47 million ten years later.

HOLLYWOOD UNDER ATTACK

The emergence of television was not the only blow suffered by the movie industry in the late 1940s. Beginning in 1947, the major studios were beset with a series of assaults from which they never fully recovered. The first attack came in 1947 when the House Committee on Un-American Activities decided to investigate alleged Communist infiltration of the movie industry. Investigations and accusations of Communist encroachment were not new to the movie community. Those of liberal persuasion in the highly visible and carefully scrutinized film industry were particularly vulnerable to the publicity-seeking, over-zealous protectors of the national security. Back in 1940, Representative Martin Dies of Texas, the chairman of the House Committee on Un-American Activities, had descended on Los Angeles in pursuit of Communists but his investigation met with little success. Three years later, some of moviedom's brightest luminaries formed the Motion Picture Alliance for the Preservation of American Ideals in an effort to exorcise the Communist spirit from Hollywood. The organization eventually included among its membership Gary Cooper, Walt Disney, Clark Gable, Adolphe Menjou, Ayn Rand, Lela Rogers (Ginger's mother), Barbara Stanwyck and John Wayne. Congressman John Rankin of Mississippi had placed himself in the movie spotlight in 1945 with accusations about subversive activities. However, even Rankin's most ardent supporters were chagrined by his blatant anti-Semitic and racist remarks. That same year, anti-Communism became the rallying standard for Roy Brewer, Los Angeles head of the International Alliance of Theatrical Stage Employees (IATSE), in his jurisdictional dispute with the Conference of Studio Unions (CSU) over who would represent set decorators. The dispute escalated into an industry-wide strike by the CSU that lasted nearly eight months. During this period, the antagonism against alleged Communist infiltrators intensified. Another CSU strike in fall of 1946, brought many more converts to the anti-Communist cause.

The anti-Communist sentiment of the first half of the 1940s had been held in check because of the United States' alignment with the Soviet Union in the fight against the Axis powers. After the war, when Soviet-American relations deteriorated, there was an upsurge in anti-Communist activity. In May 1947, a subcommittee of the House Committee on Un-American Activities held closed hearings in the Biltmore Hotel in Los Angeles, to investigate the extent of Communist influence in the movie industry. Many of the witnesses who appeared before the subcommittee were members of the Motion Picture Alliance for the Preservation of American Ideals. In September of the same year the subcommittee issued subpoenas to 41 witnesses, 19 of whom announced they would not cooperate with the investigation. The initial reaction to the subpoenas seemed to be a closing of ranks. Eric Johnston, president of the Motion Picture Association of America, stated that his organization would never countenance blacklisting. A Committee for the First Amendment was formed by William Wyler and John Huston in an effort to thwart incursions against free speech and free assembly. Its membership included Henry Fonda, Katharine Hepburn, Gregory Peck and Cornel Wilde. Any investigation into an individual's political beliefs, the Committee argued, was antithetical to the spirit and the letter of the Constitution.

On October 20, 1947, in the Caucus Room of the old House office building in Washington D.C., the subcommittee of the House Committee on Un-American Activities, chaired by Representative J. Parnell Thomas of New Jersey, began public hearings to investigate Communist infiltration of the movie industry. The other members of the subcommittee who sat behind the long table facing the witness chair were Representatives John McDowell of Pennsylvania, Richard Vail of Illinois, John Wood of Georgia and Richard Nixon of California. Scores of news-gathering agencies, many equipped with newsreel and television cameras, were on hand to cover the spectacle. Some of moviedom's best known figures, representing the Committee for the First Amendment, occupied the 300 spectator seats. Uniformed police were on guard outside the hearing room to control the crowd that congregated in the corridors to catch a glimpse of the illustrious participants.

During the first week of the hearings, 24 "friendly" witnesses testified before the subcommittee. Jack L. Warner, Robert Taylor, Louis B. Mayer, Adolphe Menjou, Leo McCarey, Walt Disney, Ayn Rand, Lela Rogers, and Gary Cooper were among those who testified. Although they produced very little evidence of subversion, they did provide some amusement. Actor Adolphe Menjou, a self-proclaimed expert on Communism, claimed that one could inject Communism into a movie by a look, an inflection, a change in voice, but he was unable to identify specific examples of such activities in motion pictures. Walt Disney told how attempts had been made to have Mickey Mouse espouse Communism. Lela Rogers explained how she had fought valiantly, but unsuccessfully, to prevent RKO from producing *None But the Lonely Heart*. She regarded the story as Communist propaganda because of its low key, moody and somber tone. Ayn Rand, author of *The Fountainhead*, testified that hardly anyone in the Soviet Union smiled.

The following week the "unfriendly" witnesses had their turn. Of the 19 recalcitrant individuals who were originally subpoenaed to appear only 11 were called, and the eleventh, Bertolt Brecht, the German playwright and poet, after denying Communist Party membership, made a precipitous retreat to East Germany, never to return. The 10 witnesses who refused to cooperate in any way with the subcommittee were: Adrian Scott, producer; Edward Dmytryk, director; and writers Alvah Bessie, Herbert Biberman, Lester Cole, Ring Lardner Jr., John Howard Lawson, Albert Maltz, Samuel Ornitz and Dalton

Trumbo. Each witness went to the stand, gave his name, address and occupation, attempted to read a prepared statement denouncing the subcommittee investigation, and then, after that had been ruled inadmissible, avoided answering the question as to whether or not he was, or ever had been, a member of the Communist Party. Only Albert Maltz had been permitted to read his entire statement. Even those opposed to the hearings must have been unnerved by the abrasiveness and insolence of many of the witnesses. John Howard Lawson, the first of the "unfriendly" witnesses to testify, appeared to be deliberately arrogant and unruly. He was dragged shouting from the witness stand. After each witness left the stand a subcommittee investigator read a lengthy dossier into the record detailing the witness's alleged Communist affiliations. For reasons which were never fully explained, Representative Thomas abruptly ended the hearings on Thursday of the second week with eight of the subpoenaed "unfriendly" witnesses still uncalled.

A barrage of protests, both pro and con, followed the hearings. On the side of the "Hollywood Ten," as the recalcitrant witnesses came to be called, were the members of the Committee for the First Amendment. The Committee's facade of courage, however, quickly collapsed. As the public pressure mounted, many of its members disavowed their roles. In the vanguard of those supporting the HUAC investigations was the American Legion which waged an all-out campaign against Communists and Communist sympathizers. The Legion along with other veterans and civic groups called for the boycotting of theatres that showed Communist associated films. In a series of front-page editorials, William Randolph Hearst lashed out at the Communist "infestation" of the movie industry, raising the recurrent specter of government censorship which has periodically plagued the industry since its very inception.

Initially, the major studios resisted the economic impulse to blacklist the Hollywood Ten. At the time of the hearings five of the "unfriendly" witnesses were under contract. Ring

Lardner Jr.'s contract with Twentieth Century-Fox expired two weeks after the hearings but was promptly renewed. Edward Dmytryk and Adrian Scott were assured by RKO's studio head, Dore Schary, that their jobs were secure; at MGM, Lester Cole and Dalton Trumbo were kept on the payroll. However, as the anti-Communist movement gathered momentum, the resistance of the industry's reigning powers weakened. On November 24, 1947, the House of Representatives voted overwhelmingly for the citation of the Hollywood Ten for contempt of Congress. On the same day, some 50 members of the movie industry's hierarchy—representing all the major companies—assembled in the Waldorf Astoria Hotel in New York City to discuss a uniform policy for dealing with the recalcitrant witnesses. The meeting was chaired by Eric Johnston, head of both the Association of Motion Picture Producers and the Motion Picture Association of America. In what has become known as the Waldorf Declaration of 1947, the major motion picture producers—all of whom were members of the Association of Motion Picture Producers—pledged that they would not knowingly employ persons believed to be Communists. The actions of the Hollywood Ten, stated the declaration, "have been a disservice to their employers and have impaired their usefulness to the industry." Those among the Ten who were still employed were either fired or suspended without pay. More than a decade would pass before they were again employable in Hollywood under their own names. The cornerstone of the motion picture blacklist had been firmly embedded. Among the industry's leaders Dore Schary, then production chief at RKO, was one of the few who consistently expressed opposition to this policy; although even he conceded that some sort of public relations gesture was necessary to counteract the adverse publicity which resulted from the hearings.

In the ensuing months, the Hollywood Ten, on a charge of contempt of Congress, were indicted, arraigned, tried, convicted, sentenced and released on bail pending appeal. John Howard Lawson was the first to be tried and found guilty.

A short time later Dalton Trumbo's trial ended with the same verdict. The general consensus was that the final outcome of their appeals would determine the fate of the entire group. In the spring of 1950, the U.S. Supreme Court refused to review their convictions. All ten went to jail to serve sentences of up to a year. Ironically, J. Parnell Thomas, who was convicted in December 1949 of padding his payroll, was sent to the Federal Corrections Institution at Danbury, Connecticut where his fellow inmates included Ring Lardner Jr. and Lester Cole.

After their release from prison, the Hollywood Ten found themselves unemployable under their own names. The only exception was director Edward Dmytryk who, upon release, avoided further reprisals by recanting his political beliefs in a "friendly" appearance before the subcommittee of House Committee on Un-American Activities in 1951. The Committee had resumed its public hearings that year with Representative John S. Wood in command. During this round, actors Howard da Silva and Will Geer, and actress Gale Sondergaard (who was married to Herbert Biberman) were among the "unfriendly" witnesses. Actor Larry Parks, who had starred in *The Jolson Story,* also appeared before the Committee. He admitted that he had been a member of the Communist Party, but when asked to name other members of the party he demurred, at least initially. In a humiliating display of expiation, Parks pleaded with the Committee not to force him "to crawl through the mud and to be an informer." Parks apparently had little choice but to give the Committee the names it sought. In 1950, the U.S. Supreme Court had ruled in *Rogers v. U.S.* that once a witness had admitted his own party membership he lost his immunity privilege under the Fifth Amendment and could not refuse to answer questions about other people's party membership. Parks later testified fully in executive session. Sterling Hayden, who also admitted he had belonged to the Communist Party, was not as timid as Parks in naming fellow Communists. Actress Karen Morley and writer-director Abraham Polonsky were among those named by Hayden. Lee

J. Cobb, Elia Kazan and Clifford Odets also cooperated with the Committee by providing names. José Ferrer and John Garfield, on the other hand, denied that they had ever been members of the Communist Party. In all, some 90 witnesses testified at the second set of hearings; about a third of them provided the subcommittee with the names of those they thought to be Communists. The rest were "unfriendly" witnesses who sought refuge under the Fifth Amendment.

As the hearings proceeded along their inevitable course, panic permeated the movie colony. Producers rushed to rid their rolls of individuals who might cause embarrassment. Once established and accepted, the practice of blacklisting spread to epidemic proportions. Uncooperative witnesses soon found themselves unemployable. Those fortunate enough to find employment were forced to work under pseudonyms for cut-rate salaries. For actors and actresses the blacklist was particularly onerous, since the principal commodity they had to sell were their identities. Many of the blacklistees turned to alcohol; a few, in total despair, committed suicide. It was a sorrowful and shameful period for the movie industry.

THE PARAMOUNT CASE

The most devastating blow of all to the movie industry's pyramid of power was not the "communist" charge, but a U.S. Supreme Court decision. In 1948 the government's antitrust suit against the eight major companies in the *Paramount* case, which was originally instituted a decade earlier, was finally settled. The Justice Department had reactivated its suit against Paramount and the seven other major companies late in the summer of 1944. The case went to trial in October of the following year before a three-judge panel of the Federal District Court in the Southern District of New York. This time, the government pressed for the separation of production and distribution from exhibition. On New Year's Eve in 1946, the district court issued a final decree in the government's nearly nine-year old antitrust suit. The court found that the distribution practices of the major companies violated the provisions of the Sherman Act and it enjoined them from such practices as forced blockbooking, co-operative theatre management and pooling, and the fixing of minimum admission prices. In an effort to end unreasonable discrimination against small independent theatres, the district court ordered a system of competitive bidding for films. It did not, however, compel the studios to divest themselves of their theatre holdings.

The district court's decision failed to satisfy either side, and both the plaintiff and the defendants appealed the case to the U.S. Supreme Court. Early in May of 1948, the High Court voted unanimously to uphold the general verdict of the lower court with respect to unfair trade practices, but rejected competitive bidding as a workable solution. The Supreme Court remanded the question of theatre ownership to the lower court for reconsideration. The district court decided in 1949 that the separation of production and distribution from exhibition was the appropriate remedy.

The five vertically integrated companies, beginning with RKO and continuing with Paramount, Warner Brothers, Twentieth Century-Fox, and Loew's-MGM signed a consent decree that broke the corporate chains linking production and distribution to exhibition. The consent decree called for the divestiture of specific theatres as well as the divorcement of theatre circuits. The divestiture of individual theatres progressed slowly, impeded by the advent of television which had drastically reduced the value of many exhibition outlets. Indeed, many theatres which were not designated for divestiture were closed anyway because of dwindling box-office receipts. Since RKO and Paramount, which did not wait for the district court's inevitable edict, were the first two of the Big Five to sign consent decrees, they obtained a major concession. The new production and distribution companies were permitted, in due course, to acquire theatres while the new theatre companies were eventually permitted to produce films so long as the reintegration did not impair competition.

The old Paramount company was dissolved and its assets were transferred to two new companies: Paramount Pictures Corporation and United Paramount Theatres. The latter company merged in 1953 with the American Broadcasting Company, and Leonard H. Goldenson, who had been president of the theatre operation, assumed the presidency of the newly formed American Broadcasting-Paramount Theatres, Inc. In July of 1965, the parent company's name was changed to the American Broadcasting Companies, Inc.

RKO, which was a holding rather than an operating company, was reorganized in 1950 into two new holding companies, the RKO Pictures Corporation, and the RKO Theatres Corporation. All of the assets related to the theatre operation, including RKO's chain of 124 movie houses, were transferred to the new theatre company. The new RKO Pictures Corporation acquired: RKO Radio Pictures, Inc., the principal feature-picture making and distributing subsidiary; RKO Pathé, which primarily produced short subjects and commercial films; and RKO's various television and real estate interests. RKO stockholders received shares in each of the new, independent companies.

The other three integrated companies—Warner Brothers, Twentieth Century-Fox and Loew's-MGM—attempted to forestall divorcement through a series of appeals, but eventually they acceded to the government's demands. Warner Brothers signed the consent decree in January, 1951 and later split into two new companies, Warner Brothers Pictures and the Stanley Warner Corporation. Six months later Twentieth Century-Fox signed the decree and transferred its 385 theatres to a new company, National Theatres, Inc. Both companies were given two years to complete the divorcement. The last of the Big Five to undergo divorcement was Loew's-MGM, whose separation was stalled because of complications in allocating the company's large debt between the production and theatre operations. The split was not finally completed until March, 1959.

Columbia, Universal and United Artists, none of which owned theatres, had filed for a separate consent decree but they were forced to submit to the same trade restrictions as the Big Five. Nevertheless, the *Paramount* decision ultimately proved to be financially advantageous to the three smaller companies. United Artists, in particular, prospered in the post-*Paramount* era.

ASCENDENCY OF UNITED ARTISTS

During the 1940s, the fortunes of United Artists had declined steadily. By the end of the decade, United Artists had little product, no profit, and banking institutions had become increasingly reluctant to advance production money to the few independent producers who were still releasing through the company. Chaplin and Pickford, who were frequently not on speaking terms with each other, were UA's sole owners. All the other member-owners had sold their shares back to the company by the mid-'40s, and by July 1950, UA had no cash reserves. At this juncture, Paul McNutt, a former governor of Indiana, and his associates, assumed managerial control of United Artists. They were given an option to buy 90 per cent of the company after two years for $5.4 million. The fortunes of United Artists continued to plummet under McNutt's administration. By the close of the year, UA had a deficit of $871,000. McNutt clearly lacked the practical experience in the movie business necessary to make the company solvent. Amid rumors of mergers, bankruptcy, and dissolution, McNutt agreed to step aside, and control of United Artists passed to lawyers Arthur Krim and Robert Benjamin, whose New York law firm, Philips, Nizer, Benjamin, and Krim specialized in movie litigation. These two lawyers, together with their associates, struck a unique bargain with the UA owners. If the new management could turn a profit within any one of the ensuing three years, Krim, Benjamin and their associates would acquire 50 per cent of the company's stock and a voting trust would give them full control of UA until 1961.

In February 1951, when Robert Benjamin and Arthur Krim assumed control of UA as, respectively, chairman and president, the company was more than $1 million in debt, and losing money at the rate of $100,000 a week. The new management team's first objective was to generate money and movies. Walter Heller, a Chicago financier perceiving a potential opportunity for profits, agreed to loan UA $1.5 million for prints and advertising and another $2 million to help finance new movies. An additional $500,000 loan came from Twentieth Century-Fox. United Artists, in turn, agreed to give its film processing work to Deluxe Laboratories, a Fox subsidiary.

In order to increase its film inventory quickly, the new management bought the distribution rights to the 300 features of the short-lived Eagle-Lion, a company which railroad magnate Robert R. Young had organized in 1943. A search through the vaults of Europe yielded some additional product. Good fortune came to the new managers in the form of Stanley Kramer, who had almost completed production on a Western before leaving United Artists for Columbia. (He returned to UA in 1955.) Since Kramer still owed one picture on his UA contract, Columbia, thinking the Western lacked action, agreed to let it be distributed by United Artists. This film, called *High Noon,* became one of the biggest box office successes of the decade. Another big picture came to United Artists from Sam Spiegel. UA assisted him in financing *African Queen,* starring Humphrey Bogart and Katharine Hepburn, in return for the U.S. distribution rights to the film. By the end of 1951, United Artists showed a profit of $313,000. It was the first time the company had been in the black since 1946. Krim and Benjamin, along with their associates, became half-owners of the company.

United Artists soon embarked on a policy of financing the motion pictures of actors and directors as well as independent producers, foreshadowing the commercial practices prevalent today. This practice was not totally new to the company. As early as 1942, United Artists had funded the independent productions of James Cagney. (Cagney had severed ties with Warner Brothers after making *Yankee Doodle Dandy* in order to set up his own company in partnership with his brother William.) But under Benjamin and Krim the policy of financing the independent productions of actors was greatly expanded. John Wayne, Burt Lancaster, Gregory Peck, and Robert Mitchum, among others, joined UA's roster of actor-producers. Many with creative talent were attracted into the UA fold by the assurance that they could make their pictures wherever and however they wished. UA provided some measure of financing, assisted in such particulars as leasing studio space and drawing contracts, and guaranteed promotion and distribution. United Artists' policy of trusting talent to make their own films with a minimum of front office interference, encouraged directors like Otto Preminger, Billy Wilder, Joseph Mankiewicz and William Wyler to release their films under the UA banner. Generally, the profits from a UA film were divided evenly—half to the producer for making the film and half to UA for distributing it. Terms, of course, varied according to the reputation of the producer and the nature of the film being produced. United Artists' gross went up from $18 million in 1951 to $43 million in 1954.

In February 1955, Charlie Chaplin (who had exiled himself in Switzerland to avoid the harassment he suffered in this country because of his alleged Communist sympathies) sold his UA stock to the Krim and Benjamin forces for $1.1 million. In 1956, they acquired Miss Pickford's stock interests for $3 million. The managing partners now owned the company outright. In the spring of 1957, United Artists offered shares to the public, and soon after the company was listed on the board of the New York Stock Exchange. United Artists' releases during the 1950s included such now historic films as Otto Preminger's *The Moon is Blue* (1953), the Hecht-Lancaster production of *Marty* (1955), and Michael Todd's *Around the World in 80 Days* (1957). Throughout this period, United Artists continued to grow in both prestige and economic statute. In 1958 alone, this company realized a profit of $3.7 million.

THE AILING LION

Not all of the movie industry's aristocracy fared equally well during the 1950s. The sales volume and profit margins of several of the major companies continued to decline. Even the once majestic Metro-Goldwyn-Mayer studio fell into trouble. By the time MGM celebrated its twenty-fifth anniversary in 1949, the company was in a state of deterioration. The slick, glossy, superficial film fare introduced by MGM's trademark of Leo the lion no longer seemed to attract the movie-going public. Shareholders were becoming increasingly alarmed over the studio's losses and many critical observers began to prepare obituaries for the debilitated lion. Louis B. Mayer, who had reigned over the studio since its founding in 1924, struggled desperately to preserve his shaken empire, but his efforts were unsuccessful. Under Dore Schary, who had been appointed production chief in July of 1948, there had been some appreciable improvement in the studio product. Such box-office successes as *Battleground, Father of the Bride, King Solomon's Mines,* and *An American in Paris* had helped to prop up the company's sagging revenues. However, Schary soon came into conflict with the aging Mayer over how the studio's rich reservoir of talent and technique should best be employed. Nicholas Schenck sided with Schary and, in 1951, Mayer, the archetype of the old-style movie mogul, angrily resigned. Under the terms of his contract settlement, Mayer received $2.6 million for his 10 per cent interest in the residual rights of all pictures produced at the studio since 1924.

Dore Schary assumed full command of the studio, but his success was short-lived. Under his regime MGM produced a number of hits, including *Ivanhoe, Singing in the Rain, Million Dollar Mermaid* and *Julius Caesar.* But the revenue from these films was not enough to compensate for the enormous financial overhead of the studio operation. Schary also had his share of failures. *Jupiter's Darling,* an Esther Williams vehicle, showed a loss of over $2 million and *Plymouth Adventure,* the story of the seventeenth century settlers who came to America, lost a reported $1.8 million. Late in 1955, 76-year old Nicholas Schenck withdrew as president to assume the newly created position of chairman of the board. Arthur Loew, the 56-year old son of the founder, reluctantly succeeded Schenck as president; but he relinquished the post after less than a year in office. He returned to his former position as head of Loew's International and also assumed the position of chairman of the board. Nicholas Schenck became MGM's honorary chairman. It was purely a nominal title, and he retired at the end of the year. After various replacements were considered, the title of president, and the task of revitalizing MGM fell to Joseph Vogel, head of Loew's theatre operation. Within a month after assuming the presidency, Vogel fired Dore Schary and appointed Benjamin Thau, MGM's long-time casting director, as administrative head of the studio.

The departure of Schary signaled an end to the old studio system. MGM, one of the last of the majors to operate with its own stock company, began to sign with independent producers and stars under short-term contracts for a limited number of pictures. The studio arranged for financing, and the producing agent invested enough of his own money in the project to qualify for the lower corporate profits taxation. Generally, the deal called for the producer to receive a percentage of the aggregate earnings from the entire package. The studio head was now relegated to determining which packages of directors, stars, and writers to put under short-term contract. Contract negotiations were, and are, of course a highly individual matter of bargain and barter. But MGM, like most of the major studios, under its standard contract generally shared

50 per cent of a picture's profit with the independent producer. MGM added up to 25 per cent on to the initial production cost (the amount depending on whether or not studio space or equipment was used) to cover the operation of its production facilities. Before any "profits" were realized, MGM as distributor received a fee of 30 per cent or even 35 per cent of the box office receipts left after the theatre owner had taken his share. The distribution fee was used, in part, to support MGM's network of 100 or so sales offices throughout the world. As distributor, MGM, like the other majors, was in the felicitous position of collecting its fee off the top, before any funds were used toward repayment of expenses.

THE NEW ORDER

Although the decisions by the U.S. Supreme Court in 1948, the U.S. District Court in the Southern District of New York in 1949, and the resultant consent decrees significantly altered the character and structure of the movie industry, they did little to prevent the development of new concentrations of control. The major theatre chains were able to continue their dominance over exhibition even though they were required to divest some of their holdings. Distribution, the key to controlling independent production, continued to be dominated by the *Paramount* defendants. Production activity appeared to become more dispersed in the 1950s, but actually the power of the major distributing companies continued unabated.

During the 1950s the trend toward independent production accelerated greatly. Actors, writers, and producers in the top income bracket, attracted by the less onerous levy of capital gains and corporate profit, began to leave the employ of the major studios to devote their energies and talents to their own productions. High taxes had swallowed up so much of their salaries that there seemed to be little incentive to remain an employee. Under the extant tax structure, an independent producer could earn income as a percentage of profits rather than as a salary, reducing his effective tax rate from 90 to 60 per cent. Some producers formed corporations for the sole purpose of making a single picture. When the project was completed, the producer would dissolve the corporation, receiving the picture in return for his stock. The film could then be sold as a capital asset, subject to only a 25 per cent capital-gains tax. Congress, however, modified the tax laws in 1950 to preclude anyone taking tax advantage through a "collapsible" corporation.

Not only individual profit incentives and the general tax base affected industry growth in this period. The whole issue of financing techniques for independent production was integral to the patterns of development. The principles and procedures for financing independent productions of course varied greatly, but at least three distinct categories of money can be identified: "first money," "second money," and completion or "end" money. These categories are distinguished by the amount of risk attached to them. The completion money—the last $90,000 or so necessary to complete the picture—is the most difficult to raise because the risk for the investor is so great. In motion picture financing, the completion money is the last to be paid from the film's gross receipts. In addition, the investor putting up the completion money must guarantee to continue to finance the production if it should go over budget. The investor who advances the completion money generally shares in the producer's profits—usually from 5 to 20 per cent, plus a penalty percentage if the film goes over budget. The second-money for the production—usually about 30 per cent—is often provided by one of the major distribution companies. In addition to financing, the distributor makes a release commitment for the film and agrees to pay for prints and advertising. The large banks generally provide the first-money, so termed because it is the first to be repaid. First-money, which generally comprises 60 per cent of a picture's total budget, is usually the last money to be raised by a producer. Banks will rarely lend money to a producer who has not secured second and completion money along with a distribution contract.

Independent producers are not nearly as "independent" as they may first appear. As a condition for a release commitment, a major distribution organization may insist that a producer rent its equipment, technical services and studio space. The distributor may also demand the right of final approval on the director, writers, actors, and anyone else rendering service on the film. The distributor, who generally receives 30 per cent of the gross for distributing the film, is much more likely to show a profit than the producer. Only about one film in four shows any profit for the independent producer. The general rule of thumb in the movie business is that a film will begin to show a profit after its gross income from distribution reaches two and half times its "negative cost"— the total cost of making the film. The distributor, however, has already made a substantial profit from its studio rental charges and its distribution fee, which are paid even before the first-money loaned by the banks. The costs for prints and advertising are also recouped prior to the bank loans.

Although by 1957 some 58 per cent of the feature films released by the major movie companies were made by independent producers it was the industry hierarchy who still determined the character and quality of these productions. Those who sought financing outside the studio nexus ran the risk of not being able to get their films distributed. In the final analysis, it became apparent that independent producers enjoyed very little independence or autonomy, and their financial rewards often did not justify the risks they incurred.

THE DEMISE OF RKO

The one member of the moviedom's hierarchy that did not survive the new order was RKO. The box-office boom during the war years had helped RKO regain its competitive position in the movie industry; however, internal conflict and individual caprice ultimately crippled the company. At first, when Floyd Odlum took uncontested control of RKO early in 1943, the company had been on the verge of collapse. RKO Radio Pictures, the company's principal film producing subsidiary, had suffered a half-million dollar loss in 1941 and was over $2 million in the red by the end of the following year. Odlum installed Charles Koerner, who had gained distinction in the company's theatre operation, as production chief. Under Koerner's stewardship, the studio turned out 23 pictures in 11 months and the entire corporation ended 1943 with a net profit after taxes of almost $7 million. One RKO release, *Hitler's Children,* an Edward Golden production which starred Tim Holt and Bonita Granville as doomed lovers in Nazi Germany, cost $175,000 to make and grossed in excess of $3 million. Another wartime bonanza for RKO was Golden's production of *Behind the Rising Sun* in which Tom Neal played a Japanese educated at an American college who returns to Japan, and caught between two cultures, ultimately degenerates totally. Both of these wartime films were directed by the same Edward Dmytryk who later became the recipient of unwelcome notoriety as one of the "Hollywood Ten."

One of the most successful film genres introduced at RKO under Koerner was the elegant cycle of low-cost horror thrillers produced by Vladimir Lewton. In the four years between 1942 and 1946, Lewton produced 11 films for RKO, nine of which fit loosely into the horror classification. Lewton's most famous film, *The Cat People,* featured Simone Simon in a supernatural tale of woman under a strange spell. Other Lewton features include *I Walked with a Zombie, The Leopard Man* and *The Body Snatcher.* Lewton's films possessed a distinctive mood, style and substance which often transcended the horror genre. In *The Curse of the Cat People,* a sequel to *Cat People,* he explored the dimensions of emotion and fantasy in lonely people. Two of Hollywood's most successful directors, Mark Robson and Robert Wise, served their directorial apprenticeships

A St. Louis theatre lobby display for Val Lewton's *The Cat People*. Lewton and his competent staff, eschewing the more blatant shocks of conventional horror films, used sound, silence and shadow to heighten tension. His highly atmospheric films were made on very small budgets. *The Cat People*, for instance, cost about $134,000 to produce; it grossed over $4 million. Lewton's low-budgeted journeys into the macabre helped considerably to rescue RKO from a sea of red ink.

under Lewton, who had promoted them from cutting room technicians.

In the postwar boom year of 1946, RKO's corporate net had reached $12 million, but the studio operation was in trouble again. Charles Koerner had died unexpectedly of leukemia earlier in the year and production was virtually at a standstill. Dore Schary who had produced films for David Selznick's Vanguard company which released through RKO, was put in charge of the RKO studio operation. During the war years, Schary had worked as a producer for MGM, turning out such low-budget successes as *Joe Smith, American, Journey for Margaret, Lassie Come Home* and *Nazi Agent.* Under Schary's stewardship, RKO developed a distinctive style with low-budget "message" films, e.g. Edward Dmytryk's *Crossfire,* a tough adult thriller in which Robert Ryan portrayed a man whose anti-Semitism leads him to become a murderer. Schary encouraged new directors by giving them a relatively free hand in their work. Among the films resulting from this policy were Joseph Losey's *The Boy with Green Hair* and Nicholas Ray's *They Live by Night.*

By the middle of 1947 Floyd Odlum, apparently fearful of the effects of the impending divorcement decrees and the increasing competition from television, had decided to sell his RKO holdings. The following May, after several months of what can only be described as bizarre negotiations, Howard Hughes bought controlling interest in RKO from Odlum for $8,825,690. In addition to movies, Hughes had investments in such diversified fields as the oil industry, transportation, aircraft, electronics, tools, and beverages. By the summer of 1948, some 700 people were dropped from the RKO payroll as Hughes installed his own people to run RKO and assumed active management of the studio operation. Noah Dietrich, president of the $80 million-plus Hughes Tool Co., replaced Odlum as RKO board chairman.

Almost immediately upon taking control of the studio, Hughes began to question Dore Schary's production judgments. A primary source of conflict was Schary's making of the movie *Battleground,* a story about the Battle of the Bulge. Hughes doubted the merit of producing a war film and ordered production stopped. Schary promptly resigned and moved back to MGM where, after purchasing the screen rights from

Hughes, his production of *Battleground,* starring Van Johnson became a smash hit. It started a new vogue in war films that lasted for several years.

During his reign at RKO, Hughes made a shambles of its production schedule. On one occasion he signed with Polan Banks Production Inc. to produce three films for RKO starring Ann Sheridan, but production on the project was delayed for such a prolonged period of time, that the company finally sued RKO for breach of contract. In another deal, Hughes apparently reneged on an oral agreement with Jack Skirball of Gold Seal Productions, Inc. to make *Appointment in Samarra,* tentatively starring Gregory Peck, for RKO release. Skirball was awarded over $375,000 in damages. In one of the most colossal financial negotiations in movie history, Hughes bought the contracts of producers Jerry Wald and Norman Krasna from Warner Brothers and signed the team up to produce 12 films a year from RKO for five years at an aggregate cost of $50 million. Wald and Krasna were paid weekly salaries of $2,500 each. In addition, they were to receive a 50 per cent equity in the forthcoming films as well as 50 per cent of their domestic and foreign earnings. The Wald-Krasna deal proved to be a financial disaster. The team, frustrated by Hughes' constant interference, barely succeeded in making four movies for RKO release (*The Blue Veil, Behave Yourself, Clash by Night,* and *Lusty Men*) before they resigned.

Despite the desperate state of the studio operation, the control of RKO proved to be a profitable venture for Howard Hughes. When RKO, under the consent decree, was required to separate production and distribution from exhibition, Hughes, as majority stockholder, had been given the choice between keeping his stock in one of the two new companies, and of either putting his shares in the other company in a nonvoting trust or selling them. He kept his stock in the new RKO Pictures Corporation and put his theatre holdings in trusteeship. In November of 1953, Hughes sold his 929,020 shares in RKO Theatres Corporation to a group headed by

David J. Greene, a New York investment counselor, for $4.75 per share.

Hughes was able to glean profits from the failing studio in other ways as well. In the fall of 1952, Hughes sold his stock in RKO Pictures to a five-member syndicate headed by Ralph E. Stolkin of Chicago for $7,093,940—$1,250,000 down with the remaining amount to be paid over a two-year period. The syndicate, apparently believing RKO was worth more as a saleable commodity than as an active producing company, planned to shut down the studio operation and sell off the film assets which included such classics as *The Informer, Gunga Din,* and *Citizen Kane.* Revelations about the shady dealings of some of the syndicate members appeared in the *Wall Street Journal* and other newspapers, and many of RKO's 15,000 disgruntled minority stockholders threatened to file suit. In February 1953, the syndicate decided to bow out, taking advantage of a six-month escape clause added to the original agreement in December. They forfeited their down payment and Hughes, over a million dollars richer, regained control of RKO.

Under Hughes' aegis, RKO was reduced to a corporate shell. From 1948 through 1952, the studio had losses totalling over $20 million. The company's financial situation had deteriorated to the point where no bank would underwrite an RKO picture unless Hughes personally guaranteed the loan. The successful re-release of RKO's film classic *King Kong* helped to minimize the company's 1952 losses, but the studio still showed a deficit of $4.8 million by the end of the third quarter and was shut down for the duration of the year. Overall, RKO recorded a net loss of more than $15 million, the largest deficit in the history of the firm. The 12 months of 1953 recorded another substantial loss for the studio. In the fall of 1953, several minority stockholders filed for receivership. One of the minority stockholder suits against Hughes accused him of running the studio with "caprice, pique, and whim." Hughes was also accused of placing various actresses under contract at excessive salaries and then neglecting to use them in pictures. Early in 1954, in a move that astounded the financial community, Hughes offered to buy all of RKO Pictures' outstanding stock at $6 per share, an amount well above the market price. On March 31, 1954, Howard Hughes wrote a personal check for $23,489,478 and became the only person in history to own the assets and operating organization of a major motion picture company outright. The studio, however, was nearly moribund. In 1954, RKO released only four studio-produced new features.

Hughes' sole ownership of the movie company was short-lived. In July of 1955, he sold the entire capital stock of RKO Radio Pictures, Inc. and five associated companies for $25 million to General Teleradio, Inc., the entertainment subsidiary of the General Tire and Rubber Company, a huge conglomerate whose far-flung interests included tiremaking, chemicals, plastics, rockets, guided-missile controls, submarines and even tennis balls (mostly sold under the Pennsylvania label). Thomas O'Neil, president of RKO Teleradio Pictures (the new General Tire subsidiary set up after the RKO takeover) quickly recouped the RKO investment by selling off the studio's backlog of some 740 feature films and 1,000 short subjects for $15.2 million to Matthew Fox's C&C Super Corporation, for television distribution. O'Neil retained the exclusive rights to televise the 740 features on RKO Teleradio's owned-and-operated stations in Boston, Hartford, Los Angeles, Memphis, New York, and West Palm Beach. He also retained the first-run network television rights to a 150 selected features. Shortly thereafter, O'Neil sold back to Hughes two unreleased RKO films (*The Conqueror* and *Jet Pilot*) for $8 million in cash, plus $4 million to be paid out of the earnings of the two films. O'Neil also sold Hughes *The Outlaw* for an undisclosed amount. Hughes, in turn, merged RKO's corporate shell, over which he had kept control, into Floyd Odlum's Atlas Corporation in exchange for Atlas stock valued at almost $10 million. The entire RKO transaction proved to be financially beneficial for all parties involved: Atlas gained a substantial tax write-off,

Hughes made a modest profit, and O'Neil more than covered his payment to Hughes by selling the films, thereby acquiring RKO's studios and distribution system for nothing.

Under O'Neil's management RKO's production apparatus moved into high gear. By the middle of 1956, five new feature films were completed and ready for release. The first movie to premiere under the new regime was *The First Traveling Saleslady,* starring Ginger Rogers, who had soared to stardom two decades earlier as Fred Astaire's dancing partner in such RKO releases as *Top Hat* and *The Gay Divorcee.* RKO made total of 13 pictures in 1956, at an aggregate cost of some $16 million. The revenue derived from the first pictures released, however, was disappointing. The Ginger Rogers vehicle, in particular, was a box-office disaster. In January 1957, O'Neil shut down RKO's entire domestic distribution organization (which had employed roughly 800 people and cost $16 million a year to operate) and arranged for Universal to distribute the remainder of the company's already completed films. Early in 1958, Desilu, the television corporation developed by two former RKO contract players, Desi Arnaz and Lucille Ball, purchased RKO's 14-acre plant in Hollywood, along with RKO-Pathé, its sprawling subsidiary in Culver City for some $6 million. RKO-Radio Pictures, the studio which produced some of the most memorable films in motion picture history, passed from existence.

THE RUSH TO TELEVISION

The film remnants of RKO proved newly profitable in the emerging medium of television. Matthew Fox released the RKO library to television through the C&C Television Corporation, a newly formed subsidiary of C&C Super Corporation. The exclusive television rights to the films were sold to individual stations in major cities throughout the country. Each station received the rights to the films in perpetuity. The films were paid for, in part, through the exchange of advertising time by the stations. By mid-1957, C&C Television had earned an estimated $25 million from the RKO library.

The sale of RKO's film inventory to a television distributor was a major breakthrough. Until then, only Monogram and Republic had released a substantial part of their film assets to the rival medium. Monogram had released some 300 features to television in 1951. That same year, Republic set up a subsidiary, Hollywood Television Service, to distribute 175 of its features to television. By the end of 1954, over 350 Republic features had been telecast. However, the industry's aristocracy had resisted the enticement of television dollars. Fox had sold some of its Charlie Chan features through Unity, a television distributor, and Paramount had unloaded 30 or so of its low budget Pine-Thomas features, but this trickling was of little consequence. However, after the RKO onslaught the dam broke. Almost immediately following the C&C purchase of the RKO library, Columbia Pictures released 104 features to television through its subsidiary, Screen Gems. Warner Brothers followed in March 1956 with the $21 million sale of 850 features (including 100 silent features) and 1,500 shorts to PRM, a Canadian-American investment firm, and Associated Artists Productions, a television distributor. The features were sold to television stations in 13 packages of 52 films each. In June 1956, MGM announced plans to release 750 features and 900 shorts to television through its own distribution company, MGM-TV. MGM decided to lease its films, rather than sell them outright. November of 1956 brought word of a $30 million-plus deal between Twentieth Century-Fox and National Telefilm Associates (NTA) for 390 features. Fox purchased half-interest in the NTA Film Network which distributed the features to television. In August 1957, Universal sold 600 of its features to Columbia's Screen Gems in return for a minimum guarantee of $20 million. The last holdout, Paramount, succumbed to the lure of television dollars in February 1958 with the sale of 750 features to Music Corporation of America (MCA) for a potential $50 million: $10 million in cash at the outset, $25 million guaranteed from television revenues, and an additional 60 per cent of the gross television receipts up to $15 million. MCA recouped its investment with astonishing speed. By the end of the decade, feature films had become a mainstay of local television program schedules.

Some of the big studios had sold their film libraries outright. Since the production costs of many of the pre-1948 features had been fully amortized from theatre revenues, the films had been carried on the company ledgers for tax purposes at a nominal value of one dollar each. From this perspective, the revenues derived from television sales must have seemed an unexpected economic windfall. In actuality, the studios had blundered badly by selling, rather than leasing, their old features. The earning power of old movies has proven to be far greater than anyone in the movie business at the time could have anticipated. MGM, one of the studios that had decided to lease its pre-1948 features to television, quickly realized the potential long-range financial worth of its old films. By March of 1957, a package of 750 MGM features had grossed $34.5 million. One MGM film, *The Wizard of Oz,* was leased separately to CBS-TV for annual showings starting in November 1956. Under the terms of the agreement, CBS paid a total of $450,000 for the first two telecasts. The network had options to show the film seven more times at $150,000 per showing. (The deal was negotiated by MGM lawyer Frank Rosenfelt, who became the movie studio's president 17 years later.) When CBS's options ran out in 1967, NBC paid MGM some $650,000 per year to televise the film once annually between 1968 and 1970 and $500,000 per year for subsequent showings through 1976. The film's value in the television market continues to rise. CBS agreed to pay MGM $4 million for the rights to televise *The Wizard of Oz* five times between 1976 and 1980.

NEW LEGAL AND UNION PROBLEMS

The initial release of theatrical features to television had raised many legal questions. One interesting legal problem concerned a featured actor's right to restrict the television use of films in which he appeared. When Republic Pictures announced plans in mid-1951 to release to television its feature films and theatrical shorts starring Roy Rogers and Gene Autry, the two musical Western stars filed separate suits in the U.S. District Court in Los Angeles for an injunction to stop the transaction. The district court granted the injunction sought by Rogers since his contract with Republic expressly forbid the use of his name, voice or likeness for advertising without his consent. The exhibition of his films upon commercially sponsored television programs, the Court held, constituted such use. The same Court, however, refused a similar request by Autry since the wording in his Republic contract differed somewhat from that of Rogers. The district court decisions were appealed by Republic and Autry respectively. In June 1954, the Federal Court of Appeals in San Francisco, ruling on both appeals, found in favor of Republic. The Court permitted editing of the films to allow for commercial insertions, and ruled that Republic, as producer and owner of the films, had the right to release them to television. The only stipulation was that the Western stars, themselves, should not appear to be endorsing specific commercial products. The U.S. Supreme Court, in October 1954, refused to review the lower court's decision. Republic released the Rogers and Autry films to television through Music Corporation of America (MCA) under a five-year contract. MCA paid Republic a $1 million advance against 60 per cent of the television gross for the length of the agreement.

The release of theatrical features for television syndication was further complicated by demands for remuneration from the various talent guilds. James C. Petrillo, the irascible president of the American Federation of Musicians (AFM) had the prescience in 1946, when television was still a fledgling, to secure from the major producers an agreement which effectively restricted films with sound tracks performed by AFM members from being telecast. Since this agreement extended through August 1951, Monogram and Republic were required by AFM to rescore their films using a full orchestra paid at union scale, prior to releasing them to television. In addition, the two studios had to pay 5 per cent of their television receipts to the AFM's trust fund.

The Screen Actors Guild (SAG) also demanded recompense for the television release of theatrical features. The movie companies were free to release pre-1948 films without negotiation or payment since standard contracts prior to that year specifically gave producers the television performance rights. However, in its 1951 contract negotiations with movie producers, SAG sought to secure a financial interest in all post-1948 features released to television. Any producer wishing to sell or lease films to television made after August 1, 1948 was required to negotiate with SAG for additional payments to actors appearing in the releases. Failure to negotiate would result in the cancellation of the producer's contract with the Guild within 60 days after the television release. This provision provided a potent inducement for most producers to negotiate with SAG since they required the acting talents of the guild's members for future productions. The Screen Directors Guild (SDG) and the Writers Guild of America (WGA) later adopted the same cancellation rights in their negotiations with movie producers.

During the 1950s, many of the talent guilds across different media amalgamated to strengthen their bargaining position in contract negotiations. In 1954, the Screen Writers Guild, the Radio Writers Guild and the Dramatists Guild were united as Writers Guild of America. This guild was divided geographically into Writers Guild, East and Writers Guild, West. In 1960, the Screen Directors Guild merged with the Radio-TV Directors Guild to form the Directors Guild of America. That same year, however, the membership of the Screen Actors Guild rejected a proposed merger with the American Federation of Television and Radio Artists (AFTRA). In an earlier jurisdictional dispute it was decided that SAG would serve as the bargaining agent for performers in all filmed television programs. AFTRA maintains jurisdiction over all performers who appear in live or videotaped shows.

Beginning in 1960, the principal talent guilds incorporated provisions into their industry-wide contracts providing for standardized payment of residuals—additional compensation to performers for the re-use of their work. That year, the Screen Actors Guild, after a six-week strike, won an agreement with movie producers providing for payments to actors when theatrical features in which their members appear are sold to television. The payment formula was revised in 1965 so that now each actor in the cast of a theatrical release sold to television is compensated on a sliding-scale based on the film's gross television earnings. The actor is assured of an irreducible minimum payment. In calculating this compensation, a base amount, ranging from $100 to $500, is established, determined by the days or weeks an actor has worked on the picture. When the picture is initially exhibited on television the actors receive 30 per cent of their base amount. Subsequent payments are based on the film's accruing gross receipts. In 1971, SAG relinquished any claim to residuals on pictures which began production prior to February 1961.

The three other talent guilds that have negotiated residual payments for theatrical releases sold to television are the Directors Guild of America, the Writers Guild of America, and the American Federation of Musicians. The residuals received by members of these three guilds, however, are computed on the basis of a given film's "accountable" receipts—the gross television earnings minus 40 per cent to cover distribution costs. Consequently, their compensation is substantially less than that of SAG's members.

OLD TECHNOLOGY USED ANEW

Although the major studios had acquiesced to television's seemingly insatiable appetite for product, the fight against the small screen competitor was not abandoned altogether. In an effort to combat the inroads made by television, movie makers had turned to technical processes they had long ignored. A number of technological innovations were introduced during the early 1950s. The process that achieved the most sensational results was Cinerama, which had been invented in the 1930s by Fred Waller. In 1937, Ralph Walker, of the architectural firm of Vorhees, Walker, Foley, and Smith, commissioned Waller to develop a film display for presentation at the 1939 World's Fair in New York City. Waller and Walker subsequently received a joint patent for the process, which they called Vitarama. Using 11 cameras and 11 projectors, Waller presented a spectacular visual history of the petroleum industry. The Vitarama Corporation was formed to develop the process for commercial use. Laurance Rockefeller bought a half-interest in the new company for $25,000. Working in some Rockefeller-owned stables which had been converted into a laboratory, Waller continued to perfect his invention. He interrupted his work during World War II to develop an aerial gunnery trainer for the Navy in which five synchronized projectors cast an image of attacking planes on a spherical screen. The trainees, equipped with earphones, sat in front of the screen and fired at the attacking planes with electronic guns. A beeping sound in the earphones signaled a hit. Waller's device proved to be an invaluable military aid.

After the war, Laurance Rockefeller joined with Time Inc. and Hazard Reeves, a sound engineer and industrial promoter, to exploit the Vitarama process commercially under the name Cinerama. This new company, the Cinerama Corporation, was licensed by the Vitarama Corporation, which was owned almost entirely by Fred Waller and Laurance Rockefeller. During the next three years, Waller developed less cumbersome equipment, employing a three-lensed camera and three electronically synchronized projectors. However, Time Inc. and Laurance Rockefeller, apparently losing faith in the project, decided to withdraw from the Cinerama Corporation and the company was liquidated; although Rockefeller continued to maintain his interest in the Vitarama Corporation. At this juncture, Hazard Reeves, who had developed Cinerama's stereophonic sound system, formed a new company to exploit the process, Cinerama Inc. A new license agreement was signed which called for Cinerama Inc. to give 5 per cent of its income to Vitarama Inc.

In the fall of 1950, Lowell Thomas, the famed radio newscaster, witnessed a Cinerama demonstration and was enthralled with what he had seen. Thomas joined with his business manager, Frank Smith, and Broadway producer Mike Todd to form Thomas-Todd Productions, Inc. to produce films using the Vitarama process. Todd, who had made no financial investment in the company that bore his name, soon came into conflict with Thomas and Smith on production policies, and he withdrew from the project. Thomas persuaded several financial backers, including Dudley Roberts of the investment firm of Roberts and Company and financier Alger B. Chapan, to support the company, which was renamed Cinerama Productions Corporation. Merian C. Cooper, producer of *King Kong,* became executive producer for the new production company. In return for a sliding scale percentage of its eventual box office receipts, Cinerama Productions received an exclusive sublicense from Cinerama Inc.

Cinerama Productions' first feature film was *This is Cinerama,* a startling two-hour kaleidoscopic travelogue of action and scenery which ranged from a roller-coaster ride to a plane trip through the Grand Canyon. The film's unveiling at the Broadway Theatre in New York City on September 30, 1952 created a sensation. The audience shrieked with terrified delight as they seemed to zoom down the chutes and around the curves of the roller-coaster in New York's Rockaway Amusement Park. The sense of participation and involvement was created by permitting the spectator to use his peripheral vision. Three crisscrossing images were projected simultaneously on three screens which were joined and curved in an arc approximately 146 degrees wide and 55 degrees high. The semicircular screen,

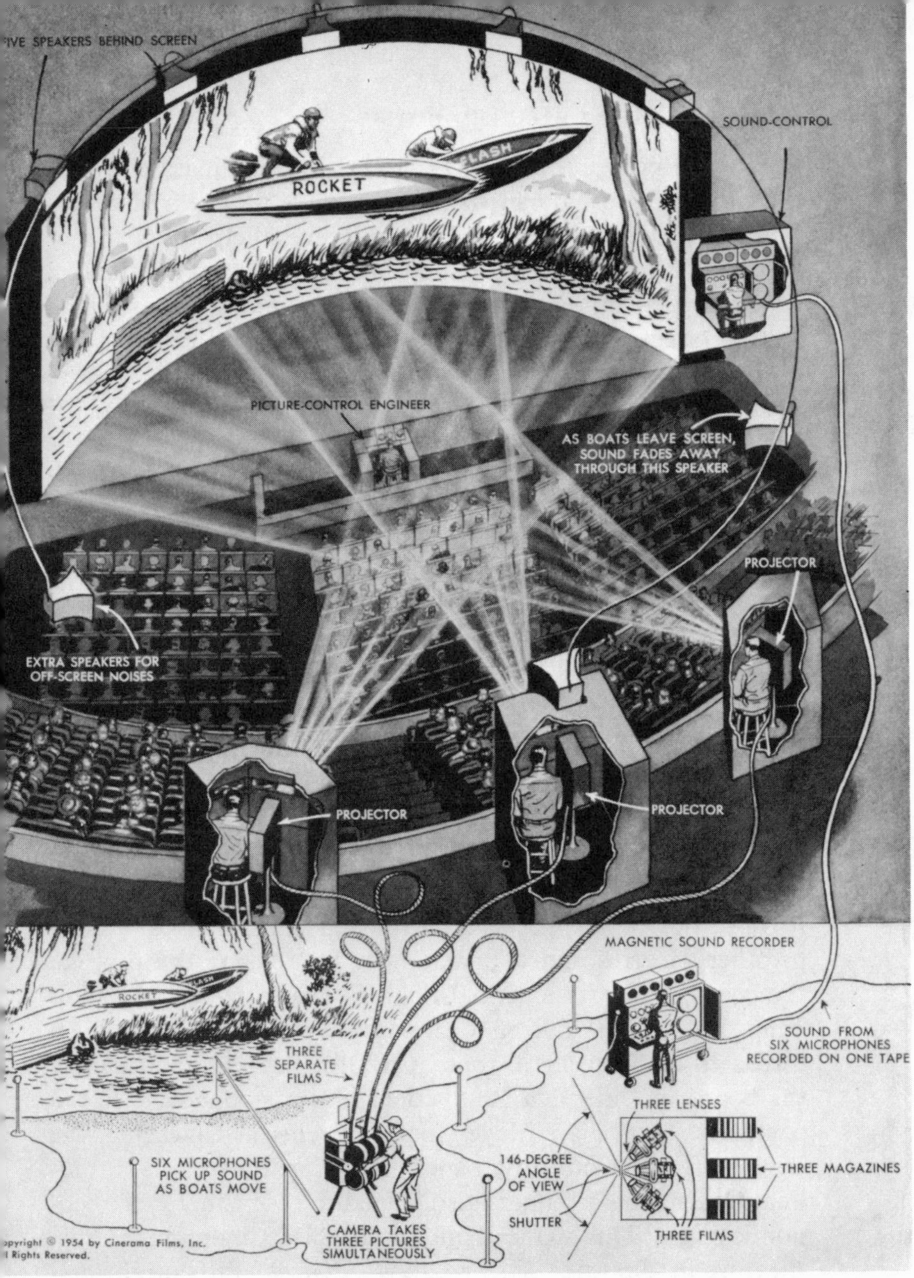
FIVE SPEAKERS BEHIND SCREEN
ROCKET
FLASH
SOUND-CONTROL
PICTURE-CONTROL ENGINEER
AS BOATS LEAVE SCREEN, SOUND FADES AWAY THROUGH THIS SPEAKER
PROJECTOR
EXTRA SPEAKERS FOR OFF-SCREEN NOISES
PROJECTOR
PROJECTOR
MAGNETIC SOUND RECORDER
ROCKET
FLASH
THREE SEPARATE FILMS
SOUND FROM SIX MICROPHONES RECORDED ON ONE TAPE
THREE LENSES
146-DEGREE ANGLE OF VIEW
THREE MAGAZINES
SIX MICROPHONES PICK UP SOUND AS BOATS MOVE
SHUTTER
THREE FILMS
CAMERA TAKES THREE PICTURES SIMULTANEOUSLY
Copyright © 1954 by Cinerama Films, Inc.
All Rights Reserved.

This schematic drawing of the Cinerama process shows the evolution of the image from photography on location to projection in the theatre. On location a three-lensed camera photographs different parts of a single scene; while in the theatre three separate projectors throw the three images on a curved screen.

which was 51 feet wide and 25 feet high, encompassed almost the entire field of human vision. The use of a system of stereophonic sound, developed by Hazard Reeves, helped to enhance the film's illusion of reality and dimension. Sound for the film was recorded on six sound tracks from microphones which were strategically placed to cover all the action. When the film was projected, speakers located throughout the theatre created the impression that each sound originated from its visual source. The clatter of the roller-coaster cars and the screech of airplane wheels reverberated off the theatre's walls in a cacophony of deafening magnitude. *This is Cinerama*'s spectacular illusions thrilled patron and critic alike. The film opened to uniformly enthusiastic reviews. Nevertheless, the process was not without its imperfections, most serious of which was that the three-screen images did not always blend and synchronize convincingly. In addition, the two dividing lines separating the three images were disconcertingly apparent to the observant viewer, and those sitting at the sides of the theatre could only see two of the three images properly.

Although the Cinerama Productions' first effort was an enormous success, the company, as a result of the great expense in launching the enterprise, was heavily in debt. In an effort to raise the capital necessary to install Cinerama equipment in other theatres and to make more films using the process, the board of directors invited Louis B. Mayer to join the company. Late in the fall of 1952, Mayer, who earlier had been forced to abdicate his throne at MGM, became chairman of the board of Cinerama Productions and a stockholder in the company. Soon after Mayer took the reins at Cinerama, the Bankers Trust Company loaned the company some $1.6 million. Other money lenders also helped to ease Cinerama's economic plight. This financial infusion enabled Cinerama to equip theatres in Detroit, Chicago, Los Angeles, Pittsburgh, and other major cities. The "roadshowing" of *This is Cinerama* reaped a record box-office harvest. While at New York's Broadway Theatre the film played to capacity crowds for over two years. A second Cinerama vehicle, *Cinerama Holiday,* was released in October of 1953. This film, too, was greeted by enthusiastic public response. A third offering, *Seven Wonders of the World,* followed. However, audience enthusiasm for the travelogue format was starting to wane. In November of 1954, Louis B. Mayer, apparently sensing that the novelty was beginning to lose its commercial value, severed his ties with the Cinerama Productions. He received a substantial settlement from the company.

Cinerama remained outside the mainstream of the movie industry throughout the 1950s. Then in 1960, MGM signed a contract with Cinerama to produce two films: *How the West Was Won* and *The Wonderful World of the Brothers Grimm.* Both films, however, were later modified for conventional showings. Cinerama Inc. shared equally with MGM in the receipts from both the Cinerama and the non-Cinerama engagements. Few theatres had the physical dimensions sufficient to accommodate the huge screen and the three projectors necessary to present Cinerama films. Since Cinerama-converted theatres (which cost between $50,000 and $70,000 to restructure) seated fewer patrons than conventional theatres, there was little financial incentive for many exhibitors to make the changeover. Although no other commercial process has yet to match Cinerama's sense of audience participation and involvement, the size requirements and the three-projector system eventually proved to be economically unfeasible. In the ensuing years, most of the specially equipped Cinerama theatres closed. During the 1960s, however, Cinerama's research division developed a single lens camera and projection system that has been used in such highly successful films as Stanley Kubrick's *2001: A Space Odyssey.* This picture, released through MGM, has grossed over $36 million in film rentals to date.

Another depth-producing process which enjoyed a brief vogue in the anxiety-ridden movie industry of the early 1950s was Natural Vision, a stereoscopic process based on the pioneer work of camera engineer Friend Baker. Although Natural Vision, like Cinerama, was nurtured outside the mainstream of the industry, it was eventually utilized by many of the major companies. The prime mover in the development of Natural Vision was Milton Gunzburg, a little-known writer, who had purchased the rights to the invention from Friend Baker for a nominal sum and the promise of a small percentage of any accruing profits. Working with his brother Julian, an eye specialist, Milton Gunzburg perfected the process. Natural Vision achieved the illusion of three dimensions by the use of a camera which took two shots of each scene through two lenses separated to correspond roughly to the distance between the right and the left eye of a human being. The images from the two lenses were recorded on separate reels of film. Two projectors, one for each eye, cast slightly overlapping images on the screen. The projected images passed through special polarized filters. The filter for the left projector permitted only vertical light wave vibrations to pass, while the filter for the right projector transmitted only horizontal vibrations. An automatic interlocking device kept the two films in synchronization as they went through the projectors. The viewer wore special polaroid spectacles which corresponded to the filters for the projectors and fused the two images stereoscopically. The result was an amazing sense of three-dimensionality.

Milton and Julian Gunzburg formed the Natural Vision Corporation to promote their stereoscopic process; but their efforts, initially at least, were unsuccessful. MGM took an option on the process but allowed it to lapse. After being spurned by several of the major companies, the Gunzburgs permitted Arch Oboler, an independent filmmaker who had achieved earlier fame as a radio dramatist, to make a movie using the Natural Vision process. The Gunzburgs had a 20 per cent interest in Oboler's film project. Using $10,000 of his own money plus some borrowed funds, Oboler produced *Bwana Devil,* an African adventure film starring Robert Stack and Barbara Britton. Although the film was ineptly made, its visual effects were startling; for example, lions appeared to leap out of the screen.

Bwana Devil opened late in the fall of 1952 at two Paramount theatres in Los Angeles. Despite its poor quality, the film was an overwhelming success. Audiences marvelled at its special effects. After a few months in independent release, the film was sold to United Artists for $500,000 plus a share of the profits. The novelty of the third dimension made *Bwana Devil* a sensation. The Polaroid Company, sole manufacturer of polaroid lenses, granted Natural Vision an exclusive contract to distribute the cardboard-framed polaroid spectacles necessary for viewing three dimensional films. Natural Vision purchased the spectacles from Polaroid for six cents a pair and sold them to exhibitors for ten cents. After the success of *Bwana Devil,* Polaroid manufactured its spectacles at the rate of six million pairs a week. The company's stock rose by 30 per cent in a matter of weeks.

Warner Brothers, whose foresight had resulted in the advent of sound movies, was the first major studio to use the Natural Vision process. Warners' first three-dimensional release, *House of Wax* starring Vincent Price, broke box-office records almost everywhere it played. The depth rush was on. By the middle of 1953, nearly all the major studios were producing three-dimensional films. Columbia's three-dimensional production, *Man in the Dark,* grossed over $1 million in its first five weeks in release. Universal offered *It Came from Outer Space* and *The Creature from the Black Lagoon,* among other three-dimensional releases. Paramount produced five films using depth photography in 1953. RKO's *Second Chance* included one of the most sensational three-dimensional sequences ever produced—a cable car hurtling down an abyss after a suspense-filled ride.

Many new three-dimensional systems were introduced; each was guaranteed to be less costly and more effective than those already in existence. However, since the market was being glutted by innumerable types of three-dimensional films, MGM decided to release *Kiss Me Kate* in both conventional and in-depth versions. (The three-dimensional version, which appeared at Radio City Music Hall, was a box-office disaster.) Warner Brothers, which had once expected to produce most of its films in Natural Vision, stopped making three-dimensional films after the release of *The Phantom of Rue Morgue* and *Dial M For Murder*. The latter film, directed by Alfred Hitchcock, was released in two versions, but most people saw it in its conventional form. The popularity of the third dimension declined steadily—possibly due to reliance on novelty to the exclusion of plot, theme and character, and probably also due to the annoyance of wearing the spectacles. By 1955 the depth rage had run its course. Despite occasional attempts to resurrect the process in such films as *The Stewardesses* and Andy Warhol's *Frankenstein,* it is rarely employed in current films.

The initial success of Cinerama and Natural Vision stimulated experimentation with other less complicated and more versatile technical processes. Supported by Bank of America and Chase Manhattan Bank among others, Twentieth Century-Fox decided to gamble its future on a wide-screen process called CinemaScope. Developed by the French physicist Henri Chrétien in the 1920s, CinemaScope (originally christened Anamorphoscope) used an anamorphic lens in the movie camera to compress a scene which was a little more than two-and-a-half times as wide as it was high onto a standard 35mm negative. A compensating lens on the theatre projector expanded the compressed image out again to the dimensions of a specially constructed elongated screen. The major advantage of Cinema-Scope was that the anamorphic lens could be screwed into an ordinary projector. Stereophonic origination of sounds from the appropriate visual source was accomplished through the use of three speakers. The total cost of converting a theatre for CinemaScope, including the lenses, the elongated screen, and the stereophonic sound system, was less than $20,000.

In the spring of 1953, Twentieth Century-Fox announced that, henceforth, all its films would be produced in CinemaScope. It made this commitment, in part, to encourage theatre owners to invest in the equipment necessary to show CinemaScope movies. To further encourage widespread use, Fox leased the CinemaScope cameras and lenses to its competitors.

In September 1953, Twentieth Century-Fox's *The Robe,* the first feature to be released in CinemaScope, opened at the Roxy Theatre in New York City. Based on Lloyd C. Douglas' piously didactic best seller about what happened to Christ's robe after the Crucifixion, *The Robe* had been shot in 52 days at a cost of $4 million. A comparatively obscure young English actor named Richard Burton was cast in the leading role of Marcellus, the soldier who won Christ's robe in a dice game. Audience reaction to *The Robe* was extremely favorable. The dramatic sweep and power of the film's panoramic scenes were ideally suited for the extremely wide, slightly curved screen. The Roxy Theatre reported a gross of $264,000 for the first week of its showing of *The Robe.* Soon the film was being shown in over a hundred theatres around the country. Within a year after the premier of *The Robe,* some 11,000 theatres were equipped to show CinemaScope productions. Several Cinema-Scope releases quickly followed *The Robe,* including *How to Marry a Millionaire, Beneath the Twelve-Mile Reef* and *King of the Khyber Rifles,* among others.

By the middle of 1954, all of the major companies, with the exception of RKO and Paramount were using the Cinema-Scope process. To get wider distribution for their product, several companies also released conventional versions (usually shot at the same time) of their wide-screen films. Warner Brothers had announced the development of its own anamorphic system, called WarnerSuperScope (later shortened to Warner-Scope), but soon abandoned the project and switched to Cine-maScope. The studio's CinemaScope releases included *A Star Is Born* and *Mr. Roberts.*

Although it offered some illusion of depth, of three dimensionality, CinemaScope was not truly stereoscopic; it was merely panoramic. In addition, CinemaScope achieved width at the expense of clarity and definition; the projected image had a slightly blurred, grainy texture. When it became increasingly apparent that the standard 35mm film was inadequate for wide-screen production, Paramount decided to experiment with its own wide-screen variant, VistaVision. Invented in 1919 by E. W. Clark, VistaVision is a process in which width is achieved by running the negative film through the camera horizontally in order to record one image across two frames of 35mm film. The double-framed image was then optically reduced and printed on a 35mm release print that could be shown with a special lens on standard projecting equipment. Paramount unveiled VistaVision in *White Christmas,* which premiered on April 27, 1954 at Radio City Music Hall. The VistaVision process resulted in an image which was sharper and brighter than CinemaScope. What's more, the VistaVision image was high as well as wide. By comparison, CinemaScope often gave the viewer the impression that he was looking at the world through a mail slot. *Strategic Air Command, The Rose Tatoo,* and *The Ten Commandments,* among others, were shot by Paramount using VistaVision. Paramount also leased its patented process to rivals in an effort to encourage widespread adoption by exhibitors.

A system called Todd-AO, which achieved even more spectacular visual results than VistaVision, was introduced in 1955 by Mike Todd. Todd's new system, developed in conjunction with Dr. Brian O'Brien of the American Optical Company, employed the use of 65mm film in the camera and a 70mm print for projection. The first Todd-AO release was the film version of Rodgers and Hammerstein's *Oklahoma,* which was shot at the MGM studios on a budget of $4 million. The film, which was initially shown at specially-equipped theatres on a "roadshow" basis, was a smash hit. After its first highly successful year in release, the film was reduced to CinemaScope form and shown in theatres with standard projectors since most exhibitors refused to purchase the equipment necessary to show the over-sized prints. The second feature shot in Todd-AO was Michael Todd's own production, *Around the World in Eighty Days.* Although the film cost nearly $6 million to produce, it was an enormous financial success. The Todd-AO process later came under the control of Twentieth Century-Fox. Eventually, most of the major studios adopted their own versions of the wide-screen process.

In addition to the wide screen, other and more ephemeral innovations were introduced to the conventional movie theatre. In the latter half of the 1950s, the dimension of "smell" was added to the motion picture. New York theatre-owner Walter Reade Jr. introduced AromaRama, a scent-yielding process conceived and developed by Charles Weiss to heighten the impact of a movie. The odors were released to the audience through the regular air circulating system. Reade added AromaRama's scents to an Italian-made travelogue on China, *Behind the Great Wall,* which opened at the DeMille Theatre in New York City on December 2, 1959. Audience reaction to the process was encouraging. The following month, Michael Todd Jr., son of the flamboyant showman, unveiled *Scent of Mystery,* a tongue-in-cheek murder mystery, which used a process called Smell-O-Vision. Developed by Swiss inventor Hans Laube, the process proved to be even more effective than AromaRama. *Scent of Mystery,* which cost $2 million to produce, premiered at Chicago's Cinestage theatre on January 12, 1960. Apparatus was installed in each seat in the theatre which released various mixtures of aromatic chemicals to correspond to the scenes on the screen. The large assortment of scents ranged from salty ocean breezes and fresh-baked bread to the villain's odoriferous pipe tobacco. The aroma of port wine permeated the theatre during a scene in which a man was crushed to death by falling wine casks. A special fan wafted away each odor before the next one was emitted into the atmosphere. Other than providing novelty appeal, the odors did little to enhance the enjoyment value of the movie. Both Aroma-Rama and Smell-O-Vision disappeared soon after their debuts.

TELEFILM PRODUCTION

While the major studios continued to search for new ways to make their theatrical releases more appealing, they also diversified their activities to include production directly intended for television. The first major studio to produce "telefilms" was Columbia, which in 1951 established Screen Gems as a wholly-owned subsidiary to make television commercials and programs. Screen Gems (recently renamed Columbia Television Inc.) was the brainchild of Ralph Cohn, the eldest son of Jack Cohn. Ralph Cohn proved to be as adept at business as his father and uncle before him. In June of 1952, he announced a $1 million deal with the Ford Motor Company to produce 39 half-hour films for the *Ford Theatre*. Screen Gems' production apparatus soon moved into high gear, turning out such popular television series as *Rin Tin Tin, Captain Midnight* and the phenomenally successful, *Father Knows Best*. Television was fast becoming a big business. By the mid-1950s, some 500 stations were sprinkled across the nation. In the face of dwindling box-office receipts all the major movie companies eventually followed Columbia's lead and turned to telefilm production. In April 1954, Walt Disney Productions and ABC-TV announced plans for a *Disneyland* series. The new program was intended to promote another Disney-ABC venture, Disneyland Park, in Anaheim, California. Following fast upon the heels of the Disney deal came word that Jack Warner was negotiating with ABC's Leonard Goldenson to produce films for that television network. In the fall of 1955, *Warner Brothers Presents* made its debut on ABC-TV. The show's title was actually an umbrella for three separate series which played on alternating weeks, *Casablanca, King's Row* and *Cheyenne*.

The latter show, which starred an unknown actor named Clint Walker, enjoyed a seven-year run on the network. The 1955–56 television season also saw the entry of *M-G-M Parade* and *Twentieth Century-Fox Hour.* Paramount was soon to join the procession to television production. Then, in the fall of 1957, United Artists, too, set up a television subsidiary for the financing and distribution of independently produced telefilms. Later UA was to absorb Ziv Television Programs, Inc., one of the most successful of the early independent television producers.

UNIVERSAL ENGULFED

The studio which eventually became the most active television producer was Universal. In the years following World War II, Universal went through several financial crises. In 1946, the Universal studio facilities had been merged with International Pictures, owned by Leo Spitz and William Goetz, to form Universal-International (UI). John Cheever Cowdin and Nate Blumberg, however, remained at the helm of Universal Pictures Company, the parent organization. The newly merged studio embarked on an ambitious, but unprofitable, program of prestige pictures such as the movie version of Lillian Hellman's play *Another Part of the Forest.* Cowdin, Universal's long-time board chairman, resigned in 1950. In November of the following year, Decca Records gained substantial stock in the company, including those shares owned by Spitz and Goetz. Within a short time, Decca owned controlling interest in Universal. Decca-president, Milton Rackmil assumed the same post at Universal, succeeding Nate Blumberg. During the 1950s, the studio operation, headed by Edward Muhl, set its sights on a broader market with a number of well-made adventure stories in combination with use of well-known performers. The studio scored at the box-office with Jimmy Stewart in such action-packed films as *Winchester 73, Bend of the River* and *Thunder Bay.* The studio was able to present big stars through a policy of offering them a percentage of the profits from their films. Tyrone Power, Gregory Peck and Alan Ladd were among the stars attracted to UI by this profit participation plan; for his work in UI's 1953 release *Desert Legion,* Alan Ladd received 50 per cent of the film's profits. In addition, low-budget series also helped to swell UI's income. One of these popular low-budget series featured Marjorie Main and Percy Kilbride as Ma and Pa Kettle. They appeared in several predictable but profitable films. Another popular UI series featured Donald O'Connor playing opposite a "talking" mule named Francis. Although Universal had few artistic triumphs during the 1950s, the studio managed to turn a profit.

As movie attendance fell catastrophically, however, Universal's revenues dropped correspondingly. In 1958, the studio suffered a $2 million loss. The following year, Decca sold the 423-acre Universal studio lot (but not the production and distribution company) to Revue Productions, the television subsidiary of MCA Inc., then a major talent agency. MCA was founded in 1924 as the Music Corporation of America by a Chicago ophthalmologist, Dr. Jules C. Stein, with a capital of $1,000. Under Stein's direction, MCA grew from a small booking agency for musical groups into one of the largest and most powerful talent representatives in the world. By the late 1930s, MCA's clients included the bands of the Dorseys, Benny Goodman, Horace Heidt, Kay Kyser and Guy Lombardo. Originally an agent solely for musical performers, MCA diversified in 1941 with the purchase of the CBS Artist Bureau, adding actors, writers, directors and commentators to its roster of talent. Four years later, MCA bought the prestigious Hayward-Deverich agency in New York for a reported $4 million. Henry Fonda, Ginger Rogers, Jimmy Stewart, Myrna Loy and Joseph Cotten were among the many star-clients acquired from this purchase. Such famous writers as Ben Hecht, Dashiell Hammett and Dorothy Parker had also been numbered among the prominent clients of Leland Hayward and Nat Deverich. The purchase of the Hayward-Deverich agency made MCA

A poster for *Francis Covers the Big Town,* a 1953 Universal-International release. The struggling studio found an unexpected goldmine in the unlikely form of a "talking" mule named Francis. The seven films in the series featured a guileless young man (played by Donald O'Connor in six of the films), who is led into and out of trouble by a droll and rather cunning mule. The low-budgeted series did big business at the box-office.

overnight the representative of the greatest galaxy of talent in the entertainment world.

As MCA grew in stature, its need for top-rank executives increased. Jules Stein carefully developed his managerial cadre from within the organization. In 1946, Lew Wasserman, whom Stein had hired as a publicist a decade earlier, became president of MCA. Although Wasserman ran the company, Stein continued to hold the controlling stock in MCA. In 1949, MCA further broadened its activities with the establishment of a

COURTESY OF UNIVERSAL

Cary Grant and Dina Merrill in a scene from the 1959 Universal-International release, *Operation Petticoat*. The studio prospered during the late 1950s and early 1960s when it released a number of highly successful light romantic comedies featuring such popular performers as Doris Day, Rock Hudson, and Cary Grant. In his extraordinary arrangement with the Universal studio, Mr. Grant was given all rights to the negatives of his pictures after seven years.

television subsidiary, Revue Productions, to produce *Stars Over Hollywood* and other shows for network television. Within four years, MCA's income from television rentals exceeded its agency commissions.

During the 1950s, MCA had to depend on rental space

for its television productions. With the purchase of the Universal studio, MCA was able to expand its television production activities considerably. Universal City became the home of *Wagon Train, Riverboat, Bachelor Father* and scores of other television programs and series. In 1961, under pressure from the Justice Department, MCA was forced to decide between being an agent and being an employer of talent. MCA's dual role was thought to constitute a serious conflict of interest. By then, however, the choice was clear. MCA moved to divest itself of its talent agency. The television production business had become so lucrative that by 1962 MCA was able to absorb both Universal Pictures and the controlling company, Decca Records.

By the end of the 1950s, the lines between the making of theatrical features and telefilms were becoming blurred. The new decade would witness far-reaching structural changes in the management, financing and control of all aspects of the entertainment industry. The outlines of corporate structure, audience constituencies and economic possibilities were already being transformed by television, the newest of the media.

Censorship: from Dolorita to Deep Throat

ALMOST from its inception the movie industry has been subjected to the scrutiny and disapproval of social reformers and moral agitators. The first glimmer of censorship came as early as 1895, when the showing of an innocuous short film, provocatively promoted as "Dolorita in the Passion Dance," caused a flurry of excitement at a Kinetoscope parlor on the boardwalk at Atlantic City; the film was promptly removed to appease local authorities. The following year a Vitascope presentation of the prolonged kiss between May Irwin and John C. Rice from their Broadway hit, *The Widow Jones,* produced a storm of moral agitation. In New York City a showing of the short film *Orange Blossoms,* which featured a pantomime of a young bride preparing for her wedding night by deftly disrobing so as to reveal very little flesh, was closed in 1897 by court order. The presiding judge denounced the film as "offensive to public decency."

Early in the twentieth century, as nickelodeons multiplied throughout the country, the institutions of social control—churches, reform groups, police, segments of the press—intensified their efforts to exert influence over the content of the new medium. The first municipal censorship ordinance was passed in Chicago, in 1907. It not only empowered the superintendent of police to issue permits for the exhibition of motion pictures, but also invested him with the right to withhold or deny such permission for films deemed "immoral" or "obscene." Standards for judgment were determined by the personal predilections of the local authorities. Beginning in 1911, state censorship boards began to appear. The first state to pass a censorship law was Pennsylvania; Ohio and Kansas followed in 1913; Maryland in 1916; New York in 1921; and Virginia in 1922.

NATIONAL BOARD OF REVIEW

The first national system of voluntary censorship was attempted in March of 1909, when the members of the Motion Picture Patents Company joined forces with Dr. Charles Sprague Smith of the People's Institute of New York, an institution for adult education and social research. The resultant National Board of Censorship was created in response to a direct threat against the financial welfare of the fledgling movie industry. In December of the previous year, Mayor George B. McClellan of New York, under pressure from local church and civic leaders, had ordered all movie houses in the city closed. The stated purpose for this action was to inspect the theatre dwellings for safety hazards, but the mayor announced that he would issue new licenses only on the condition that exhibitors agreed, in writing, to remain closed on Sundays. The mayor also threatened to revoke the licenses of exhibitors who showed films that tended "to degrade or injure the morals of the community." Exhibitors successfully petitioned the courts for injunctions allowing the theatres to open; meanwhile the movie hierarchy decided that decisive action was necessary to forestall any further such intimidative activity. The members of the Motion Picture Patents Company, who produced about two-thirds of the films made in the United States, agreed to submit all their films to the Board for pre-release inspection.

The newly created National Board of Censorship (later changed to the less foreboding National Board of Review) was comprised of social workers, educators, church people and other public-spirited citizens. Authority within the organization rested in a General Committee of 20 members chosen from civic and educational organizations. A number of censoring subcommittees, selected by the General Committee, previewed and evaluated films to determine their suitability for public viewing. Initially, the Board charged a fee of $3.50 for each thousand feet of film negative it examined. Producers agreed to abide by the decisions of the censorship committee, subject to a right of appeal to the General Committee. Often the Board required that certain scenes be excised before it gave its seal of approval—originally an open pair of scissors superimposed on a four-pointed star. Judgment of a particular film was based on the presumed effects its content would have on a large heterogeneous audience. Reviewed films were listed in the Board's weekly bulletin and classified as "Passed," or "Passed with changes as specified," or "Condemned." Although the Board lacked the legal authority to compel compliance with its recommendations, it wielded some influence on the national level through the police chiefs, mayors and local civic organizations throughout the country who received its weekly list of films. Producers who received the Board's seal of approval were generally assured that their films would be shown in those cities and states without official censorship boards. The industry-supported Board, however, eventually came under external fire for its liberal policies and its opposition to official censorship. Many began to question whether its function was to oversee or to overlook. Among the Board's detractors was the Reverend Clifford Trombley, Rector of St. James Church in Lancaster, Pennsylvania, who conducted a study which compared 228 films examined by both the Pennsylvania

Board of Censors and the National Board of Review. Trombley found that the state censor had required 1,464 deletions in the 228 films, while the Board had recommended only 47 deletions. The Board also lost many supporters as a result of its active campaign against proposed censorship legislation in several states. Included among the defectors was the influential General Federation of Women's Clubs. It soon became apparent that the Board was not strong enough to overcome the mounting pressure from public organizations for more official censorship.

MOVIES NOT PROTECTED

Pressure groups working for legal censorship had received new impetus in 1915 when the U.S. Supreme Court in the *Mutual* case, unanimously upheld Ohio's censorship law. Harry E. Aitken Mutual Film Corporation, a Detroit-based company, had sought to enjoin enforcement of the law because it failed to set up precise standards by which films were to be approved or rejected. The Ohio censorship board, which functioned under the authority and supervision of the state's Industrial Commission, could only approve those films which they determined were of a ". . . moral, educational or amusing and harmless character." Mutual asserted that the statute violated the free speech guarantee of the Ohio Constitution and the First Amendment. Indeed, had this sort of prior restraint been applied to the press, it would doubtless have been unconstitutional. The Supreme Court dismissed the question of federal protection entirely saying, in upholding the Ohio law, that the exhibition of motion pictures was a "business pure and simple, originated and conducted for profit like other spectacles, not to be regarded by the Ohio Constitution, . . . as part of the press of the country or as organs of public opinion." The First Amendment didn't become applicable to the states until a decade later. In 1925 the U.S. Supreme Court, in the

Gitlow case, ruled that freedom of speech and press are among those unspecified "privileges" and "immunities" protected from impairment by the states under the due process clause of the Fourteenth Amendment. Nevertheless, the High Court's decision in the *Mutual* case stood for nearly four decades.

Given the absence of constitutional safeguards, movie producers had to tread cautiously, displaying a marked solicitude for the institutions of social control. Censors, using the many potentialities of their power, grew increasingly hostile to any manifestation of cinematic eccentricity. In 1915, Representative Dudley M. Hughes of Georgia, Chairman of the House Education Committee, introduced a bill to establish a five-member Federal Motion Picture Commission which would examine, censor and license all films prior to their interstate shipment. The cost of the Commission was to be borne by the movie industry. Although the bill was defeated, it alerted industry leaders to the need for a strong national organization to avert federal censorship. In the summer of 1916 the leading producers and distributors formed the National Association of the Movie Industry. This organization eventually proposed a constitutional amendment providing for freedom of the screen, but it was defeated in Congressional committee. In March of 1921, the industry's reigning powers, under the benign aegis of the National Association of the Motion Picture Industry, adopted a 13-point code to serve as a yardstick for the production and exhibition of motion pictures. Subject matter proscribed by the code included: exploitive use of sex, white slavery, illicit love, nakedness or scanty attire, prolonged expressions of passionate love, vice, the presentation of gambling or drunkenness in an attractive light, the depreciation of governmental authority or religion, undue bloodshed and violence, the display of vulgar or improper gestures and attitudes, and the use of salacious advertising matter. All segments of the Association agreed to adhere to these resolutions. Members who violated the code's dictates were threatened with expulsion.

This self-regulatory code was adopted by the industry in an effort to stem the rise of criticism against motion pictures. In the period following World War I there had been a general relaxation of moral standards which was mildly reflected on the screen. Since the profits of the major companies depended on maintaining a large heterogeneous audience, they were compelled to adhere to accepted fashions and forms of behavior. As a result, the complexion of motion pictures was probably more conservative than revolutionary. Nevertheless innuendoes of sex, seduction, divorce, and the use of alcohol and narcotics were introduced into the early post-war films.

It soon became apparent that the "thirteen points" of propriety codified by the National Association of the Motion Picture Industry were not being effectively enforced. The organization fell into further disrepute when it badly bungled an attempt to thwart the passage of censorship legislation which was pending in the New York State legislature. Entreaties and supplications to the Governor also met with failure. Such incursions into state politics proved to be the National Association's undoing. In August 1921, the same month the New York Censorship Board began its work, Senator Henry L. Myers of South Dakota requested the Senate Judiciary Committee to conduct an investigation into the political activities of the movie industry. Both the National Association of the Motion Picture Industry and the National Board of Review were mentioned unfavorably in the resolution. Although nothing official ever came of the Myers resolution, it served to weaken the two organizations further in the censorship battle. In the early months of 1922, censorship bills were introduced in more than two dozen state legislatures.

SCANDAL ERUPTS

A succession of scandals had served to further exacerbate the movie industry's plight. The first hint of scandal came early in 1920 when Mary Pickford, "America's Sweetheart," established residence in Nevada and secured a divorce from her husband, actor Owen Moore. A short time later, she and Douglas Fairbanks were married in California. The attorney general in Nevada made headlines when he filed suit to set aside Miss Pickford's divorce decree because of alleged "collusion, fraud and untruthful testimony." The Nevada Supreme Court eventually upheld the divorce, but Miss Pickford's fall from grace provided more fuel for the legislative locomotive of the professional reformers.

As other and more serious allegations of moral dereliction and degeneracy were inflated by the tabloids into national scandals the attack against the movie industry intensified. Late in the summer of 1921, popular comedian Roscoe "Fatty" Arbuckle, who had shortly before signed a three-year $3 million dollar contract with Paramount, became involved in a scandal that shook the foundations of the movie industry. On Labor Day weekend in 1921 Arbuckle, with another actor and a director, had rented three adjoining suites at the St. Francis Hotel in San Francisco for a party. During the festivities one of the guests, a minor screen actress named Virginia Rappe, was found fatally ill in a bedroom, her clothes tattered and torn. She later died in a hospital from peritonitis caused by the rupture of her bladder. Testimony from Mrs. Bambina Maude Delmont, a friend of Miss Rappe's, placed Arbuckle alone with the young woman in the locked bedroom. Screams were reported to have been heard through the door. Arbuckle was indicted for manslaughter and tried three times (the first two trials resulted in hung juries). Newspapers across the country gave the case front-page coverage. Although Arbuckle was eventually acquitted, his acting career was destroyed. Protests from community groups caused his earlier films to be withdrawn from distribution, and three pictures completed before his arrest were not released. Paramount had to write-off a million-dollar loss from the unreleased pictures.

In this 1933 photograph, Fatty Arbuckle and his third wife, the former Addie McPhail, wave goodbye as they leave Newark Airport on route to Hollywood. The once-popular comedian was to begin a series of two-reel comedy productions under the Warner banner. Arbuckle had been barred from the movies as a performer almost twelve years earlier, when he was indicted for manslaughter in the death of a minor screen actress. In the ensuring years, he had turned to directing, using the name William Goodrich. His screen comeback ended abruptly on June 29, 1933 with his untimely death. Formerly extremely wealthy, he left an estate of only $2,000.

MUSEUM OF MODERN ART/FILM STILLS ARCHIVE

RISING STORM

While the Arbuckle case was being tried on the front pages of newspapers throughout the country, moviedom's emerging aristocracy recognized that immediate and decisive action was necessary to stem the swelling tide of moral criticism against the movie industry. The major companies decided that a new trade association should be created to supersede earlier, less effective attempts at unity. The person to head this new organization needed to be someone above reproach, an individual who could lend his personal prestige, dignity and respectability to the business of movie-making. In addition, he would have to be a good administrator, with strong political contacts, so that he could effectually stave off any further attempts at state or federal regulation. All of these attributes seemed to be embodied in one man, Will Hays, President Harding's Postmaster General. Early in 1922, in a letter signed by moviedom's most powerful monarchs—including Adolph Zukor, William Fox, Samuel Goldwyn and Carl Laemmle—Hays was offered a three-year contract at an annual salary of $100,000. He accepted and on March 12, 1922, the Motion Picture Producers and Distributors of America (MPPDA), as the new trade association was officially called, was incorporated in New York State. Hays was formally appointed as president, chairman of the board of directors and chairman of the executive committee. Under the bylaws, Hays had the power of veto over all decisions by the board of directors; a two-thirds vote by the board was required to override his veto. The new organization, which was comprised of all the major movie companies, was financed by a small percentage of the gross receipts of its members.

While Will Hays was preparing to assume his new post, another scandal erupted in the movie community. On the night of February 1, 1922, William Desmond Taylor, a director with Famous Players-Lasky, was shot to death at his home. Newspapers quickly increased their circulation by insinuating that the case involved sex and drugs. Evidence was found in the house that romantically linked the murdered director with actress Mary Miles Minter. Comedienne Mabel Normand, another of Taylor's amours, was known to be one of the last people to see him alive. Further investigation uncovered that Taylor was not his real name, that he had deserted a wife and daughter in New York. The mystery became more intriguing when it was revealed that Taylor had also been involved with Miss Minter's mother. The murder was never solved and, although Normand and Minter were eventually cleared of suspicion, their careers were ruined by the scandal.

By the middle of 1922, more than half the states in the union were considering some form of censorship legislation. In March of 1922, while the MPPDA was taking form, the General Assembly of Virginia passed a censorship law that empowered a State Board of Censors to censor films that were obscene or likely to incite crime. In Massachusetts the legislature had passed a censorship bill in 1920, but it was vetoed by the state's governor, Calvin Coolidge. A similar bill was passed the following year, however, and exhibitors in the state managed to collect enough petitions to force a referendum on the censorship legislation in the November elections of 1922. Since this was the first test of the general public's attitude about censorship, Hays decided to launch a fierce campaign under the banner of "free speech" to defeat the legislation. The result of the referendum was a resounding victory for Hays; the censorship bill was defeated by a vote of almost three to one. By the end of the year, the pressure for censorship legislation seemed to abate.

In his efforts to quell the rising storm of public criticism against the movie industry, Hays had successfully enlisted the support of numerous national agencies committed to social reform. A few months after taking office, he arranged a conference at the old Waldorf Hotel in New York with those religious, civic, welfare and educational organizations most concerned about motion pictures. He urged them to abandon all support for censorship legislation and to help the industry reform itself. More than 200 persons attended, representing such groups as the Boy Scouts of America, the National Council of Catholic Women, the National Congress of Parents and Teachers, and the Daughters of American Revolution.

This conference resulted in the formation of the Committee on Public Relations, an independent coalition which was comprised of representatives from the various national organizations. The committee's first chairman was Lee F. Hammer, director of recreation for the Russell Sage Foundation. Colonel Jason S. Joy, former national director of the American Red

Cross and a prominent Methodist layman, was appointed executive secretary. For almost three years the committee served as intermediary between the movie industry and the various national organizations. Its purpose was twofold: It registered complaints with the industry about those films it found objectionable; and it encouraged the civic and religious organizations to publicize those films it found worthwhile. In an effort to establish closer contact between the public and the movie industry, the Committee on Public Relations was dissolved by mutual agreement in March, 1925 and its functions were assumed by the newly created Department of Public Relations within the MPPDA. Colonel Jason Joy was placed in charge of this new division.

The first tentative attempts at formalized self-regulation began in July 1924, when the board of directors of the MPPDA passed a resolution requiring that a synopsis of all plays, novels and stories be submitted for approval before they were filmed. This policy, however, did not apply to original scripts and adherence to MPPDA's recommendations was strictly voluntary. The only means of enforcement was Hays' persuasive power, since he did not attempt to bring public pressure to bear on the producers. Responsible members of the public were encouraged, however, to bring their complaints or suggestions to the attention of the MPPDA through what Hays called the "open door" policy of the Department of Public Relations.

In the effort to encourage greater co-operation from the major producers, Hays sent Colonel Jason Joy to Hollywood in December 1926 to set up a Studio Relations Committee within the Association of Motion Picture Producers (AMPP). The AMPP was, it should be recalled, the West Coast affiliate of the MPPDA, established in 1924 to handle management-labor negotiations. Industry leaders had decided to set up another trade organization in Hollywood in order to keep their labor problems separate from the public relations activities of the MPPDA. One of the major accomplishments of the AMPP was its creation and operation of the Central Casting

Corporation, which beginning in 1926, registered all of the available "extra" players in the movie industry. Central Casting, which was given the exclusive right to furnish extras to the studios, soon became one of the largest placement agencies in the country.

Colonel Joy worked with the studios on a voluntary basis, advising them on the attitudes of the various national reform organizations and state and municipal censorship boards. The studio heads soon realized that when they followed Colonel Joy's recommendations, their distribution outlets experienced fewer problems with the censor boards. In June 1927, the activities of Colonel Joy's Studio Relations Department were formalized. A study conducted by a committee of the MPPDA on the specific rejections and deletions made by state censorship boards resulted in the codification of two lists of admonitions. Known as the "Don'ts" and "Be Carefuls," they were unanimously adopted by the members of the Association of Motion Picture Producers. The list of "Don'ts" contained 11 items which could not be shown on the screen. Included were pointed profanity—by either title or lip, licentious or suggestive nudity, illegal drug traffic, any inference of sexual perversion, white slavery, miscegenation (sex relations between white and black races), sex hygiene and venereal diseases, childbirth, children's sex organs, ridicule of the clergy and willful offense to any nation, race or creed. The list of "Be Carefuls" was comprised of 25 subjects, concerning which the producers agreed to exercise special care "to the end that vulgarity and suggestiveness may be eliminated and that good taste may be emphasized." Included on this list were such things as the use of the flag, international relations, arson, firearms, theft, robbery, brutality, murder techniques, methods of smuggling, hangings or electrocutions, sympathy for criminals, sedition, cruelty to children or animals, the sale of women, rape or attempted rape, first-night scenes, man and woman in bed together, deliberate seduction of girls, the institution of marriage, surgical operations, the use of drugs, and excessive or lustful kissing.

Although the new code was widely heralded by the MPPDA as an indication of the movie industry's ability to regulate itself, the manifest weight of the evidence contradicted such a claim. The new code differed from the earlier "thirteen points" of the defunct National Association of the Motion Picture Industry primarily in its greater length. As in earlier efforts at self-regulation, the "Dont's and Be Carefuls" were broad and general in character and lacked any enforcement machinery. With the general introduction of sound in 1929, the criticism of movie content increased in intensity. It soon became apparent that more substantial self-regulatory fortifications were needed to avert the threat of official censorship.

PRODUCTION CODE

One of the most outspoken and influential agitators for motion picture reform was Martin Quigley, a Catholic layman and publisher of the important trade magazine *Motion Picture Herald.* Quigley was critical of the vague, generalized character of the existing code. He enlisted the support of Daniel A. Lord, a Jesuit priest who had been a technical advisor on the biblical epic, *The King of Kings,* to draft a new, more elaborate self-regulatory code. Quigley and Lord conferred with Will Hays on several occasions prior to presenting him with the final draft of their expanded and revised code late in 1929. After suggesting some minor modifications and additions, Hays, promoted the Quigley-Lord code to the industry's leaders and managed to secure its adoption early in 1930. The members of the Association of Motion Picture Producers agreed to submit every film they produced to the Studio Relations Committee before it was sent to the laboratory for printing. If a film violated the Motion Picture Production Code, as the new canons of morality were officially called, it could not be released until the necessary changes were made. A panel composed of three members selected on a rotation basis from the AMPP's Production Committee, served as an appeals board with the power to overrule the decisions of the Studio Relations Committee. Initially, the submission of pre-production scripts was optional. This practice became compulsory in October 1931. Effective in June 1930, the studios were also required to submit their advertising copy for approval.

Like its predecessors, the 1930 Motion Picture Production Code was highly moralistic and restrictive in nature, prohibiting a wide range of human expression and experience from being presented in motion pictures. The Code was divided into two parts. Part one includes a preamble, general principles, and particular applications; while part two contains the philosophical rationale for each of the sections of the first part. The preamble of the Code acknowledges the high trust and confidence placed in motion picture producers and their recognition of responsibility to the public. At the same time it asks for the public's sympathetic understanding of the problems involved and for co-operation in solving them so that producers will have "the freedom and opportunity necessary to bring the motion picture to a still higher level of wholesome entertainment." The preamble is followed by three general principles. The first proscribes the production of any picture that "will lower the moral standards of those who see it. Hence the sympathy of the audience shall never be thrown to the side of crime, wrong-doing, evil or sin." The second requires the presentation of "correct standards of life, subject only to the requirements of drama and entertainment." The third principle says: "Law, natural or human, shall not be ridiculed, nor shall sympathy be created for its violation."

The main body of the Code consisted of the section on "particular applications" which is sub-divided into 12 categories. Section I (Crime), for example, says that crime "shall never be presented in such a way as to throw sympathy with the crime as against law and justice or to inspire others with a desire for imitation." There are four classifications under crime: murder, methods of crime, illegal drug traffic, and the use of liquor (the code was written when the Volstead Act ("prohibition") was still in effect). These sub-sections are further divided. Thus, the subsection under murder states that "the technique of murder must be presented in a way that will not inspire imitation"; that "brutal killings are not to be presented in detail"; that "revenge in modern times shall not be justified."

Section II (Sex) declares that "the sanctity of the institution of marriage and the home shall be upheld. Pictures shall not infer that low forms of sex relationship are the accepted or common thing." Under this general heading are sub-sections covering adultery and illicit sex, scenes of passion, seduction or rape, sex perversion, white slavery, miscegenation, sex hygiene and venereal diseases, actual childbirth, and exposure of children's sex organs. Each of these areas is briefly amplified. Thus, the sub-section under scenes of passion states that "these should not be introduced except where they are definitely essential to the plot"; that "excessive or lustful kissing, lustful embraces, suggestive postures and gestures are not to be shown"; that "in general, passion should be treated in such manner as not to stimulate the lower and baser emotions."

Under Section III (Vulgarity), the Code says that "the treatment of low, disgusting, unpleasant, though not necessarily evil, subjects should be guided always by the dictates of good taste and a proper regard for the sensibilities of the audience." And Obscenity (Section IV), states the Code, "in word, gesture, reference, song, joke, or by suggestion (even when likely to be understood only by part of the audience) is forbidden." Other sections of the Code cover profanity, costume, dance, religion, locations, national feelings, titles, and repellent subjects. The latter category includes such topics as actual hangings or electrocutions, third-degree methods, brutality and possible gruesomeness, branding of people or animals, apparent cruelty to children or animals, the sale of women, or a woman selling her virtue, and surgical operations. These subjects were to be "treated within the careful limits of good taste."

When the Motion Picture Production Code was first unveiled in April 1930, part one was presented as the entire document. There was no mention of the philosophical rationales underlying the preamble, general principles, and particular applications. Nor was attention given to the role played by Martin Quigley and Father Daniel A. Lord in recasting the "Don'ts and Be Carefuls" and furnishing them a philosophical foundation. The apparent reason for initially trying to obscure the Code's rationale and authorship was to minimize the growing criticism that the MPPDA was becoming dominated by the dictates of the Catholic Church. (The entire Code, including the philosophical sections, may be found in the Appendix.)

The enforcement mechanism for the new code, however, once again proved to be weak. Since all its decisions could be appealed to the AMPP's Production Committee, the Studio Relations Committee had, in fact very little power. The rotating panel of producers hesitated to condemn rival productions since they knew their own films might eventually come under the scrutiny of the panel.

A number of incidents during the early 1930s helped to tarnish the image of the new self-regulatory mechanism in the eyes of many reformers and censorship advocates. Soon after the Code had been ratified by the MPPDA, the Federal Council of Churches charged that many civic, club and church leaders were actually subsidized by the industry-sponsored MPPDA. As a result of these accusations, there was a rash of resignations in the various educational and religious organizations. Although no specific wrongdoing had been documented, the circumstances caused embarrassment to the Hays organization, and gave credence to the belief that the Code was a defensive stratagem intended solely to avert federal censorship. The seeds of discontent germinated quickly, fertilized by the movie industry's apparent disregard for the spirit, if not the letter, of the Code. As the full impact of the Depression began to be felt in the movie industry, producers grew increasingly more audacious in their efforts to offset losses. Paramount

Cary Grant and Mae West in a scene from the early 1933 Paramount release, *She Done Him Wrong.* Miss West's sexual repartee became a focus of agitation among reform-minded groups and contributed greatly to the demand for stricter screen censorship.

COURTESY OF UNIVERSAL

caused the greatest stir when it released several features starring the splendidly vulgar Mae West. In such vehicles as *Night After Night* (1932), *She Done Him Wrong* (1933) and *I'm No Angel* (1933), Miss West's sexual repartee (she wrote the screenplays for the latter two films) left little doubt in the minds of reformers that the Code was merely camouflage to permit producers to test the limits of public taste. The public responded enthusiastically to the West films; Miss West soared to the top in lists of box-office favorites. Her delightful mockery of morality is represented in one of her most famous lines from *Night After Night.* When a cloakroom attendant exclaims, "Goodness, what lovely diamonds," Miss West drawls, "Goodness has nothing to do with it." The lines themselves, of course, cannot account for the erotic enticement of Miss West's delivery. Everything she said sounded sexually suggestive. After the release of *She Done Him Wrong* in March 1933, Miss West became one of the principal targets of the reform crusaders. In her every word and gesture, she was thought to be a living mockery of the Code's pieties. Paramount's executives, however, found solace in the fact that the film broke box-office

Jean Harlow as she appeared at the height of her fame in the 1930s. Despite the effusion of speculative gossip that surrounded her husband's suicide, Miss Harlow's screen career continued to flourish. Early in 1937, when she was making *Saratoga,* she fell ill. For a time, she seemed to rally, and then she was fatally stricken with acute uremic poisoning. She was only 26 at the time of her death.

records, grossing more than $2 million in the first three months of its release. Still, as the reform movement gained momentum, the major studios became ever more sensitive to the demands of these special interest groups.

The image of Hollywood's lifestyle reached yet one more low ebb when a scandal involving another of the screen's sex sirens erupted on the national scene. In September of 1932, Paul Bern, who had recently married Jean Harlow, was found dead in their home, an apparent suicide. The revolver that had killed him was found several feet away from his naked body. The unusual circumstances surrounding the case added even more grist to the scandalmongers' mill. Bern had been casting director for MGM. The butler who discovered the body called the studio, instead of notifying the police. Mayer and Thalberg arrived at the scene before the police were summoned, giving rise to the rumor that they removed incriminating evidence to prevent a possible murder indictment against Jean Harlow, who was under contract to MGM. Mayer later returned a suicide note which Bern had allegedly written before taking his life. The death was officially ruled as a suicide, but rumors of wrongdoing persisted, providing ammunition for the growing army of reformers.

OPPOSITION MOUNTS

One of the most damaging blows to the movie industry's code of good conduct came early in 1933, when the results of a four-year study on the influence of motion pictures on youth were made public. The research had been initiated by the Reverend William H. Short, executive director of the Motion Picture Research Council, under a $200,000 grant from the Payne Study and Experiment Fund, a private foundation. In all, a series of 12 studies had been done by psychologists, sociologists, and educators under the direction of Dr. W. W. Charters of the Bureau of Educational Research at Ohio State

University. The studies were published in nine volumes in 1933 and 1934. Utilizing such methods as physiological experiments, rating scales, questionnaires and interviews, the research team found that a wide agglomeration of factors determined the effects of a motion picture. Age, sex, economic and social status, cultural background were among the many variables that contributed to an individual's response to motion pictures. Several of the researchers found that the viewing of certain motion pictures had a deleterious effect on some youngsters under certain circumstances; still these conclusions were cautiously qualified. However, the common preface to each volume, written by Dr. Charters, reflected a subtle hostility toward motion pictures. The motives of Dr. Charters and the Motion Picture Research Council became even more suspect when they cooperated fully with journalist Henry James Forman in the publication of a book, *Our Movie-Made Children,* based on the studies. Forman's book, which was published in 1933, presented a misleading summarization and popularization of the findings which tended to confirm some of the worst suspicions of the self-appointed guardians of the public welfare. In his distillation of the research findings Forman had failed to represent the facts fully and impartially. The major weakness of the Payne Fund studies was that they treated movies in isolation—divorcing them from the influence of comic strips, newspapers, magazines, radio and all other forms of communication which impinge on a child's psyche. Whereas many of the researchers had been cautious to qualify their findings, Forman treated them as gospel intended to bring moviemakers to redemption.

As the attack against the movie industry mounted, the MPPDA's Board of Directors met to reaffirm their original 1922 dedication to "establish and maintain the highest possible moral and artistic standards." Although producers pledged to work toward the production of "better" films, it soon became apparent the MPPDA would have to tighten up the enforcement mechanism of its self-regulatory code. Colonel Joy, who had given up the fight in 1932 to accept an executive position in the movie industry, had been replaced as head of the Studio Relations Committee by Dr. James Wingate, a former member of the censorship board in New York State. Wingate's promises of reform, however, had done little to stave off organized protest.

The most vigorous campaign for motion picture reform was initiated by the hierarchy of the Catholic Church which apparently had become disillusioned by the Hays organization's unkept promises. The first public indication of a Catholic reform movement came in October 1933 when the newly arrived apostolic delegate to the United States, Archbishop Amleto Giovanni Cicognani, addressed the National Conference of Catholic Charities in New York City. The Archbishop rallied Catholics "to a united and vigorous campaign for the purification of the cinema, which has become a deadly menace to morals." One month later, at the annual American Bishops' Convention, the Catholic bishops decided to organize the National Legion of Decency to carry out the Archbishop's mandate. An Episcopal Committee on Motion Pictures was appointed to organize the reform movement. The following April, the Episcopal Committee officially launched its campaign against objectionable motion pictures. The bishops of each of the Catholic Church's 104 dioceses nationwide were to recruit members for the "Legion of Decency." Catholics in each diocese were entreated to repeat or sign a pledge which condemned absolutely "those salacious motion pictures which, with other degrading agencies, are corrupting public morals and promoting a sex mania in our land." A rising storm of moral protest swept across the country. In Philadelphia, Cardinal Dougherty called for boycott by Catholics of all motion picture theatres in the city. The Cardinal's call to arms brought national attention to the Legion of Decency's campaign. Theatre boycotts were threatened in St. Louis, Boston, and other major cities. An estimated seven to nine million Catholics formally pledged to stay away from "indecent and immoral films." Numerous non-Catholic religious, civic, and educational groups, including the United Presbyterian Assembly, the Massachusetts Civic League, the Christian Endeavor Union, the National Conference of Christian and Jews and the Federal Council of Churches of Christ in America, joined the swelling ranks of those pledged to support the fight against objectionable films. The marshaling of such a large and solid body of highly influential public opinion strongly and actively opposed to alleged improprieties in motion pictures could not be ignored by the movie industry without serious economic consequences. Motion picture producers, already caught in the throes of the Depression, heeded the call to repent.

ENFORCEMENT

In the summer of 1934, less than three months after the formation of the Legion of Decency, the MPPDA abolished the Studio Relations Committee and replaced it with the more formidable Production Code Administration (PCA). The AMPP's rotating appeals panel was also eliminated, leaving only an appeal directly from the new PCA to the Board of Directors of the MPPDA. Joseph Breen, a devout Catholic, father of six children, former newspaper and publicity man, was placed in charge of the PCA at an annual salary of $20,000. The members of the MPPDA agreed not to release or distribute any film unless it received a certificate of approval signed by the director of PCA. The PCA was financed separately from the other activities of the MPPDA. Producers were charged a fee based on the total production cost of each picture submitted for approval. A resolution was passed empowering the PCA to impose a $25,000 fine against any MPPDA member who sold, distributed or exhibited any film not bearing the seal of approval. The Advertising Code (see Appendix) also became binding the following year with a fine ranging from $1,000 to $5,000 for failure to honor its dictates. In addition, the MPPDA's Title Registration Bureau, which had been established in 1925 to eliminate the duplication of motion picture titles, was now given the authority to prohibit the use of salacious, indecent or obscene titles.

By the end of 1934 the impact of the new enforcement mechanism had already become apparent. The PCA closely followed productions from script to preview. Producers often consulted with Breen's staff on story material even before a property was purchased. The new regulatory structure made a changed woman of Mae West. It was not a change for the better. The title of her latest film, *It Ain't No Sin,* was transformed to *Belle of the Nineties* and her scintillating repartee and sexual independence were toned down considerably. Jean Harlow suffered the same fate. Her newest picture went through several title changes before it was released—from *One Hundred Per Cent Pure* to *Born to be Kissed* to, finally, *The Girl from Missouri.* Her film *Reckless* had to be reworked several times before it received Code approval. The PCA's interpretation of the Code's provisions sometimes bordered on the absurd. While Ernst Lubitsch's *The Merry Widow* was in production, the PCA objected to a scene in which Maurice Chevalier took Jeanette MacDonald in his arms and, carrying her across the room (kissing her as he did so), placed her on the sofa. The PCA agreed to pass the film only "if Miss MacDonald keeps her feet on the floor as she is placed on the sofa." The PCA, operating under a self-imposed set of taboos, soon became more restrictive than many of the state and municipal censors.

Within a remarkably short period of time, the Catholic Church had obtained what reform-minded groups had sought since the Kinetoscope first appeared—the power to exert a profound influence on motion picture content. The Legion of Decency, which the Catholic bishops had formally resolved to make a permanent institution in November 1934, continued to wield great power over the movie industry for more than a quarter of a century. Beginning in February 1936, the Catholic Church systematically reviewed and classified motion pictures.

The task of assigning moral ratings to films was given to the International Federation of Catholic Alumnae. A film was placed in one of four categories: A-1, morally unobjectionable for general patronage; A-2, morally unobjectionable for adults; B, morally objectionable in part for all; C, condemned. Since a film which received a moral rating of "C" was thought to be doomed to box-office failure, the major studios were generally cautious not to offend the Catholic Church.

Not all Legion of Decency campaigns were aimed at curtailing cinematic sex and sin. The Catholic Church on occasion entered into the political arena. It strongly opposed the showing of Walter Wanger's 1938 production, *Blockade,* a mildly pro-loyalist film dealing with the Spanish civil war. The Knights of Columbus and other pro-Franco Catholic groups actively boycotted and picketed theatres showing the film. As a result of Catholic pressure, the film was banned in several cities. Confrontations of this type between Catholics and the movie industry were infrequent, however, since the producers generally eschewed political controversy.

In those few instances when the Legion of Decency and the major studios came into conflict it was usually over sexual matters. MGM's 1941 release of *Two-Faced Woman,* a comedy of errors in which Greta Garbo played identical twins, caused a mild furor when the film received a "condemned" rating even though the PCA had given it a certificate of approval. The picture dealt with a plain-looking wife's attempt to entice her indifferent husband by impersonating her more glamorous twin sister. To win Catholic approval, MGM agreed to shoot a completely new scene in which the husband receives a telephone call apprising him of the masquerade. The rest of the film is senselessly played as though he didn't know the glamorous sister he is pursuing is really his wife.

The controversy surrounding *Two-Faced Woman* had occurred in Joseph Breen's absence. Breen had left the PCA in June 1941 to serve as production head at RKO. While he was away, Geoffrey Shurlock, an English-born Episcopalian who had joined the Studio Relations Committee in 1932, served as acting director of the PCA. Breen returned to the PCA in June of 1942. That same year, the MPPDA passed an amendment which freed its membership of the threat of a $25,000 levy for exhibiting films without PCA approval. (The fine for recalcitrant producers and distributors remained in effect until 1956). The fine, in cases of exhibition, was rescinded because it was thought to be in violation of the antitrust laws. The change had little immediate effect since the oligarchical structure of the movie industry assured continued adherence to the Production Code. Throughout the 1940s, the PCA reviewed and approved over 95 per cent of the films exhibited throughout the United States.

In September of 1945, Eric Johnston, president of the U.S. Chamber of Commerce, succeeded the aging Will Hays as president of the MPPDA. Johnston received an annual salary of $150,000, plus an additional $50,000 for expenses. Three months after taking command, Johnston changed the name of the organization to the more succinct Motion Picture Association of America (MPAA).

THE OUTLAW

The first serious court challenge to the production and advertising codes of the Motion Picture Association came from Howard Hughes. In 1940, after an eight-year absence from the movie business, Hughes began production on a film entitled *The Outlaw,* a fictional account of the escapades of Billy the Kid. For the role of Billy, Hughes chose an unknown actor named Jack Buetel. The female leading role, Rio, was played by another unknown, 19-year old Jane Russell. These two novices were supported by veteran character actors Walter Huston and Thomas Mitchell. Filming for *The Outlaw* began on location in Arizona under the direction of Howard Hawks. Each day's footage was flown back to Hughes in Los Angeles by

An early 1940s publicity still of Jane Russell. When Howard Hughes selected Miss Russell to play the female lead in *The Outlaw,* he hired publicist Russell Birdwell to paper the United States with her pictures. Within a two-year period, some 43,000 different photographs of Miss Russell were distributed to newspapers and magazines throughout the nation.

MUSEUM OF MODERN ART/FILM STILLS ARCHIVE

private plane. Hughes, after viewing the rushes, would send his criticisms and suggestions back to Hawks. Hawks, noted for his fierce independence, objected to the interference. He resigned and went to Warner Brothers where he made *Sergeant York.* Hughes' chartered train moved the entire company of 250 actors and technicians from Arizona back to Los Angeles where Hughes himself directed the film.

In one scene Miss Russell, the victim of Indian torture, was tied by leather thongs between two trees. Hughes, the aeronautical expert, designed a special brassiere for Miss Russell to emphasize her unusual contours as she writhed about, as if in agony. In another scene, the camera eye lingers on Miss Russell's anatomy as she is leaning over Billy's bed in a loosely fitting blouse to treat his wounds. Indeed, throughout the film Miss Russell was often bending over for one reason or another.

A publicity campaign was launched for *The Outlaw* even before shooting began. Hughes hired Russell Birdwell, the press agent who handled publicity for *Gone With the Wind,* to promote *The Outlaw.* Birdwell flooded the newspapers and magazines with provocative pictures of Jane Russell. She became a celebrity before the public ever saw her on the screen.

In the spring of 1941, a print of the finished picture was submitted to the Production Code Administration for approval. After screening the film, Joseph Breen wrote to Hughes explaining why *The Outlaw* could not be approved. Breen objected especially to "the countless shots of Rio, in which her breasts are not fully covered." He suggested several changes. Hughes made some revisions and resubmitted the film. Following additional screenings of *The Outlaw,* the PCA outlined specifically the cuts necessary to bring the picture into conformity with the Production Code. Hughes appealed the PCA's decision, and was granted a hearing before the MPPDA's board of directors in New York City. At the hearing, Russell Birdwell, Hughes' publicity director, displayed stills of Jean Harlow, Norma Shearer, Rita Hayworth, Ann Sheridan, and Marlene Dietrich among others. A mathematician, using calipers, demonstrated that proportionately the amount of anatomical exposure in the objectionable stills of Miss Russell was no greater than that shown in the stills taken from the PCA approved movies of the other actresses. Hughes eventually agreed to the removal of some additional footage from the controversial scenes and a certificate of approval was issued to *The Outlaw.* Hughes continued to work on the film. He even personally directed production on the excerpts used for the "coming attractions." By the time Hughes was ready to release *The Outlaw,* Twentieth Century–Fox, the company scheduled to distribute the film, had cancelled its agreement. On February 5, 1943, the first public exhibition of *The Outlaw* began at a single theatre in San Francisco. Provocative poses of Miss Russell were displayed on billboards throughout the San Francisco area. The advertising for the film's debut created an uproar and resulted in a flood of protest. Arrests were threatened and the offensive posters were withdrawn. The publicity campaign was a resounding success. *The Outlaw* played to record-breaking numbers of people for ten straight weeks. Hughes then withdrew the film and concerned himself with the war effort.

Early in 1946, United Artists, which at the time was not a member of MPAA, released *The Outlaw* nationwide. Once again, Hughes launched a massive advertising campaign. Newspapers, magazines, billboards and even sky writing proclaimed the attributes of Jane Russell. An airplane wrote the words "The Outlaw" in the sky over Pasadena, and then made two enormous circles with a dot in the middle of each. Newspaper advertisements for the movie asked such provocative questions as "How would you like to tussle with Russell?" and "What are the two reasons for Jane Russell's rise to stardom?" and some contained the false and misleading statement, "Exactly as filmed—not a scene cut." Many of the advertisements used in the publicity campaign had not been submitted to the Code Authority for approval, or had been rejected after being submitted.

In what was then an unprecedented action, the Motion Picture Association moved to withdraw its previously issued seal of approval. The Hughes Tool Company, owner of Hughes Productions, filed suit against the MPAA in the U.S. District Court in the Southern District of New York charging violation of the antitrust laws, restraint of trade, and contravention of the First Amendment guarantee of free expression. The Hughes complaint requested damages totalling $6 million. The suit was brought before the district court on April 22, 1946. A temporary restraining order was issued prohibiting the MPAA from revoking its certificate of approval. In June, the district court vacated the restraining order and denied Hughes' motion to enjoin the MPAA from voiding its certificate of approval until the case was tried on its merits. Judge John Bright, in rendering his decision, outlined the events leading up to the MPAA's revocation of its seal of approval. He found no evidence that the policies of the trade association tended to reduce or destroy competition in the production, distribution or exhibition of motion pictures. Nor did he find that the MPAA's practices were aimed or designed to achieve such an effect. With regard to Hughes' meretricious advertising activities, Judge Bright held that "the industry can suffer as much from indecent advertising as from indecent pictures. Once a picture has been approved the public may properly assume that the advertisement and promotional matter of the picture are likewise approved. The blame for improper, salacious or false advertising is placed as much at the door of the defendant as of the producer." Hughes appealed this decision to the U.S. Circuit Court of Appeals for the Second Circuit, but his request for a stay was again denied. On September 6, 1946, Hughes Productions was ordered to return the certificate of approval for *The Outlaw* and to remove the MPAA's seal from all prints of the motion picture.

Since the MPAA's $25,000 fine no longer applied to exhibition, a number of theatres were willing to show *The Outlaw* even though it lacked a certificate of approval. Many state and municipal censorship boards, however, insisted upon alterations and deletions before the picture was permitted to be shown. A Maryland judge upheld a complete ban on the picture, and noted that Jane Russell's breasts "hung over the picture like a thunderstorm spread out over a summer landscape." Hughes' widely publicized difficulties with the censors had a salutary effect on the box office. United Artists was able to secure enough play dates by 1948 to enable the film to earn over $3 million.

THE HIGH COURT

The power of state and municipal censors to control film exhibition in any way they saw fit was substantially diminished beginning in 1952, when the U.S. Supreme Court finally brought motion pictures within the scope of free speech and free press guaranteed by the First Amendment and made applicable to the states by the Fourteenth. The case to come before the High Court involved an Italian-made movie called *The Miracle,* which was written and directed by Roberto Rossellini and starred Anna Magnani. The film concerned a peasant woman who is seduced by a bearded stranger she believes to be Saint Joseph. Later she conceives a male child whom she imagines is Jesus Christ. The motion picture division of the New York Education Department, which since 1927 had been vested with the full authority to preview all movies shown in the state, licensed the film, first without English subtitles, then with subtitles, in 1949 and 1950 respectively. *The Miracle* opened at the Paris Theatre in New York City on December 12, 1950, with two French films as part of a trilogy called *The Ways of Love.* Twelve days later, New York City Commissioner of Licenses, Edward T. McCaffrey, declared *The Miracle* "officially and personally blasphemous" and ordered it removed from the screen. The New York Supreme Court, however, ruled that McCaffrey had exceeded his authority. In the meantime, the Legion of Decency had condemned *The Miracle* as a "sacrilegious and blasphemous mockery of Christian and religious truth." Cardinal Spellman, Archbishop of New York, also denounced the film and enjoined Catholics not to patronize theatres where it was scheduled to be shown. Following the Cardinal's denunciation, members of the Catholic War Veterans picketed the Paris Theatre. The theatre even received bomb threats.

Claiming to have been deluged with hundreds of letters, postcards and telegrams protesting the showing of *The Mira-*

cle, the New York Board of Regents ordered a special three-member subcommittee to review the film. When the committee found *The Miracle* to be "sacrilegious," i.e., in violation of state law, Joseph Burstyn, the American distributor of the film, was ordered to appear before the Board of Regents to show cause why his license should not be rescinded. Burstyn refused to appear on the ground that the board lacked the authority to revoke a license once it had been granted. After reviewing the film, the full board unanimously agreed that it was sacrilegious, and revoked its license. Burstyn appealed the board's decision in the courts. The Appellate Division of the New York Supreme Court and the New York Court of Appeals both upheld the action of the Board of Regents. Late in May of 1952, a unanimous U.S. Supreme Court, in reversing the lower court decision, ruled that the New York law was an unconstitutional abridgement of free speech and free press. The standard of "sacrilegious," stated the court, was "far from the kind of narrow exception to freedom of expression which a state may carve out to satisfy the adverse demands of other interests of society." Furthermore, said the court, "In seeking to apply the broad and all-inclusive definition of 'sacrilegious' given by the New York courts, the censor is set adrift upon a boundless sea amid a myriad of conflicting currents of religious views, with no charts but those provided by the most vocal and powerful orthodoxies." The court further held that the state had no legitimate interest in protecting the various religions from distasteful views, sufficient to justify prior restraint. The U.S. Supreme Court, however, did not deal with the broader issue of whether all prior licensing of motion pictures is in itself unconstitutional.

Throughout the 1950s, the U.S. Supreme Court, in a series of cases, continued to reduce the powers of the censors. By 1959, only four states had censorship boards—Kansas, Maryland, New York and Virginia. Finally, the court in 1961 ruled on the constitutional status of licensing *per se* in a case involving *Don Juan,* a film version of Mozart's opera *Don Giovanni.*

The film's distributor, Times Film Corporation, apparently had decided to challenge Chicago's censorship law. After paying the license fee, the distributor refused to submit the film to Chicago's superintendent of police for previewing. When the city refused to grant a license for exhibition, Times appealed the decision in the federal courts, charging that Chicago's licensing system and all prior restraint of motion pictures was unconstitutional. Both the district court and court of appeals dismissed the complaint. In a 5-to-4 decision, the U.S. Supreme Court upheld the city's power to license films and ruled that prior censorship of motion pictures was not unconstitutional. Motion pictures, said the court, are not "necessarily subject to the precise rules governing any other particular method of expression. Each method . . . tends to present its own peculiar problems." Taking care to limit the scope of its ruling, the court said that no "unreasonable strictures on individual liberty" should result from prior restraint. Chief Justice Warren, in a heated dissent, cited historical examples of the abuses of prior restraint and concluded that the majority's decision "officially unleashes the censor and permits him to roam at will, limited only by an ordinance which contains some standards that, although concededly not before us in this case, are patently imprecise."

The U.S. Supreme Court attempted to clarify its position on prior restraint of motion pictures in the 1965 *Freedman* case. The court unanimously reversed the conviction of Ronald Freedman, a Baltimore theatre manager, for exhibiting the film *Revenge at Daybreak* without a license. Although the court recognized the exercise of licensing power, it held that Maryland did not provide adequate procedural safeguards "against undue inhibition of expression." The court shifted the burden of proof to the censors and required swift judicial review of licensing decisions in future cases.

When the U.S. Supreme Court began to erect a constitutional bulwark against the actions of state and municipal censorship boards, the guardians of the public welfare, in their efforts to control motion picture content, turned to the nation's obscenity laws. Both state and federal jurisdictions have consistently maintained that obscenity is beyond the pale of the constitutional protection intended to safeguard freedom of speech and press. However, beginning in 1957, the Supreme Court, in attempting to define obscenity and to set standards for applying that definition, has continuously increased the diversity of subject matter covered by the shield of the First Amendment, oftentimes to topics previously thought to be obscene. The High Court handed down its first major decision on obscenity in the 1957 *Roth* case. Although the court ruled in a five-to-four decision that "obscenity is not within the area of constitutionally protected speech and press," it qualified its judgment by stating that "sex and obscenity are not synonymous." Obscene material, stated the court, deals with sex in a manner "appealing to the prurient interest." The Court rejected the British *Hicklin* test of obscenity which allowed material to be judged merely by the effect of an isolated excerpt upon particularly susceptible persons, and sanctioned the test which had been evolving in the federal and state courts: "whether to the average person, applying contemporary community standards, the dominant theme of the work taken as a whole appeals to the prurient interest." The court included under the protection of the Constitution "all ideas having even the slightest redeeming social importance." Although the *Roth* case dealt specifically with printed matter, its impact was felt on all communications media.

Throughout the 1960s, the High Court continued to refine its definition of obscenity. In 1964 the Supreme Court applied its obscenity standards directly to the motion picture medium in the *Jacobellis* case. Nico Jacobellis, a Cleveland Heights, Ohio theatre manager, had been convicted on two counts of possessing and exhibiting an obscene film, *The Lovers.* The film, which contained a short but explicit love scene, had already been shown in a number of cities in the United States including Columbus and Toledo, Ohio. At least two critics of major importance rated it among the ten best films of the year in which it was released. In a six to three decision, the Supreme Court ruled that the film was not obscene within the standards enunciated in the *Roth* case since it was not "utterly without redeeming social importance." Justice Brennan, writing the judgment for the court, stated that "material dealing with sex in a manner that advocates ideas . . . or has literary or scientific or artistic value or any other forms of social importance may not be branded as obscenity and denied constitutional protection." Justice Brennan, whose opinion was joined only by Justice Goldberg, held without qualification that a national standard should be used in applying the test for obscenity. In particular he saw the inherent danger in localized standards—that is inhibition of expression, since sellers and exhibitors might be reluctant to risk criminal conviction by testing the variations of taste among different locales. The four other prevailing Justices concurred separately without addressing themselves to the issue of national versus local standards.

Two years later, the Supreme Court further clarified its definition of obscenity in the *Memoirs* case. The Superior Court of Suffolk County, Massachusetts had found the book *Memoirs of a Woman of Pleasure,* more commonly known as "Fanny Hill," to be obscene. This decision was upheld by the Supreme Court of Massachusetts. The U.S. Supreme Court, however, ruled that the Massachusetts courts had failed to consider the "redeeming social value" of the work. Justice Brennan, in his opinion for the Court in which Chief Justice Warren and Justice Fortas joined, stated that the test for obscenity requires the coalescence of three elements. It must be established "that (a) the dominant theme of the material taken as a whole appeals to a prurient interest in sex; (b) the material is patently offensive because it affronts contemporary community standards relating to the description or representation of sexual matters; (c) the material is utterly without redeeming social value." Each of the three criteria, said Justice Brennan, must be applied independently. One cannot be weighed against or cancelled by another. It should be noted that Justice Brennan substituted the word "value" for "importance." Although seemingly a fine distinction, social value is a broader, more general test which suggests value of any degree, important or unimportant. The "social value" criterion appeared to permit minimal standards for determination of literary, scientific or artistic worth. Although Justices Douglas, Black and Stewart, in concurring with the reversal, offered separate opinions, the social value criterion seemed to have the support of a majority of the Court.

BREAKDOWN

The legal freedom thus accorded the motion picture, coupled with the threat of television, and the court-imposed dismantling of the vertical structures of distribution and exhibition, caused an inevitable breakdown in the enforcement machinery of the MPAA's Production Code. In 1953, United Artists decided to release Otto Preminger's *The Moon Is Blue* even though the film had been denied a seal of approval by the MPAA's Production Code Administration. This innocuous comedy—essentially a light-hearted look at seduction and adultery—had also been condemned by the National Legion of Decency. The prevailing belief, i.e., that defiance of the dictates of the Catholic Church and the Code Authority spelled economic disaster for a motion picture, was shattered when *The Moon Is Blue* reaped a box-office bonanza. By the end of 1953, the film, made on a budget of $450,000, had played in some 4,200 theatres and earned over $3 million.

Since United Artists had not been a member of the MPAA at the time *The Moon Is Blue* was released, the Code Authority could not impose its $25,000 fine against the intractable company. The opportunity to fine a full-fledged MPAA member came late in 1953 when RKO decided to release a three-dimensional film that had been refused a seal of approval. This was

The French Line starring Jane Russell. The sequence which the PCA found most offensive occurred during the picture's finale when Miss Russell, wearing a one-piece black-satin tights outfit with three large leaf-shaped pieces cut from the midriff area, did a provocative bump-and-grind dance while singing the song "Lookin' for Trouble." When *The French Line* made its debut in St. Louis, the archbishop of that city forbid all Catholics to attend the movie, under pain of mortal sin. The PCA imposed a $25,000 fine against RKO for releasing the film without a seal. The offending film was withdrawn, slightly re-edited, and released nationwide in mid-1954. Advertisements for the picture proclaimed, "Jane Russell in 3-D . . . it'll knock *both* your eyes out!" Late in 1955, the PCA and RKO finally reached a compromise after some of the objectionable material

RKO decided to release *The French Line* (1953) without revision, even though the film had been condemned by the Legion of Decency and refused approval by the Production Code Administration.

was cut. The film received the seal of approval and the unpaid fine was rescinded.

The notoriety caused by RKO's unauthorized release of *The French Line* undoubtedly put another dent in PCA's enforcement machinery. A more crushing blow to the MPAA's antiquated Production Code came early in 1956 when United Artists, without the seal of approval, released Otto Preminger's *The Man with the Golden Arm,* which starred Frank Sinatra as a heroin addict. Based on a novel by Nelson Algren, the film graphically depicted the problems of drug addiction. Geoffrey Shurlock, who had succeeded an ailing Joseph Breen as head of the PCA in the autumn of 1954, later conceded that the film should have received approval. But at the time he had little choice since the Production Code specifically prohibited "scenes which show the use of illegal drugs, or their effects, in detail." United Artists, which had rejoined the MPAA, once again withdrew from the association, while simultaneously battling to have the Code changed to permit movies on narcotics addiction. *The Man with the Golden Arm* was approved by the New York Board of Censors after Otto Preminger had cut only 37 seconds of a scene from the film in which Frank Sinatra prepared heroin in a spoon. Pressure to modify the Production Code continued to mount since the Code Authority still would not grant its seal of approval. The executive committee of the MPAA's board of directors did, however, set up a four-member review committee, under the chairmanship of Eric Johnston, to study the entire Production Code.

The Legion of Decency, meanwhile, had not condemned *The Man with the Golden Arm,* even though it had been released without the PCA's imprimatur. The Catholic Church was not so much concerned with a detailed depiction of drug addiction as with what the Church regarded as a growing tendency on the part of the Code Authority to allow greater explicitness in the film treatment of sexual matters. Beginning in the middle 1950s, the major movie companies had released a number of

PCA-approved pictures that brought them into increasing conflict with the Catholic Church. In 1955 alone, some 33 per cent of the films reviewed by the Legion of Decency received a "B" rating—Morally Objectionable in Part for All. This figure represented an 11 per cent increase over the previous year. The Catholic hierarchy looked with particular disfavor on British-born Geoffrey Shurlock, a Protestant, who was thought to interpret the Production Code's provisions more liberally than his Catholic predecessor. Early in 1956, the Catholic Committee of Bishops launched a new campaign against "objectionable" motion pictures, which was intended to "reach into every one of the church's 131 archdioceses and dioceses to correct the apathy of many people and to arouse Catholics to vigorous action."

The Catholic campaign against the "rising tide of moral laxity in films" intensified in the winter of 1956 when the PCA approved Warner Brothers' release of Elia Kazan's *Baby Doll*. Based on two short plays by Tennessee Williams, the film starred Carroll Baker as a child-wife who, though nearly 20-years old, sleeps in a crib, sucks her thumb and has yet to consummate her marriage with her lusting, middle-aged husband. The film was promptly condemned by the Legion of Decency on the ground that its subject matter was "morally repellent both in theme and treatment." The Legion further charged that "carnal suggestiveness" pervaded the film's action, dialogue and costuming. Cardinal Spellman of the Archdiocese of New York, singled out the picture for special condemnation. On Sunday, December 16, 1956, the outraged prelate mounted the pulpit at Saint Patrick's Cathedral to denounce the film and to enjoin Catholics to stay away from it "under pain of sin." Cardinal Spellman's stinging denunciation sparked a Catholic crusade against *Baby Doll* throughout the country. In several cities, Catholic organizations set up picket lines at theatres showing the film. In some dioceses, bishops imposed a general economic boycott against theatres where *Baby Doll* was playing. Exhibitors again received bomb threats.

Carroll Baker, in the title role of *Baby Doll,* sleeps in an old crib surrounded by a litter of soft-drink bottles, pulp magazines and other symbols of her arrested mental state. The film became the censorship *cause célèbre* of 1956.

Although Catholic condemnations of *Baby Doll* unquestionably reduced the film's national exposure (the film only secured an estimated 25 per cent of its potential bookings), the resultant controversy provided ammunition for those who were critical of the Church's encroachment on motion picture content. Reverend James Pike, then Dean of New York's Protestant Episcopal Cathedral of St. John the Divine, took strong issue with Cardinal Spellman's condemnation of the film. "Those who do not want the sexual aspect of life included in the portrayal of real-life situations" said Reverend Pike, "had better burn their Bibles as well as abstain from the movies." Critics of the Catholic use of general boycotts included the American Civil Liberties Union, who called this type of action "contrary to the spirit of free expression in the First Amendment. It can threaten a theatre's existence, and may deny to other groups within the community a chance to see films of their choice."

The fragile link between the Catholic Church and the movie industry had remained intact as long as profits were high. With the general decline in theatre attendance during the 1950s, Hollywood's disaffection with the dictates of the Legion of Decency intensified. The hierarchy of the Catholic Church, however, was not easily deterred from its efforts to organize actions against those films it regarded as objectionable. Nevertheless, the *Baby Doll* incident had marked a turning point in the Legion of Decency's influence on motion picture content. Beginning in 1958, the Catholic Church's grip on the movie industry was gradually weakened. In an apparent attempt to accommodate the increasing independence and sophistication of American Catholics, the Legion expanded its movie classification system late in 1957 and again in 1963 to allow for greater flexibility in the assignment of ratings. In 1966, the Legion of Decency was renamed the National Catholic Office of Motion Pictures in a further attempt to emphasize the organization's more adaptive approach to motion pictures.

CHANGES

The power of the Production Code Administration also began to diminish toward the end of the 1950s. From its inception in 1930, the Motion Picture Production Code had undergone only minor changes. Late in 1956, as an aftermath of *The Man with the Golden Arm* controversy, MPAA president Eric Johnston announced significant revisions in the Production Code. The Code was simplified and its language was made more precise. Certain of its provisions were rearranged into more logical order and new provisions were added to deal with topics not previously treated. Most important, the MPAA modified the Code to allow greater latitude in the treatment of such topics as drug addiction, miscegenation, prostitution and abortion. At the same time, new restrictions were placed on mercy killing, blasphemy, and the details of physical violence. Although the changes in the Code were not dramatic, they permitted a certain flexibility of interpretation. In the fall of 1957, the right to reverse a PCA ruling was vested in a newly created appeals committee, the Production Code Review Board. This marked a significant departure from past practice since the new review board included exhibitors and independent producers as well as representatives from the major production-distribution companies. Four years later, interpretation of the Code's provision which forbade "sexual perversion or any reference to it" was broadened by the board of directors of the MPAA to permit the release of such films as William Wyler's *The Children's Hour* (which dealt with lesbianism), and Otto Preminger's *Advise and Consent* (which had a homosexual theme).

Despite substantive and procedural changes in the administration of the Production Code, PCA rulings still continued to be out of harmony with the changing temper of the times. United Artists' 1959 release, *Happy Anniversary,* was initially denied Code approval because of its cavalier treatment of a prenuptial tryst. In the film, David Niven and Mitzi Gaynor portrayed a long-married couple who recall a sexual liaison prior to their wedding. United Artists, which had once again rejoined the MPAA, appealed the Code Authority's adverse ruling to the Production Code Review Board, but announced in advance that it would release the picture regardless of the outcome. A curious compromise was reached when it was agreed that an off-camera soliloquy would be added to the film's sound track in which the Niven character repented by saying: "I was wrong. I never should have taken Alice to that hotel room before we were married. What could I have been thinking of?" Such absurd applications of the Production Code only served to subject the Code Authority to further derision.

The United States was one of the few countries in the western world that did employ some sort of uniform national system of advisory ratings. Critics of the Code's outdated manners and morals called for a classification system restricting certain films to adults. It was hoped that such a system would allow for the treatment of more mature and sophisticated themes in motion pictures. Even religious and civic groups began to rally for an MPAA classification system. United Artists once again took the lead when it promoted its 1960 release, *Elmer Gantry,* as intended for "adults only." Based on a 1927 novel by Sinclair Lewis, the film starred Burt Lancaster as a charlatan evangelist. The trade publication, *Variety,* reported that because United Artists had released *Elmer Gantry* with an advisory, the film received a "B" rating from the Legion of Decency; without the "adults only" admonition it would surely have been condemned. Although *Elmer Gantry* received critical acclaim, the film was not a box-office success. UA executives attributed the film's disappointing returns to its restricted audience designation.

After careful consideration, the board of directors of the MPAA decided against replacing the Production Code with a formalized classification system. Eric Johnston instead proposed increased circulation and publicity for the *Green Sheet,* a publication of film ratings. This monthly publication first appeared in 1933 and was distributed by the MPAA-supported Film Board of National Organizations (FBNA). The ten organizations represented in the FBNA amalgram included the American Library Association, the Daughters of the American Revolution, the American Jewish Committee, the National Congress of Parents and Teachers, and the Protestant Motion Picture Council. The editor of the *Green Sheet,* whose office was located in the New York headquarters of the MPAA, prepared, for each film considered, a complete rating based on the reviews submitted by representatives of the member organizations. Until 1963, only PCA-approved films were rated. Beginning that year, coverage was expanded to include nationally distributed non-seal films. Films were rated in the *Green Sheet* according to their suitability for five age designations: adults, mature young people, young people, general audience, and children. Although the *Green Sheet,* which was last published in December 1969, was disseminated to newspapers, schools, libraries, and churches, it had a minimal impact on movie attendance.

Eric Johnston died unexpectedly in 1963, leaving the MPAA temporarily without a leader of national stature. Ralph Hetzel filled in as acting president while the MPAA's board of directors sought someone who would add prestige to the organization. In the spring of 1966, the MPAA hierarchy selected Jack Valenti, a presidential assistant to Lyndon Johnson, as their new head. Valenti was given a seven-year contract at an annual salary of $150,000, plus expenses.

Almost immediately upon taking command of his new post, Valenti was confronted with a major challenge to the rigid restrictions of the Production Code. Warner Brothers, one of the industry's most powerful studios, had submitted its $7 million-plus production of Edward Albee's award-winning play *Who's Afraid of Virginia Woolf?* for Code Authority approval. The film's dialogue employed language that was clearly in direct violation of the Code's provision on profanity, and contained expressions such as "hump-the-hostess" that the faithful framers of the Production Code never imagined would be at issue. The PCA initially denied its seal but, on appeal, the film was approved when Warner Brothers made several concessions. In addition to modifying or cutting some of the objectionable dialogue ("hump-the-hostess" was not deleted), the studio agreed to advertise the film with the cautionary statement, "Suggested for Mature Audiences." More significant, Warner Brothers inserted a clause into all contracts with exhibitors prohibiting them from allowing anyone under

18 to see the film unless accompanied by a parent. This innovation was a huge success. Even the National Catholic Office for Motion Pictures, reflecting its new found liberal tendencies, rated the film "morally unobjectionable for adults, with reservations."

The MPAA's decision to approve *Who's Afraid of Virginia Woolf?* for restricted audiences foreshadowed the movie industry's general acceptance of the need for a classification system. In September of 1966, the MPAA's board of directors replaced the original Production Code with a more simplified version that authorized the labeling of certain approved films as "Suggested for Mature Audiences." Although the new Code reflected the increasing sophistication in the tastes and sensibilities of the movie theatre audience to some extent, it still fell far short of allowing artistic expression of the full range of human experience. Michelangelo Antonioni's *Blow-Up,* which included some sex scenes that were bland by contemporary standards, was denied PCA approval soon after the new Code took effect. MGM, the film's distributor and a prominent member of the MPAA, decided to release *Blow-Up* without a seal through a wholly-owned subsidiary, Premier Films. Since the subsidiary company was not a signatory of the Code agreement, MGM technically had not violated its pledge not to release films denied a seal of approval. This practice was not uncommon among the majors. Such hypocrisy on the part of the MPAA members soon undermined the effectiveness of the new Code in restricting films intended for mature audiences.

RATING SYSTEM

The impetus for industry-wide adoption of an effective classification system for motion pictures came in April 1968 when the U.S. Supreme Court, in two cases handed down on the same day, ruled that state and local authorities have the right to protect minors from exposure to subject matter deemed permissible for adults. In one decision, *Ginsberg v. New York,* the High Court upheld the constitutionality of a New York criminal obscenity statute prohibiting the sale of obscene material to minors under 17 years of age, even though the material in question (magazines which depicted female nudity) would not be considered obscene for adults. Justice Brennan, writing for the six-to-three majority, affirmed that the authority of the state over the conduct of minors is broader than its authority over adults. The Court's recognition of the constitutionality of variable standards of obscenity, one standard for adults and another for children, was perceived as having far-reaching significance in the regulation of motion picture content.

The second decision, even more important to the movie industry, was *Interstate Circuit, Inc. v. Dallas,* in which the Supreme Court ruled on the constitutionality of motion picture classification. The city of Dallas, Texas had adopted an ordinance in 1965 which established a Motion Picture Classification Board. The board classified films as "suitable for young persons" or "not suitable for young persons." A "young person" was defined as anyone who had not attained his sixteenth birthday. Interstate Circuit, a major theatre chain in the southwest, challenged the ordinance as being unconstitutionally vague. Ignoring the board's ruling that a United Artists release, *Viva Maria,* starring Brigitte Bardot and Jeanne Moreau, was "not suitable for young persons," Interstate deliberately exhibited the film without imposing age restrictions on the audience. A county court upheld the municipal classification board's determination and the Texas Court of Civil Appeals affirmed the lower court ruling. The U.S. Supreme Court, in reversing the decision, declared that where expression is subjected to licensing there must be rigorous insistence upon procedural safeguards for judicial superintendence of the censor's action. While agreeing with Interstate Circuit that the Dallas classification system was too vague, the Court did not preclude the acceptance of a more carefully drafted age classification scheme for proscribing minors from viewing certain films. Echoing the ruling in the *Ginsberg* case, Justice Marshall, writing for an eight-to-one majority, emphasized that a state "may regulate the dissemination to juveniles of, and their access to, material objectionable as to them, but which a state clearly could not regulate as to adults."

The potential impact of the two Supreme Court decisions was not lost on the MPAA's reigning powers. Unless the movie industry took decisive action the proliferation of state and municipal classification boards seemed inevitable. The changing structure of the motion picture business, however, now required more than the cooperation of the major producer-distributors in order to effect a meaningful change in the industry's self-regulatory scheme. Two new forces had emerged that would have to be reckoned with, the International Film Importers and Distributors of America Inc. (IFIDA) and the National Association of Theatre Owners (NATO). The latter organization represented the owners of 70 per cent of all the movie theatres in the United States. In order to accommodate these disparate groups, Jack Valenti was called upon to use his talents as a negotiator. His skill stood him in good stead, and, after extensive discussions, the IFIDA and NATO joined with the MPAA to establish a national system of voluntary classification.

On October 7, 1968, within six months of the *Interstate* decision, the Motion Picture Rating System was publicly unveiled. Under this new system (which took effect on November 1, 1968), the members of MPAA agreed to submit each film produced or distributed for rating prior to commercial release. The rating system, which is operated under the joint supervision of the MPAA, the IFIDA and the NATO, is open to all producers and distributors on the same basis as members of MPAA.

With the introduction of a rating system, the Production Code Administration was replaced by the newly created Code and Rating Administration (CARA). Originally films submitted to CARA were classified into one of four designations: "G," suggested for general audiences; "M," suggested for mature audiences—adults and mature young people; "R," restricted, persons under 16 not admitted, unless accompanied by parent or adult guardian; "X," persons under 16 not admitted. Early in 1970, the M rating, which was thought to be confusing, was changed to "GP," general audience—parental guidance suggested. At the same time, the R and X age limits were increased to 17. Two years later GP was changed to the current designation, "PG," parental guidance suggested—some material may not be suitable for pre-teenagers.

The Code and Rating Administration, which is located in Hollywood, is comprised of seven members who serve for an indeterminate period of time. CARA's chairperson is selected by the MPAA's president. The chairperson, in turn, selects the other six members who serve on the rating board. The president of the MPAA (this post is still held by Jack Valenti) does not participate in, nor may he overrule, CARA's decisions. The MPAA estimates that about 99 per cent of the "responsible" (i.e. non exploitative) films made each year are submitted to CARA for a rating. According to Jack Valenti, most makers of "pornographic movies" avoid the formal rating procedure by simply self-applying an X rating rather than having the MPAA do so. The other symbols, G, PG and R, may not be self-applied since they are registered with the U.S. Patent and Trademark Office. The MPAA's seal—which validates the rating, is withheld from any film which receives an X designation. The association is committed to defend any G, PG or R film.

In determining a film's rating, CARA evaluates thematic content, visual treatment, and use of such elements as language, violence, sex, or nudity. If a company desires a less restrictive rating, it may resubmit film in edited form. A film company not satisfied with a rating may appeal for a less restrictive rating to an appeals board consisting of representatives of MPAA, NATO, and IFIDA. The board is the final arbiter for ratings. The appeals board, which meets in New York, is comprised of a total of 22 representatives from the three organizations. The president of the MPAA presides as chairman of the appeals board. After the film in question is screened, the chairman calls on a representative of the company appealing CARA's decision to explain why the rating received was inappropriate. The chairman of CARA is then asked to explain the rating board's reasons for its determination. The company representative is given an opportunity for rebuttal. When the members of the appeals board have had a chance to question the two opposing parties, both contenders are asked to leave the room. Following this, the appeals board discusses the appeal and then takes a secret ballot.

Originally, a two-thirds vote of the board was required to *sustain* an X rating. This provision caused the rating system to come under fire when CARA's assignment of an X rating to *Drive, He Said,* a Columbia release, was overturned by only eight members of the Code and Ratings Appeals Board. The film had received an X rating because of some male nudity, excessive profanity, and a suggestive sex scene. Columbia appealed the rating and engaged Ramsay Clark, the former U.S. Attorney General, to present the studio's case before the appeals board. Clark argued that the X rating was prejudicial since the picture was moral and serious in intent. Clark further held that the only rightful censor is the parent refusing to allow a child to see the film. When the vote was cast 20 members of the appeals board were present. The vote was 12 to uphold the X rating and 8 to reclassify the film into the R category. As a two-thirds vote was necessary to sustain the X rating, 8 votes out of 20 prevailed and a rating of R was granted. Subsequently, the bylaws were amended to require a two-thirds vote to reverse any rating board decision.

When the Code and Rating Administration came into existence Eugene Dougherty, a 26-year veteran of the old PCA, became head of the new agency. Dougherty's leadership was conservative, but fair minded. During his tenure, the rating

A poster for *If It's Tuesday, This Must be Belgium,* a comedy about the adventures and misadventures of a busload of tourists who visit seven European cities in 18 days. The elimination of a minute or so from a bedroom scene in this picture, resulted in a change from "GP" to a "G" rating.

board allowed unprecedented latitude in the treatment of diversified subject matter to those film-makers who were aiming at a general audience. At the same time, themes, language, and visual content oriented to an adult audience were restricted to the R and X categories. Since, however, most films are not easily classifiable into one of four simple categories, it was inevitable that the rating board decisions would soon become controversial. Exhibitors were particularly sensitive to patron complaints about offensive material in such G-rated films as *Popi,* a charming story of poverty in the ghetto, and *If It's Tuesday, This Must Be Belgium,* an amusing comedy of Americans on tour abroad. Films in the G category were apparently expected by some patrons to be free of even the slightest offense.

By the latter half of the 1960s, the U.S. Congress had found traffic in obscenity across all media to be "a matter of national concern." In October 1967, Congress created a Commission of Obscenity and Pornography, whose members were appointed by President Johnson. In 1970—after two years of intensive study—the Commission's findings were released. Charles H. Keating, Jr., in his minority report to the Commission singled out current film fare as having an especially harmful effect on society. "Thanks to Jack Valenti," said Keating, "we have a condition in the motion picture industry today that literally constitutes a course of instruction in decadence, perversion, and immorality." The majority report, however, advocated that "federal, state and local legislation prohibiting the sale, exhibition and distribution of sexual materials to consenting adults should be repealed." On the basis of exhaustive documented research, surveys, and empirical investigations, the Commission had found no reliable evidence that exposure to explicit sexual materials plays a significant role in the causation of social or individual harms. President Nixon repudiated the Commission's report and recommendations, saying that even stronger obscenity laws were desirable. "American morality" said President Nixon, "is not to be trifled with." The Senate, in turn, voted overwhelmingly to disregard the Commission's findings.

In this climate it was inevitable that the Code and Rating Administration's alleged leniency in classifying films would come under attack from the church community. In May of 1971, the National Catholic Office of Motion Pictures, and the Broadcasting and Film Commission of the National Council of Churches withdrew their support from the movie industry's rating system, charging that CARA's film classifications were too lenient and unreliable. Within two months after this action by the church councils, Eugene Dougherty was replaced as head of CARA by Dr. Aaron Stern, a psychiatrist on the faculty at Columbia University's College of Physicians and Surgeons. Stern had served as a consultant to the rating board since 1969. Jack Valenti's appointment of Dr. Stern to the top post at CARA, signified for many observers a shift within the movie industry toward greater emphasis on thematic content in assigning ratings. Stern was a vocal proponent of restricting audiences for films that significantly challenged the conventional wisdom of right and wrong. His conservative influence on the rating board helped to mollify the moral critics of the industry's classification system. When Dr. Stern resigned his post as CARA's chairman in April 1974, he was succeeded by Richard D. Heffner, a communications consultant and an adjunct professor at Rutgers University.

The rating board is able to exert influence over the movie industry through its power to impose restrictive ratings. A big-budgeted film that receives an R or an X rating is often destined to financial failure. When David Lean's $10 million production of *Ryan's Daughter* received a R rating, MGM, the film's distributor, threatened to withdraw from the MPAA unless the rating was changed. At the time, MGM was on the verge of economic collapse and it was feared that the limited box-office returns resulting from the film's restrictive rating would bring the studio down. CARA had assigned *Ryan's Daughter* to the R category because of an explicit sex scene in the picture. Although the appeals board changed the film's rating to GP, the incident alerted less prestigious producers to the economic dangers of violating the rating board's moral proscriptions.

Many of the major movie companies are particularly sensitive to the stigma of an X rating. It has become common practice for the large studios to include a "ratings clause" in their distribution contracts with independent producers stipulating that all films must receive either an R or a less restrictive rating. The producer is obligated to make any changes in the film necessary to receive an acceptable rating. Many of the industry's aristocracy refuse to release an X-rated film. In addition to reducing box-office revenues, the taint of an X rating often precludes the possibility of selling a film in the television market. When the CBS television network decided to present Luchino Visconti's *The Damned,* an X-rated film about pre-World War II decadence among the German aristocracy, Warner Bros., the film's distributor, had already cut 25 minutes of potentially offensive material from the original 154 minutes. CBS, in turn, cut another 11 minutes before the movie was telecast on the network in the late evening hours. Despite these massive cuts, the network received a large number of protests and several affiliated stations refused to carry the film. Some of the refusals to "clear" the film were effected before the local station management had even seen the edited version. The three major networks are now reluctant to risk a reduction in revenues by showing another X-rated film. In the television industry, not unlike the movie business, profits take priority over artistic expression.

SEX OFFENSIVE

Not all film-makers, however, are interested in artistic expression, or require unrestricted audiences to realize large profits. The Supreme Court's assault on movie censorship had wrought dramatic changes in motion picture content. By 1970, only the state of Maryland and the city of Chicago still had active censorship boards and the rigorous procedural requirements established by the Supreme Court in the *Freedman* case for censoring films had rendered these boards almost wholly ineffective. By the early 1970s, even hard-core sex films were receiving nation-wide distribution. *Deep Throat,* a 1972 release starring Linda Lovelace, played in some 70 cities and grossed more than $3 million by January 1973. Made by Gerard Damiano in six days on a budget of about $25,000, the film featured actual copulation, fellatio and cunnilingus, with close-ups of genitals filling the screen. Linda Lovelace was propelled into the national spotlight. She appeared on the cover of *Esquire* and was the subject of a photographic essay in *Playboy.* Pornography soon became chic. Another of Damiano's hard-core sex films, *The Devil in Miss Jones* starring Georgina Spelvin, ranked sixth in box-office grosses in 1973 among all films released in the United States.

The exhibition of "sexploitation" films did not go unchallenged. A number of state and municipal prosecutors brought those involved in the production and exhibition of *Deep Throat* into the courts. In New York City, the film itself was confiscated by the police under a warrant from the New York County Criminal Court soon after its premiere in June 1972 at the New Mature World Theatre. The court calendar was crowded, however, and the trial against the theatre operator, Mature Enterprises Inc., was delayed for almost six months. Since New York requires an adversary hearing before a film can be seized, the print was returned. While the theatre operator was awaiting trial, *Deep Throat* played to record-breaking crowds. Mature Enterprises was charged with two counts of promoting obscenity, each carrying a maximum fine of $5,000 on conviction.

The *Deep Throat* case finally came before Judge Joel E. Tyler on December 19, 1972. The spectacular ten-day trial that followed became a curiosity-piquing event that received nationwide coverage. More than a thousand pages of testimony accumulated during the trial. Among the witnesses who testified on behalf of the film was movie historian Arthur Knight who stated that *Deep Throat* had redeeming social value because it might encourage people to expand their sexual horizons. A witness for the prosecution, sociologist Ernest van den Haag, on the other hand, testified that the film was highly antisocial because it showed "the physical use of people's bodies divorced from emotional relationships." Professor van den Haag spent four hours on the stand describing his objections to the film. After weighing the evidence, Judge Tyler found *Deep Throat* to be "indisputably obscene by any legal measurement." He described the film as "a feast of carrion and squalor . . . a Sodom and Gomorrah gone wild before the fire . . . one throat that deserves to be cut."

Prosecutors throughout the nation, however, have found it increasingly difficult to persuade juries to curtail the exhibition of films depicting explicit sexual activity. In such diverse communities as Binghamton, New York; Cincinnati, Ohio; Houston, Texas; and Sioux Falls, South Dakota; prosecutions against the showing of *Deep Throat* have resulted in acquittals or hung juries. Other sexually oriented films have enjoyed similar success in the courts. In Los Angeles, the trial against the exhibitor of *Behind the Green Door,* a sexual romp starring Ivory Snow-model Marilyn Chambers, ended in a jury verdict of acquittal. Apparently there is a growing public tolerance of the right of adults to see whatever they wish; this appears to have deterred many law enforcement officials from seeking further obscenity prosecutions. In his July 1974 report to the California legislature recommending the decriminalization of dissemination of sexually explicit materials to forewarned adults, Burt Pines, the Los Angeles City Attorney, described the enforcement of obscenity laws as "unworkable, ineffective and expensive."

On June 21, 1973, those advocating legal prohibitions of the right of adults to read or see explicit sexual materials seemed to receive new incentive in their fight against obscenity. On that day, the U.S. Supreme Court, which by then included four Nixon appointees, rendered several major decisions that established new guidelines for obscenity legislation and control. In the principal case, *Miller v. California,* a five member majority, composed of the Nixon appointees, Chief Justice Burger, and Justices Blackmun, Powell and Rehnquist, together with Justice White, a Kennedy appointee, handed down tougher, more restrictive standards for determining obscenity. In so doing, the Court expressly rejected the social value criterion from the 1966 *Memoirs* decision. Chief Justice Burger, writing for the majority, set forth revised considerations that determine obscenity: "(1) whether the average person, applying contemporary community standards, would find that the work taken as a whole appeals to the prurient interest; (2) whether the work depicts or describes in a patently offensive way, sexual conduct specifically defined by the applicable state law; (3) whether the work taken as a whole lacks serious literary, artistic, political or scientific value."

At first glance, the Court's new frame of reference for dealing with criteria for determining obscenity does not seem significantly different from the three-fold definition of the *Memoirs* case. Upon closer inspection, however, it becomes apparent that "serious literary, artistic, political or scientific value," the so-called "LAPS" test, hampers law enforcement officials far less in their endeavors to curtail exhibition of obscene films, than the *Memoirs* criterion of "utterly without redeeming social value." The latter test had placed an almost impossible burden on the prosecution. Under the *Miller* standard, a prosecutor is only required to demonstrate that a work is patently offensive and lacks serious value. Perhaps of even more significance is the court's judgment that determination of whether material "appeals to the prurient interest" or is "patently offensive" need not be based on uniform national standards. The Court specifically permitted state-wide standards and implied that even local communities could make their own determinations regarding a work's alleged obscenity.

The Court further limited the scope of permissible expression in four related cases, decided on the same day as the *Miller* ruling. In *Paris Adult Theatre I v. Slaton,* the Court ruled that the exhibition of obscene films in an "adult theatre" is not protected by the First Amendment, even when the theatre management effectively restricts viewing to consenting adults and does not engage in "pandering or obtrusive advertising." In rendering its decision, the Court said that expert affirmative testimony that a work is obscene is not necessary. The films themselves, said the Court are the best evidence of what they represent. By so ruling, the Court seemed to shift to the defense the burden of proving a work's value. In *United States v. Orito,* the Court held that the constitutional protection of the possession of obscene materials in one's home does not extend to transporting them on a common carrier, even when they are intended for private use. The decision in *Kaplan v. California* held that books without pictorial content may be judged obscene under the First Amendment. In the final case, *United States v. Twelve 200-Foot Reels of Super 8mm Film,* the Court ruled that the commerce clause of the Constitution empowers Congress to ban importation of obscene material even though it may be intended for private use in the home. The same five-Justice majority prevailed in all five cases.

The Court's guidelines ultimately were no more effectually definitive than those they replaced in permitting state and local authorities to determine what is obscene. Only 11 days after the June decisions, the Georgia Supreme Court upheld a local jury's conviction of an Albany, Georgia theatre manager, Billy Jenkins, for exhibiting Mike Nichols' critically acclaimed film *Carnal Knowledge* in violation of the state's anti-obscenity laws. The Georgia court's decision was appealed by the MPAA to the U.S. Supreme Court in the hope that the justices would reconsider their position allowing varying community standards of judgment. In June 1974, the Supreme Court, in *Jenkins v. Georgia* unanimously ruled that *Carnal Knowledge* was not obscene. Justice Rehnquist, writing for the Court, said that juries do not have "unbridled discretion in determining what is 'patently offensive'." In discussing *Carnal Knowledge* he noted that, although there were scenes of nudity in the film, "nudity alone is not enough to make material legally obscene under the *Miller* standards." Once again, however, the Court offered no clear guidelines for determining what does constitute obscenity. Justice Brennan identified the most serious flaw in the *Miller* test when he pointed out that "one cannot say with certainty that material is obscene until at least five members of this Court, applying inevitably obscure standards, have pronounced it so." Echoing his dissenting opinion in *Paris Adult*

Theatre I, Justice Brennan adhered to his view that "at least in the absence of distribution to juveniles or obtrusive exposure to unconsenting adults, the First and Fourteenth Amendments prohibit the State and Federal Governments from attempting wholly to suppress sexually oriented materials on the basis of their allegedly 'obscene' contents."

It would seem that obscenity defies legal definition. Under the High Court's 1973 standards the nature of obscene materials continues to be as intractable and elusive as ever. Although all 50 states have introduced obscenity legislation since the *Miller* rulings, uncertainty, confusion, and inconsistency still prevail. A number of states—i.e., Colorado, Montana, South Dakota, West Virginia, Alaska, Iowa, New Mexico and Vermont—have pragmatically limited application of their obscenity laws to minors. When weighed against the many compelling needs within American society, it would seem that expenditure of limited law enforcement and judicial resources to prosecute obscenity cases involving forewarned, consenting adults does not warrant a high priority.

The trinity of forces—industry self-regulators, organized religious groups and governmental censorship boards—which have traditionally controlled motion picture content no longer wield the influence they once did. Following in the wake of the post-*Miller* decisions, even the attempts by local law enforcement officials to suppress allegedly obscene movies seem to have diminished. In striking a balance between the conflicting demands for totally unrestricted expression and outright censorship, the MPAA's rating system has proven to be a reasonable compromise. It is clear that the incredible changes in the sexual mores of much of the world in the last decade preclude the possibility of returning to the moral strictures of the past.

The Direction of the Future

THE 1960s witnessed a change in the whole definition and character of the communications media as the movie and television industries began to coalesce into larger, increasingly complex corporate structures. The erratic earnings record of the big movie studios, dating from the advent of television, made them particularly susceptible to mergers and corporate takeovers as well as proxy fights instigated by dissatisfied stockholders. Since voting stock in most of the movie companies had become widely dispersed, managerial cadres at the studios had a tenuous hold on the corporate reins. The glamour of the industry, the fact that many people felt that moving picture making was not a mysterious expertise, and the obvious imminence of a breakdown and realignment of corporate structures—all of these contributed to a turbulent, constantly shifting ebb and flow of managerial personnel throughout the 1960s and, in fact, into the present. The increased television activities of the big studios made the movie industry particularly appealing to expansion-minded conglomerates—those corporate empires that operate in a number of different and unrelated markets. Although most of the movie companies' operations had not been consistently profitable, those seeking to gain control of these companies were attracted by the potential profits in ownership of film libraries, real estate assets, and musical and literary copyrights. Confusion and disorganization prevailed throughout the movie industry.

CORPORATE UPHEAVAL

The company that suffered most from internal strife and disorder was the once-mighty MGM. Louis B. Mayer had attempted to regain control of the studio from Joseph Vogel in 1957, by joining forces with Joseph Tomlinson, a Canadian road builder, who was then the company's largest stockholder, and Stanley Meyer, a minor Hollywood producer who had worked on the *Dragnet* series. The Mayer-Tomlinson-Meyer triumvirate was ultimately unsuccessful in its bid for power, but the Vogel forces had little time to celebrate. The studio had been saved from ruin in 1959 by the release of a highly profitable remake of *Ben-Hur,* but MGM's fortunes continued to decline steadily. Most of the revenues from *Ben-Hur* were squandered on a lavish remake of *Mutiny on the Bounty,* starring Marlon Brando. Made at a cost of some $30 million, the film was a box-office disaster; by the early 1960s, the ailing lion had become arthritic and enfeebled. Joseph Vogel was moved upstairs to the chairmanship in 1963. He was replaced as president by Robert H. O'Brien, a former commissioner with the Securities and Exchange Commission. Under O'Brien's ministrations, the old lion gradually regained his strength. Thanks to O'Brien's sound fiscal management and the studio's profitable output of films MGM ended fiscal 1964 with a $7.3 million profit. During the next several years the studio's earnings continued to climb, but calm did not prevail for very long. Philip Levin, a wealthy builder and real estate developer, had begun to accumulate MGM stock in 1964.

Within a year, he had become the studio's largest single stockholder, controlling approximately 14 per cent of the outstanding
shares. Almost immediately, Levin initiated a takeover campaign. In 1965, he became a member of the MGM board and
executive committee. He attempted to pressure the company's
management team, headed by Robert O'Brien, into a program
of diversification and acquisition, a reduction in operating costs
and an accelerated schedule of low-budget film production.
Levin also advocated the conversion of MGM's valuable Culver
City studio property—more than 180 acres—into a profitable
real estate development. These proposals, however, received
little support from the other members of the board. On the
contrary, they openly praised O'Brien's three-year record of
rising corporate profits. In fiscal 1965 alone, MGM reported
earnings of $7.8 million. Since O'Brien had assumed command,
the company's stock had more than doubled in price.

Regardless of O'Brien's impressive record, Levin continued to wage a proxy fight to seize the reins of control. Charging
the O'Brien regime with "poor fiscal management," Levin cir-
culated to MGM stockholders a critical financial report prepared by Price, Waterhouse & Company. The report lost its
credibility when the accounting firm admitted that its financial
analysis had overlooked the revenues from 16 of MGM's most
recent releases, including *Doctor Zhivago,* which eventually
grossed over $46 million in domestic film rentals. Although
the O'Brien group owned more MGM stock than Levin and
his supporters—40 per cent versus 34 per cent—the balance
of power rested with several large mutual funds that controlled
more than 20 per cent of the stock. When the votes were
tallied in March of 1967, the O'Brien forces had emerged
victorious.

After being defeated, Levin gave up, in August, 1967, and
sold his stock to Edgar Bronfman, the magnate of the Seagram
liquor empire. Time, Inc. also acquired substantial stock in
the movie company. The Bronfman and Time, Inc. forces,
after putting representatives on the MGM board, instituted

an extensive search for a "bright young executive" to succeed Robert O'Brien as president. This search resulted in the selection of Louis J. Polk. The 39-year-old Polk, a graduate of Harvard Business School, had evidenced considerable ability as an executive at General Motors, but was looking for an opportunity to advance more rapidly. When Polk assumed the MGM presidency, O'Brien moved to the nominal position of chairman, where he remained only a few months before resigning. Change followed upon change in rapid succession. Within ten months, Polk was ousted by Kirk Kerkorian, a Las Vegas based airlines and casino owner, who had accumulated substantial stock holdings in MGM. Polk was rumored to have received a $2 million settlement for the termination of his five-year contract. The studio that Kerkorian had won, however, was once again in serious economic trouble. MGM's losses for the year ending August 31, 1969, came to $35.4 million.

After Kerkorian took command of the studio he appointed James T. Aubrey, former head of CBS-TV, as MGM's $208,000 a year president. At the time of his appointment, Aubrey was one of the most colorful and talked about people in the entertainment industry. During his years at CBS, the Princeton-educated Aubrey's cold decisiveness and unsentimental detachment, coupled with his almost inaudible voice, had earned him the sobriquet of "the Smiling Cobra." When long-time CBS executive Hubbell Robinson, who had been summarily fired by Aubrey, heard the news of Aubrey's appointment as MGM president, he dryly noted, "They're going to have to teach Leo the lion to hiss."

At MGM, Aubrey lived up to his reputation. He brusquely canceled 15 imminent film projects, including a prestigious $10 million Carlo Ponti-Fred Zinneman production of André Malraux's *Man's Fate* which was within a few days of going before the cameras; he turned over the company's 46-year old collection of props, costumes, and other musty memorabilia to the Davis Weisz Company, an international auction house, for $1.4 million; and he sold MGM-owned land in Culver City as well as theatres in Australia, South Africa and England. Aubrey's zealous cost-cutting and his selling of property put the company in the black by the end of 1971. But under his rigid cost controls, MGM, the studio that once boasted of having "More Stars Than There Are in Heaven," produced mainly slick, low-budgeted pictures of little merit with few major stars or prominent directors. Some of the Aubrey-spawned movies were big money makers; for example *Shaft,* which was made for about $1 million, grossed more than 12 times that amount. For the greater part, his program of low-budgeted films failed. During his years at CBS, Aubrey had made the television network's ratings soar with such programs as *The Beverly Hillbillies,* and *Petticoat Junction,* but as a movie executive he never succeeded in finding their theatrical equivalent.

By the fall of 1973 MGM decided to withdraw from film distribution, assigning its domestic distribution rights to United Artists for ten years and its foreign distribution rights to Cinema International, a joint venture of Paramount and Universal. Aubrey announced that the studio would only make six to eight "special" movies per year. A short time later, Aubrey was replaced as president by Frank Rosenfelt, a Cornell Law School graduate who had worked in MGM's legal department. At present, MGM concentrates mainly on television programming and Las Vegas hotel and gambling operations. The company makes almost as much money from a single hotel, the MGM Grand in Las Vegas, as it does from all its feature films and television programs put together. The once proud lion, although prosperous in his old age, now presides over roulette wheels, crap games and slot machines.

CORPORATE SUITORS

Paramount Pictures in the early 1960s was equally vulnerable to a corporate takeover. By the spring of 1965, the studio had become nearly moribund. The founder of the company,

Adolph Zukor, who was in his nineties, served as chairman emeritus. Paramount's chairman, Barney Balaban, was in his late seventies. The average age of the board members was about 75. The studio was suffering heavy losses on its theatrical releases, telefilm production was almost nonexistent and old movies were being leased to television for less than their market value. Paramount's elderly executives had attempted to augment earnings by selling off assets, including not only some of the television stations the company had acquired but also the Paramount Building in New York City's Times Square area, yet the company's revenues continued to decline steadily. George Weltner, who had succeeded Balaban as president, struggled desperately to maintain the stability of the company. Despite its problems, Paramount was attractive to corporate outsiders. The studio's library of recent movies alone, at then current prices, had a potential worth in the television market of some $200 million. Paramount's stock, because of the company's poor earning record, had slumped badly and was undervalued, leading many corporate suitors to covet its assets. In the battle for control of the company, Charles Bluhdorn emerged victorious. In the fall of 1966, Paramount was merged into Bluhdorn's Gulf & Western Industries, an enormous conglomerate with holdings in automotive parts, zinc mining, cigars, and meat packing. Bluhdorn installed himself as Paramount's president and reshuffled the company's management, keeping Balaban and Zukor in essentially honorary, nonfunctioning positions. Thirty-six year-old Robert Evans, who had had both acting experience and a successful business career, was put in charge of the studio operation. This was a sagacious selection on Bluhdorn's part. Under the direction of Evans, the studio's filming schedule was soon at its highest level in more than a decade. Paramount moved seriously into television production in 1967 with the acquisition of Desilu Productions for $17 million. The coalesence of the movie and television industries was accelerating at an unprecedented rate.

There had been an upsurge in the financial fortunes of

most of the big studios in the middle 1960s as television became an increasingly profitable outlet for their products. NBC had been the first network to show theatrical features on a regular basis. In the fall of 1961, NBC inaugurated "Saturday Night at the Movies" with the television premiere of Fox's *How to Marry a Millionaire.* By 1965, all three of the major television networks had incorporated theatrical features into their program schedules. The average price paid for a picture by the networks grew steadily, culminating in 1966 with ABC's payment of $2 million to Columbia Pictures for two showings of *The Bridge on the River Kwai.* Even at that inflated price, the network got a bargain. The Ford Motor Company, to provide a showcase for its 1967 models, paid ABC $1.8 million to sponsor the first telecast of the film. An estimated 60 million viewers watched *The Bridge on the River Kwai* when it was first shown over the ABC television network on a Sunday evening late in September of 1966.

This telecast marked a watershed in Columbia's fortunes. In the early 1960s, Columbia, too, was ripe for a corporate takeover. Harry Cohn, the studio's tyrannical ruler, had died in 1958, two years after his brother. Harry's crown passed to Abe Schneider, who had joined Columbia in the late 1920s as an accountant in the bookkeeping division. Next in command was Leo Jaffe who had come to the studio in 1930. In the years following Harry Cohn's death, Columbia had floundered. Although the studio made contracts with such prestigious independent producers as Stanley Kramer and Sam Spiegel, their pictures too often did not fare well at the box-office. Only Screen Gems, Columbia's television subsidiary, consistently showed high profits. In 1966 alone, the television operation earned some $4.5 million. However, the rest of the studio that year showed a deficit of $2.2 million. Nevertheless, even though Columbia's earnings had been disappointing, its film assets were rising in value. The studio's film inventory included 50 features that had not yet been released to television. Such box-office hits as *Suddenly Last Summer, Guns of Navarone* and *Lawrence of Arabia,* among others, promised handsome returns in the television market. In addition, the company's real estate holdings included 11 acres in Hollywood and another 40 in Burbank.

In mid-1966, two groups attempted to wrest control of Columbia from the Schneider regime. Maurice Clairmont, of Lee National Corporation, a well-known corporate raider, acquired a considerable amount of Columbia's stock in an apparent attempt to gain control of the company. Immediately thereafter, Clairmont began to criticize the operational tactics of Abe Schneider and his managerial team. Then Clairmont began negotiations with representatives from the largest investment bank in Europe, the Banque de Paris et des Pays-Bas, which had acquired some 20 per cent of Columbia's outstanding stock. In a move that was regarded by many industry observers as a co-ordinated action, the French bank bid to obtain another 18 per cent of Columbia's shares. The combined stock of these two outside groups would have enabled them to seize control from the Schneider management. Attorneys for the Bank de Paris, however, had failed to take into consideration Section 310(a) of the Communications Act of 1934 which prohibits aliens from owning more than one-fifth of the capital stock of any American company with broadcasting interests. This was a critical oversight, since Columbia's subsidiary, Screen Gems, held several television licenses. The Federal Communications Commission eventually permitted the French bank to acquire the additional shares and place them in trust; but the Commission's approval carried conditions designed to prevent the bank's takeover of Columbia. The principal condition the FCC attached to its approval of the new acquisition required that the bank refrain from "any action looking toward an assertion of control by it alone or in concert with any other person over Columbia." After months of negotiations the Banque de Paris agreed to the FCC-imposed conditions and pledged its support to the incumbent management. In mid-1967, the French bank sold its Columbia stock, at a handsome profit, to investors supportive of the Schneider regime.

The late 1960s brought record profits to Columbia. The studio's string of hits included *Oliver!, Guess Who's Coming to Dinner, To Sir, With Love, Divorce American Style* and *In Cold Blood.* Much of the studio's success was attributable to Mike Frankovich, who had served as production head from 1964. Frankovich relinquished his post in 1968 to become an independent producer with a long-term Columbia contract. He was succeeded by Stanley Schneider, whose father, Abe, headed the company. Another of Abe's sons, Bert Schneider, scored heavily in 1969, when he and Robert Rafelson co-produced *Easy Rider,* which became one of the biggest financial successes in Columbia's history. The film odyssey of two cocain dealers who motorcycle across the Southwestern United States searching for meaning in their lives, had been conceived by Peter Fonda, and marked Dennis Hopper's debut as a director. Hopper and Fonda also appeared in starring roles. A then little-known, Jack Nicholson, played a key supporting role as an alcoholic Southern lawyer. Schneider and Rafelson had financed *Easy Rider* with their own money. They approached Columbia only after the film had been completed. Made for about $400,000, the film grossed over $25 million and skyrocketed its players into major box-office attractions.

A succession of box-office failures, however, soon consumed the company's *Easy Rider* profits. Within the next few years Columbia experienced several managerial changes as the last remnants of the old Cohn regime fell from power. Abe Schneider assumed the non-functioning title of honorary chairman and Leo Jaffe was given the nominal position of chairman of the board. By the time Alan J. Hirshfield, a former Wall Street investment banker with Allen & Co., joined Columbia in July 1973 as president and chief executive officer, the company had a three-year fiscal loss of some $82 million. (Allen & Co., a powerful Wall Street investment firm, had acquired a substantial amount of Columbia's stock in 1973.) Columbia's bank debts totaled more than $160 million. Big-budgeted box-office disasters like the 1973 release of a new version of *Lost Horizon* persuaded the new management to impose tight cost controls on movie budgets. David Begelman, a powerful, wheeler-dealer talent agent, was brought in to revamp the motion picture division. Buoyed by the general boom in movie attendance beginning in 1974, the Yale-educated Begelman managed to steer the studio on a sound financial course. Such Begelman-sponsored films as *Funny Lady, Shampoo, Tommy, The Deep* and *Close Encounters of the Third Kind* scored heavily at the box-office.

Nevertheless Begelman's stewardship of the studio operation came into controversy when it was revealed that he had misappropriated about $61,000 in company funds between January 1975 and May 1977. About $40,000 of this amount was allegedly stolen through check forgeries. In one instance, Begelman cashed a fraudulently endorsed $10,000 check from Columbia made out to actor Cliff Robertson. When found out, Begelman admitted his guilt. The entire affair caused considerable embarrassment for Columbia. Begelman was stripped of his corporate posts of director and senior vice-president and was suspended as studio chief. In the movie industry, however, economic considerations take priority over moral values. Columbia's directors apparently decided that Begelman's contributions to the studio outweighed his fiscal sins. In December 1977, they reinstated him as president of the company's motion picture and television operations. (He remained in this post for only a few months.)

In Begelman's absence, Alan Hirschfield had taken command of the studio, but he clearly lacked the experience necessary for the job. Hirschfield's expertise is in the area of high finance. As president of the parent company, Columbia Pictures Industries, he has proven himself to be a skilled financier. To enable Columbia to reduce its bank loans, Hirschfield sold the company's music publishing division to EMI Ltd. of Britain for $23.5 million. The sale of its New Orleans television station to Gaylord Broadcasting brought Columbia another $13.5 million. To prop up earnings in the record division, Hirschfield hired the controversial Clive Davis to head a brand new record subsidiary, Arista Records. Although Davis had been dismissed from CBS for allegedly misappropriating corporate funds, he was also regarded by many as among the most astute operators in the highly competitive record industry. Hirschfield also attempted to ensure a steadier, more predictable income for Columbia, by initiating a vigorous diversification program. The capstone of this plan was placed, in December 1976, by Columbia's purchase of privately-owned D. Gottlieb & Company, the largest pinball machine manufacturer in the country. Columbia's entry fee into the booming coin-operated pinball machine market was a reported $50 million.

Columbia's gradual fiscal turnaround had been facilitated by the extant tax law which permitted those in the upper income brackets to defer tax payments by declaring losses in film investments. Under a so-called movie "tax-shelter," an investor in the film industry was entitled to deduct film depreciation (a large percentage was allowed within the first year) and investment tax credits to offset income from other sources. The temporary financial gain from this type of transaction operated, in effect, as a tax-free loan from the government. If the movie was a hit (only a small percentage of pictures turn a profit), the investor's return could be enormous. In the more likely event that the movie failed at the box-office, the investor had the temporary use of tax-free funds for other ventures. The influx of tax-shelter investments created by this loophole in the law benefitted Columbia greatly since the company's heavy losses and huge debts made more conventional forms of financing difficult to secure. By the time Congress enacted the Tax Reform Act of 1976, which restricted movie tax shelters, Columbia appeared to be well on the road to recovery. The change in the law, however, may have an adverse effect on smaller movie companies whose only regularly available source of capital came from tax-shelter investments.

COMPETITION

Several low-budget production companies had prospered during the 1960s as the composition of film audiences changed and the techniques of movie-making became increasingly more simplified. The trend in design and manufacture of film equipment has been toward miniaturization and compactness. Cameras, for instance, have become less expensive, lighter in weight, and trimmer in line. Fouad Said, an Egyptian-born cinematographer, had developed a vehicle called the "Cinemobile" for on-location shooting which replaced a whole motorcade of trucks, trailers and cars. His highly mobile "location studio" contains cameras, lights, sound gear, dressing rooms, lavatories, kitchens, and wardrobe space. Some models even have a compartment for cast and technicians. Said's specially-designed vehicles were first used on television's *I Spy* series. He set up Fouad Said Productions to exploit his invention commercially. This venture proved to be so successful that in November 1968, Said was able to sell his company to Taft Broadcasting for $5.1 million in stock.

The advent of this type of compact vehicle for filming, combined with lightweight portable equipment, encouraged many small companies without studio facilities to shoot wherever the locale and economic advantages were most attractive. Many of these low-budgeted enterprises were able to bypass altogether the nexus of the large studios and theatre chains by showing their cheaply produced pictures on a theatre-by-theatre basis. Under this form of marketing, called "four-walling," a theatre is rented by the producer for a flat fee as is any other piece of real estate. Many of these ventures have proven to be quite profitable. Russell Neihart, Robert Crosier, and Frank Olsen, who later formed American National Enterprises, demonstrated the earning potential of the four-walling technique in 1965 by traveling around the country promoting a low-budgeted hunting film they called *Alaska Safari*. The film eventually grossed over $15 million. Even after subtracting the costs of media advertising, theatre rentals, prints and other incidentals, their profits were enormous. Pacific International Enterprises, another small operation, using saturation advertising, and renting theatres in which to show the film, also had a gross return of over $10 million from *American Wilderness,* which had been shot for about $50,000.

One of the most successful of the smaller companies has been American International Pictures (AIP). This relatively late comer to the movie business initially thrived by taking advantage of a totally new market, the drive-in theatre. From a mere 100 in 1946, drive-in theatres increased in number to over 4,000 during the post-war years. Samuel Arkoff and the late James Nicholson had pooled their efforts and modest resources in 1954, creating what became AIP to supply inexpensive double bills for this predominantly youthful audience. AIP's low-cost, hastily-made film blend of science-fiction, horror and melodrama proved to be extraordinarily successful. Between 1954 and 1960, not one AIP film lost money. The company's first big moneymaker, *The Beast with 1,000 Eyes* directed by Roger Corman, was made in eight days on a budget of $35,000. Corman churned out a remarkable number of cheap 70 minute features which ranged in cost from $50,000 to $150,000 each. *I Was a Teenage Werewolf,* a 1957 release starring Michael Landon as a high-school youth who sprouts fangs, was filmed for about $123,000 and grossed more than $2 million.

AIP initially released its pictures through independent distributors under the state's rights system. As the company prospered it eventually took over many of these exchanges establishing its own national distribution network. AIP's dominance over exploitative, low-budget features became threatened by 1959 when imitators began to saturate the movie market with similar cheaply made black-and-white double bills. To gain a competitive edge, AIP imported a number of Italian-made color features. Released under such titles as *Sign of the Gladiator* and *Goliath and the Barbarians,* these films proved to be quite profitable. The success of the latter picture, which grossed about $1.8 million, led inevitably to a series of epics of the *"Goliath and the . . ."* type. Increasing its per-film budget to $400,000, AIP produced Edgar Allan Poe's *Fall of the House of Usher,* a 1960 release starring Vincent Price. Since Poe's works are in the public domain, AIP did not have to pay any original story costs. The film was so successful that several more Poe pictures followed. The Poe features, competently directed by the seemingly indefatigable Roger Corman, gave work to such talented character actors as Peter Lorre, Lon Chaney, Jr. and Boris Karloff. Later AIP films provided a showcase for such now popular actors as Jack Nicholson, Peter Fonda, Bruce Dern, Mike Connors and a host of others. Talented directors like Peter Bogdanovich, Francis Ford Coppola and Martin Scorsese all served an apprenticeship at AIP. Cinematographer Laszlo Kovacs, whose impressive camera work can be seen in many films, among them *Easy Rider, Five Easy Pieces, Paper Moon* and *New York, New York,* is also an AIP alumnus.

During the 1960s, AIP released a plethora of inane but highly profitable beach pictures *(Beach Party, Muscle Beach Party, Bikini Beach, How to Stuff a Wild Bikini, Beach Blanket Bingo,* etc.) starring singer Frankie Avalon and ex-mouseketeer Annette Funicello. Each film cost between $500,000 and $750,000 to produce. Tantalizing, but essentially misleading advertising (e.g., "Bikini Beach where bare-as-you-dare is the rule! . . . What happens when 10,000 kids meet on 5,000 beach blankets?"), helped to lure young people to the theatres. Always trend conscious, AIP has attempted to appeal to all segments of the mercurially changing teenage market. From innocuous beach pictures, the company went to stories about rebellious youth. AIP made a number of profitable films about motorcycle gangs featuring Fonda, Nicholson and Hopper at differing times prior to their joint fame in *Easy Rider.* One low-budgeted AIP release, *The Wild Angels,* which starred Peter Fonda as the leader of an outlaw motorcycle gang, grossed over $5 million. *Easy Rider* itself had almost appeared as an AIP picture, but Samuel Arkoff balked at the idea of giving the directorial reins to Dennis Hopper who had a reputation for unreliability.

Other youth oriented features produced by AIP included *The Trip* (drug use) and *Wild in the Streets* (teenage tyranny). AIP was also quick to exploit the new genre of black supermen and superwomen pictures by releasing such hard action melodramas as *Black Caesar, Foxy Brown* and *Truck Tanner.* The company has also distributed a dozen or so Kung Fu movies *(Shanghai Killers, Screaming Tigers, Deep Thrust,* etc.). Occasionally, AIP releases a film of some artistic merit. *Cooley High,* a $750,000 production based on the work of black writer Eric Monte, offered a sensitive, often poignant portrayal of the experiences of black teenagers growing up in Chicago.

Even AIP's more recent "big-budget" features, however, were produced under very economically exacting circumstances. The company, which does not own any production facilities, finds locations or rents studio space as its needs dictate. The prime ingredient in AIP's financial success is its capacity to estimate the interests of its market. AIP helped to pioneer what has become standard merchandising technique of releasing a film to hundreds of theatres simultaneously in what is known as "saturation booking." The impression given is that a particular film is everywhere and, consequently, must be worth seeing.

The prospect of big profits provided the incentive for many other firms to make movies. Fabergé Inc., Mattel Toys, Quaker Oats and Playboy Enterprises were among the companies who, at one time or another, invested in motion pictures. The Jicarilla Apaches of New Mexico, an Indian tribe that made its money from gas leases and mineral rights, financed Kirk Douglas' $2 million production of *A Gunfight.* Two of the major television networks also took a stab at theatrical production. In February 1967, CBS paid $9.5 million for the 70-acre production facilities of the old Republic studio. (Republic had gone out of the movie business in 1959.) The network formed Cinema Center Films to make features intended for theatre showing. ABC, too, set up a subsidiary for theatrical feature film production. Most companies that have gone into motion picture financing and production without guaranteed access to the main lines of distribution have ultimately foundered. Since neither CBS nor ABC had distributed their own features, relying instead on National General (one of the country's biggest theatre operators) and Cinerama Releasing (a subsidiary of Cinerama Inc.), respectively to handle their product, the CBS and ABC theatrical ventures were not financial successes.

CHANGING FORTUNES

Several of the well established major companies were at their economic nadir by the dawn of the 1970s. Their problems were in part related to television, which had yielded a rich harvest for all of the companies, following the phenomenal success of ABC's presentation of *The Bridge on the River Kwai*. At the outset, the three major networks had vied with each other for the rights to the big box-office successes. ABC paid Twentieth Century-Fox $19.5 million for television rights to only 17 films. Included in this package was *Cleopatra*, which brought $5 million for two telecasts. Three other Fox films, *The Longest Day, Those Magnificent Men in Their Flying Machines* and *The Agony and the Ecstasy*, fetched $2.5 million apiece. For the rest ABC paid a little more than $500,000 each. The same network paid Paramount $20 million for the rights to televise 32 features, an average of $625,000 per picture. MGM received $52.8 million from CBS for television rights to 51 films that had already been shown in theatres. The studio also guaranteed CBS the right to televise 18 films that had not yet been made. Theatrical features had become a very saleable commodity. Wisely, the studios no longer sold their films outright. Television showings became an extension of the box-office, part of the projected earnings for a picture.

The big studios became ever more dependent upon the television medium to keep their ledgers in the black. Universal made an arrangement with NBC for the co-financing of a number of two-hour long feature films made expressly for television. The first of these so-called "World Premiere" films, a mystery-comedy titled *Fame Is the Name of the Game,* made its debut on Thanksgiving weekend in 1966. This feature was the source of a new television show, called simply *The Name of the Game,* which ran on the network for four years. The "World Premiere" movies proved to be an expedient and resourceful way of testing the potential of possible new series. More than 30 NBC series were developed in this manner, including *Rockford, Columbo,* and *McCloud.*

The balloon, alas, could not rise forever. The record prices the studios had received for the sale of feature-film rights were short-lived as the networks acquired enough pictures to last several years. The need for telefilms had also declined. At one time nearly every network television series consisted of 39 original episodes, and 13 reruns usually played during the summer months. By the late 1960s, "summer" began in March. Before the winter snows melted, some episodes had already been repeated. The average network series now telecasts only about 22 original episodes each year, resulting in considerable reduction in revenue for the program suppliers. Moreover, producers of most prime-time television shows rarely make back their production costs on the initial network sale since the license fee paid by the network covers only about 75 per cent of the production cost. However, after two showings on the network, the property generally reverts back to the producing company. The producer's deficit is recouped through overseas sales. Assuming the show is a hit, the producer can later make syndication deals—selling the program on a station-by-station basis—this represents almost solid profit. A 100-program package, for example, may bring as much as $18 million in syndication sales. The period from initial network presentation to eventual profits from syndication is, however, a long one. A show must generally run on the network at least four seasons before there are enough episodes to make it saleable to local stations.

Still, the most significant problem that confronted the major movie companies was not dwindling or delayed television revenues, but rather, a general box-office slump, particularly for big-budget pictures. The studios were encumbered by large inventories of expensive movies that lacked appeal in the entertainment market. Five of the major companies, as a result of write-downs and write-offs of this unsaleable inventory, reported a combined paper loss of $110 million in 1969. That year Twentieth Century-Fox, alone, had a deficit of $36.8 million. Fox's earnings, throughout the decade had been, to say the least, erratic. Aging monarch, Spyros Skouras, who had ruled the studio since the death of Sidney Kent, in 1942, was toppled from power in 1962. The last years of his reign had been plagued by mismanagement and misfortune. To balance Fox's losses on movie production, Skouras sold the company's 260-acre West Los Angeles studio in April 1961 to Aluminum Company of America (ALCOA) for $43 million. The land was developed into a commercial and residential complex called Century City. The film company leased back 80 acres of its former property from Alcoa for $1.5 million a year on a 99-year lease. Under the agreement, Fox was permitted to develop its leased land for commercial use after four years. Skouras further offset operating losses through the sale of post-1950 color features to NBC-TV. When fiscal 1961 came to a close, Fox's earnings had nose-dived to $2.9 million, down from $6.2 million the previous year. The Skouras regime's biggest disaster had been its trouble-ridden production of *Cleopatra,* starring Elizabeth Taylor and Richard Burton. Originally budgeted at $2 million, the film's production cost had escalated to more than $30 million. The studio seemed unlikely to recoup its investment since to show a profit the film would have to bring in some $60 million—about twice its negative cost. Generally, films must earn two and a half times their negative cost to turn a profit, but very high budgeted films have a lower multiple to determine their break-even point.

Skouras relinquished his throne to Darryl Zanuck in July

1962 (a year before *Cleopatra's* premiere). Zanuck, the studio's co-founder and a large stockholder, had resigned his production post at Fox six years earlier to form his own independent production company, DFZ Productions. Most of his independently produced films (*The Sun Also Rises* and *The Roots of Heaven,* among others), had fared poorly at the box-office. Although his independent productions had fared badly, Zanuck attributed this to poor distribution practices. He had just finished a film which everyone declared would be a major financial triumph, *The Longest Day,* and was anxious to see changes at Twentieth Century-Fox which would assure efficient handling of this film. He was also, as has been mentioned above, a major stockholder in the company. Soon after taking the reins from Skouras, Zanuck temporarily closed down the studio, and concentrated on editing *Cleopatra* into a marketable commodity. About half of the studio's 600 employees were laid off without salary. Despite all these measures, Fox recorded a loss of some $39.8 million in 1962. Production at the studio resumed in the spring of 1963. Disregarding charges of nepotism from dissident stockholders, 27-year old Richard Zanuck, Darryl's only son, was put in charge of the studio operation. Under the direction of the Zanuck father and son team, the Fox studio was soon operating in the black, thanks to revenues from *The Longest Day;* tangible prosperity came to the studio in the form of Robert Wise's 1965 production of *The Sound of Music.* Although panned by the critics, this innocuous and somewhat saccharine film, made at a cost of about $8 million, eventually brought theatre rental revenues to Fox of over $78 million from just the domestic—i.e., United States–Canada—market alone. The success of *Sound of Music* set Fox on a catastrophic course of undertaking big-budget productions, such as *Dr. Doolittle, Hello Dolly!, Tora! Tora! Tora!*—none of which were able to duplicate the performance of *Sound of Music* at the box-office. These vast expenditures, which were not recouped at the box-office, plunged the company from its pinnacle of prosperity to a state of near-bankruptcy. The company's fiscal losses in 1969 were followed by an even more devastating deficit the following year, of some $77.4 million. Richard Zanuck, who had succeeded to the Fox presidency in 1969, attempted to re-organize and diversify the company. His actions, however, caused a rift with his father, Darryl, who had retained the positions of chairman of the board and chief executive officer. Young Zanuck apparently had decided that the time had come for his father to relinquish the throne. He joined forces with David Brown, then a Fox story editor, to wrest control from his progenitor. The schism between the father and son gradually widened; in the summer of 1970, they were barely speaking to each other. Meanwhile the company's losses were mounting. In an effort to protect the company against stockholder suits and takeover attempts, the board requested the resignations of both Richard Zanuck and David Brown. Dennis Stanfill, a corporate finance specialist, replaced young Zanuck as president. Stanfill had joined the company a short time earlier at the suggestion of Lehman Brothers, Fox's longtime investment bankers.

In April of the following year, the fading Darryl Zanuck withdrew from the field of battle, giving up the title of executive officer. He retired from the company two months later. William Gossett, head of Fox's executive committee, temporarily inherited Zanuck's mantle. Dennis Stanfill, whom Gossett had been instrumental in bringing to the company, soon took over as chairman and chief executive. The posts of president and chief operating officer were assumed by Gordon Stulberg, who had headed CBS's short-lived Cinema Center Films. After having quelled an abortive insurrection in mid-1971 by dissatisfied stockholders, Twentieth Century-Fox management began a fiscal turnaround. With the release of such profitable films as *The French Connection* and *The Poseidon Adventure,* the company earnings gradually improved. Several successful real estate ventures have also helped considerably to augment Fox's earnings. Revenues from television series production, film laboratory operations, Australian and New Zealand theatres, three television stations, 20th Century Records, 20th Century Music Corporation, a ski resort operation and a Midwest Coca-Cola bottling franchise have all contributed to the upturn in Fox's financial fortunes.

In order to tighten financial controls, Stanfill made several organizational and managerial shifts within the company, creating a new tier of top management. Gordon Stulberg departed late in 1974 because of what were reported as "policy differences." Alan Livingston, former chairman of Capitol Records, was put in charge of a newly formed entertainment group; while Alan Ladd Jr. (son of the famous actor) was elevated from senior vice-president to president of the feature film group.

The feature film group had begun to founder again with the release of such expensive box-office failures as *Bluebird, At Long Last Love, Lucky Lady* and *The Duchess and the Dirtwater Fox*. During 1976, however, Fox turned out several substantial box-office draws, including *Silver Streak, Silent Movie* and *The Omen*. The latter film cost about $5 million and grossed some $35 million. In March of 1976, Ladd persuaded Fox's board of directors to commit $8.5 million for the production of George Lucas' intergalactic fantasy, *Star Wars*. The film, released in mid-1977, made movie history, breaking box-office records almost everywhere it played.

Not only were film-makers assuming more complex corporate structures, talent representatives in their own right have come to play an increasingly important part in the industry, with a concomitant change in management structure. The success of *Star Wars* serves to point up this shift in function. *Star Wars'* writer-director, George Lucas, is represented by International Creative Management (ICM), the principal subsidiary of Marvin Josephson Associates. As Lucas' representative, ICM stands to make millions of dollars since it will receive the standard 10 per cent of all his earnings from the picture. Lucas is to receive 40 per cent of *Star Wars'* profits; ICM's share should be substantial. The company has had highly profitable indirect interests in many films. For the 1975 smash hit, *Jaws,* ICM represented the producers, the director, and the screenwriter. Its earnings from this film alone already exceed $4 million. Among ICM's clients are such stars as Woody Allen, Sean Connery, Faye Dunaway, Steve McQueen, and Barbra Streisand. ICM also represents people like John Chancellor, Harry Reasoner, and even Henry Kissinger. Marvin Josephson, who founded the company bearing his name, had been a lawyer in CBS's contract division when he decided to become an independent agent. Beginning as an agency representing television talent, his company grew primarily through mergers and acquisitions. Josephson greatly expanded his business activities in 1969 with the purchase of California-based Ashley Famous Agency. Five years later, Josephson acquired Creative Management Associates. The latter purchase brought superagent Sue Mengers into the Josephson fold. Under her contract with ICM, Miss Mengers, who represents some of the most successful talent in the movie industry, makes more than $300,000 a year. ICM is now second in size only to the long-established William Morris Agency, founded in 1898 as a representative for talent in legitimate theatre and vaudeville. In addition to handling individual talent, large agencies like William Morris and ICM also represent producing companies and packagers, and they assemble talent packages. When in the 1950s, the big film companies began to finance independent producers, the talent agencies, who represented the major stars and leading directors, became an evermore powerful force in the movie industry. Under the new order, agents are now the mighty makers of deals. Talent representation, too, has assumed the characteristics of big business.

MEDIA CONGLOMERATION

The trend of the middle 1960s continued towards the close of the decade as several additional conglomerates entered the movie business. In 1967, United Artists was merged into Trans-

A British-based movie company headed by Harry Saltzman and Albert R. Broccoli helped to swell United Artists' profits with the production of a series of films based on the exploits of Ian Fleming's fictional super-spy, James Bond. The seemingly indestructable Bond first came to the screen in the person of Sean Connery in UA's 1962 release *Doctor No*. The latest Bond is Roger Moore, who in his third appearance in the role scored heavily with *The Spy Who Loved Me*. This 1977 film was produced by Albert Broccoli as a solo effort, since he had earlier dissolved his partnership with Saltzman. Mr. Saltzman's interests in the rights to produce *Bond* pictures were sold to United Artists.

america, a giant corporation with interests in insurance and other financial services. The acquisition by Transamerica, which left the existing UA management intact gave United Artists the advantage of a better market evaluation for its earnings and provided a larger reservoir from which to finance its movie and television productions. The movie company had continued to prosper throughout the 1960s, capturing the coveted Oscar for "best picture" five times during the decade with *The Apartment, West Side Story, Tom Jones, In the Heat of the Night* and *Midnight Cowboy*. The movie business, however, is capricious and volatile. Directly after this stellar period, United Artists showed a heavy loss for fiscal 1970. Heavy losses in the movie industry, however, are frequently misleading. In January 1970, when Arthur Krim (who had been on partial leave from UA to serve as a White House advisor) studied the film inventory which had been accumulated late in 1968 and 1969, he decided that these pictures would show a very substantial loss. His evaluation was corroborated by his colleagues and a large write-off was indicated. The decision to take the write-off in 1970 was initiated by Krim and concurred in by all of management. Under normal long-term practices, UA would have taken this write-off over the ensuing three-year period when the pictures were in actual distribution. However, since another Transamerica subsidiary, Occidential Life Insurance, had a large write-up available in 1970, UA decided to take its entire write-off that same year. The movie company recorded a pretax loss of nearly $35 million, and wrote-off another $50 million. In the ensuing years, UA has shown a dramatic upturn in its revenues. Indeed, by 1974, the company had re-established its long-term history of high profits; it has since enjoyed record success. UA's worldwide theatrical film rentals for 1977 reached an astonishing $318 million, a new high for the movie industry.

Overall, United Artists has had one of the longest histories of continuity of management in the movie industry, with virtually all management changes coming from within the company. In 1968 and 1969, both Arthur Krim and Robert Benjamin took partial leaves of absence; Krim, as previously noted, to work at the White House (and later to assist President Johnson in the post-White House transition), and Benjamin to serve as one of the U.S. representatives at the United Nations. In the summer of 1969 it was announced that Krim and Benjamin would be co-chairmen of the board of United Artists and David Picker, who had been executive vice president, would become president. The announcement of the co-chairmenship was revised with Krim becoming chairman and chief executive officer while Benjamin continued as co-chairman. In 1973, Krim and Benjamin selected David Picker to be chief executive but Picker remained in the post only a few months. Picker formed his own production company which contracted to make pictures exclusively for UA release. He was succeeded by Eric Pleskow, another UA executive of long-time standing, who became president and later chief executive officer. Krim remained chairman of the board and Benjamin became chairman of the finance committee.

In recent years, relations between UA's senior officers and the management of Transamerica had become increasingly strained. After UA's financial reversal in 1970, Transamerica imposed tighter controls on the movie company. When UA once again became strong and prosperous, its executives demanded greater autonomy in managing its affairs. Executive remuneration became a particularly sensitive issue. UA's top officials felt that executives and employees within the company were not being adequately compensated for their efforts. To rectify this situation, Arthur Krim had twice proposed some type of UA spin-off to Transamerica's board of directors; the matter was studied and rejected. The dispute culminated in January 1978 with the resignations of Arthur Krim, Robert Benjamin and Eric Pleskow. Andy Albeck, who had been UA's senior vice president of operations, became president and chief executive officer of the motion picture company. James Harvey, vice president of Transamerica's leisure time group, was named to the additional post of UA chairman.

Ironically, United Artists, the company that produced

COURTESY OF UNITED ARTISTS

United Artists triumphed at the box-office with its late 1975 release, *One Flew Over the Cuckoo's Nest* (left). This film has taken in over $163 million worldwide, making it the largest grossing picture in the company's history. The film company scored again late the following year with the release of *Rocky* (right), a low-budget film written by and starring Sylvester Stallone. This film has grossed about $79 million in the domestic market alone. Both these UA-distributed films won Academy Awards for best picture—for the years 1975 and 1976, respectively.

no movies *per se,* now controls one of the largest inventories of feature films in the entire industry. Through its purchase of Associated Artists Productions, in late 1957, UA gained control of some 700 pre-1948 Warner films. Continuing over the years to build up its inventory, UA acquired, in 1973, the United States and Canadian theatrical and television syndication rights to 1,200 MGM films for a period of ten years.

Under terms of the agreement, MGM retained the rights to sell to networks, but gave the rights to sell to individual stations, and to distribute new productions for theatrical showings to United Artists. This, in essence, makes UA the distributor for most MGM films, although a few valuable properties were held back from this agreement. These include *Gone With the Wind, Wizard of Oz, Doctor Zhivago* and *2001: A Space Odyssey.* United Artists is owned, almost totally, by Transamerica, whose largest single stockholder was, at one time, Kirk Kerkorian. The Armenian-descended Kerkorian divested himself of his Transamerica holdings when he intended to acquire controlling interest of MGM. After paying off his debts, he had planned to borrow additional money for the MGM purchase from a subsidiary of Transamerica—the Transamerica Financial Corporation. The management of MGM at that time felt that this constituted a violation of antitrust laws, and took the matter to court, where they were supported by the judicial decision. Kerkorian then raised the money from several European banks, and bought into MGM. The structure and the control of the movie industry were, indeed, becoming increasingly complex.

In the same year that United Artists merged into Transamerica, Kalvex Inc., a manufacturer and distributor of motor homes, men's wear, and other consumer goods, used its ownership of 52 per cent of Allied Artists Corporation's preferred stock to elect a majority of the members of that movie company's board. Allied Artists was an outgrowth of the old Monogram studio, having been formed in the 1940s as a subsidiary company to handle some of Monogram's more expensively produced films. Monogram was subsumed by its own subsidiary in 1953. Allied Artists produced an occasional film of merit during the 1950s, including *Friendly Persuasion* and *Love in the Afternoon.* The company, however, fell on bad times in the 1960s. Production was halted and Allied functioned primarily as a distributor of imported films. During the early 1970s, Allied released such big-budgeted hits as *Cabaret* and *Papillon.* Kalvex and Allied were merged in January 1976 to form Allied

Artists' Industries, a holding company which controls the units of the two former companies.

In June of 1968, Joseph E. Levine's small but prosperous Embassy Pictures came under the corporate umbrella of Avco, a mammoth corporation involved in the manufacture of a variety of defense and aerospace equipment, with holding interests in such diversified fields as consumer loans, land development and broadcasting. Levine had been a moderately successful theatre owner and regional distributor in Boston until 1959 when he paid $120,000 for the United States and Canadian distribution rights to an Italian-made spectacle called *Hercules*. The film, as a result of a $1.5 million advertising campaign launched by Levine, grossed over $20 million at the box-office. In the years immediately following, Levine imported such crit-

Steve Reeves as he appeared in the title role of *Hercules,* the much-publicized Italian-made film imported by entrepreneur Joseph E. Levine. This film was distributed in the United States by Warners, who paid Levine an advance of $300,000 against 25 per cent of the gross rentals for the distribution rights.

ically-acclaimed films as Carlo Ponti's *Two Women*. Working primarily with Paramount, Levine also turned out profitable trifles like *Zulu* and *Carpetbaggers*. As a subsidiary of Avco, Joseph E. Levine's newly named Avco-Embassy Pictures became a major force in the movie industry. One of the company's films, *The Graduate,* with Dustin Hoffman in his first leading role, cost less than $3 million to produce and grossed over $100 million.

Under the corporate umbrella of Gulf & Western, Paramount eventually returned to the ranks of the prosperous, particularly with the release of Albert Ruddy's production of *The Godfather*. This movie was based on Mario Puzo's best-selling novel which the studio had purchased for a mere $10,000 before it became a smash hit. (Escalator clauses eventually brought Puzo's remuneration up to $80,000.) Paramount's profits from the film were immense. Although advertising for the film cost about $1 million a week, the money was well spent. Nationwide ticket sales for *The Godfather,* which was released early in 1972, totaled some $26 million in the first 26 days. The film went on to become one of the biggest financial successes in the history of the movie industry. NBC paid an unprecedented $10 million for the rights to telecast *The Godfather* in 1974. *Godfather II,* also released by Paramount, did almost as well as its precursor at the box-office. NBC reportedly paid $15 million for its four-part presentation of the entire *Godfather* story in November 1977.

The success of *The Godfather* put its director, Francis Ford Coppola, in the forefront of American film-makers. Coppola had first distinguished himself as a screen writer when he was a graduate student at the UCLA film school. While there he won the Samuel Goldwyn writing award. One of his first jobs was assistant to Roger Corman on such low-budget thrillers as *Tower of London* and *Premature Burial*. He also worked as a staff writer at Seven Arts. His work on *Is Paris Burning?* led to a writing job with the Fox studio as the co-author of the screenplay for *Patton*. For the latter assignment he won an Oscar. His initial efforts at directing, however, were less successful. *You're a Big Boy Now, Finian's Rainbow* and *The Rain People* were neither critical nor financial successes, although the latter film showed artistic promise. With the assistance of Warners, Coppola in 1969 set up, in San Francisco, a sophisticated studio and technical facility which he called American Zoetrope. The one film to emerge from this enterprise was George Lucas' futuristic THX *1138*. When it flopped at the box-office, Warners pulled out of Zoetrope leaving Coppola heavily in debt. Financial salvation came to him in the form of *The Godfather*. For his work on the picture Coppola received 6 per cent of the profits, these proving to be quite substantial. *Godfather II* brought Coppola 13 per cent of the gross and made him a very wealthy man.

The financial fortunes of Paramount had been guided by Frank Yablans whom Charles Bluhdorn had appointed president in 1971. Yablans had first worked as a sales representative for Warners; he later held similar posts at Disney, then Filmways, finally joining Paramount in 1969. Before Bluhdorn made him president of the company, Yablans' sales expertise had helped Paramount recoup its investment from such expensive mishaps as *Paint Your Wagon* and *Catch-22*. Under his presidency, the studio's profits soared to $38.7 million in 1973. Much of the credit for Paramount's success, of course, was also due to Robert Evans who ruled the studio operations. While the Yablans/Evans team had their share of failures (*Jonathan Livingston Seagull* and *The Little Prince,* among others), profits from successful films more than canceled out the occasional losers. In addition to the *Godfather* duo, films like *Love Story, Serpico, Death Wish,* and *Chinatown* have been enormously profitable for the studio. For the latter film, Yablans and Evans each received a reported 10 per cent of the profits. Evans has since become an independent producer for Paramount, so that he can share directly in all the film projects he brings to fruition. Yablans, on the other hand, apparently fell into disfavor with Bluhdorn. Late in 1974, Barry Diller, formerly a programming vice president for ABC-TV, was appointed as Paramount's chairman and chief executive officer, superseding Yablans as the company's active head. Seven weeks after Diller's appointment, Yablans, who had seven years remaining on an eight-year employment contract, resigned as Paramount's president.

One of Paramount's most fortuitous associations has been with independent producer Dino De Laurentiis, a highly successful Italian film-maker. He has supervised the production of some of the studio's biggest moneymakers, including *Serpico* and *Death Wish*. In recent years, De Laurentiis' productions have become increasingly more ambitious. His 1976 remake of *King Kong*, for example, cost $22 million to produce, mainly due to special effects costs. (The original production of *King Kong*, it will be recalled, was made on a budget of $650,000.) Some $2 million was spent just to construct a 40-foot-high mechanical ape. A 300-foot-long, 50-foot-high wall, used in only one scene, was built on MGM's backlot at a cost of $800,000. Even with such extravagances, the new version of *King Kong* proved to be a modestly profitable venture.

The one major movie company that has been almost consistently profitable is Walt Disney Productions. Roy Disney very wisely realized early in the 1950s that the key to prosperity under the new order was distribution. The Disney organization broke with the faltering RKO in 1953 to form its own national distribution outlet called Buena Vista (named after the street where the Disney studio was located). This subsidiary was initially comprised of 8 district sales offices and 15 sub-branches. The actual physical delivery of Disney's prints was handled by National Film Service. By setting up Buena Vista, Disney reduced its distribution costs from 30 per cent to an estimated 15 per cent of the gross rentals. The first film released by the new distribution operation was *The Living Desert*, an absorbing live-action animal documentary. Made at a cost of $300,000 the film earned some $4 million. Thereafter all Disney films were distributed by Buena Vista. The rising labor and production costs of animation led Disney to concentrate more on live-action features. Such live-action fictional features as *20,000 Leagues Under the Sea* and *Mary Poppins* were spectacularly successful. The latter film grossed some $30 million-plus domestically and more than $45 million worldwide. Profits in fiscal 1965 soared to $11 million.

The Disney organization continues to prosper by concentrating on family films, television programming and the operation of amusement parks. Reissues of old films add to Disney's profits. In 1976, *Snow White and the Seven Dwarfs*, which began its fifth reissue during Christmas of the previous year, grossed $1.7 million in West Germany alone. The merchandising of music, records, publications and character rights also bring substantial revenues to the company. Disney's amusement park ventures, too, have become increasingly more profitable. In October 1971, Walt Disney World, now a $700 million-plus complex of display pavilions, parks, hotels and man-made lakes, opened on a huge tract of land near Orlando, in central Florida. The company's latest marvel is called EPCOT, Experimental Prototype Community of Tomorrow, which will include a permanent world's fair and will be constructed a few miles from Walt Disney World's Magic Kingdom. Walt Disney died in 1966, followed five years later by his brother Roy, but their heirs are still involved with the operation of Walt Disney Productions. The company, unlike most of the others, has remained immune from all outside corporate threats.

For other companies, though, the relentless pursuit of profits was still shaping broad changes in insecure corporate structures. Warner Brothers, in March 1967, had merged with Seven Arts Productions Ltd., a Canadian distributor of films to television. The new corporation was titled Warner Bros.-Seven Arts. Seventy-five-year-old Jack L. Warner, one of the last vestiges of old-line movie moguls, was given the essentially honorary titles of director and vice-chairman of the board in the new agglomeration. (Jack Warner received a reported $32 million for his one-third interest in the Warner studio.) Two years later, this enterprise merged with Kinney National, a New York City-based service industry conglomerate that had its inception in 1897 operating a funeral parlor. When Kinney absorbed Jack Warner's old company, that last of the brothers to remain active in movies had to leave the Burbank studio. (Jack Warner released some independent productions through Columbia before retiring.) Kinney National, under the direction of Steven J. Ross, the company's president, was fast becoming one of the most powerful forces in the entertainment industry. The corporation had made a number of media-related acquisitions. In addition to the Warner studio, Kinney had acquired, within a two-year period, Ashley Famous Agency, a talent firm headed by Ted Ashley; National Periodical Publications (publishers of some 50 magazines including *Mad, Superman* and *Batman,* and distributors of numerous others ranging from *Yachting* to *Playboy*); and Panavision, a company that leases movie equipment. The acquisition of Warner-Seven Arts also gave Kinney two profitable record companies, Warner Reprise and Atlantic Recording. In July 1971, Kinney's entertainment complex was transferred into a separate, superordinate sister company called Warner Communications.

Prior to completing the Warner deal, Kinney had disposed of the talent agency to avoid violation of the antitrust laws. Ted Ashley was put in charge of Warner Bros. (Seven Arts was dropped from the corporate title) at an annual salary of $156,000. The studio, which had been losing money, was completely overhauled. Within a few years, Warner Bros. was turning a healthy profit. Such low-budget releases as *Woodstock* and *Summer of '42* helped to swell corporate earnings. The latter film, made for little more than $1 million, grossed 20 times that amount. Substantial revenues came to the studio from many diverse film projects. For example, Warner Bros. financed and distributed John Wayne's Batjac company production of *Chisum.* For starring in this picture, Wayne received an acting fee of $1 million against ten per cent of the gross receipts. Made at a cost of $4.5 million, *Chisum* eventually grossed over $20 million. Such films as *Deliverance* and *What's Up, Doc.?,* two 1972 releases, also grossed around $20 million each in the domestic market. The most profitable film in Warner's history thus far has been its 1974 release of *The Exorcist,* based on William Blatty's best-selling novel about demonic possession. Originally budgeted at $5 million, the film's production costs, due in large part to the special effects employed, inflated to almost three times that amount. Blatty, who wrote the screenplay and functioned as the picture's producer, drove a hard bargain. His contract called for him to receive 35.1 per cent of the net profits. Director William Friedkin received 10 per cent; another 5 per cent went to Paul Monash, a producer who was involved in the early stages of the project. Despite such participation deals, Warner's earnings from the picture were immense. The studio's gross from theatrical film rental revenues soared from $77 million in 1971 to some $275 million by 1974. The theatrical features division continues to prosper with such releases as *All the President's Men, Dog Day Afternoon, A Star Is Born* and *The Late Show.* Warner has also expanded its television activities. Late in 1976, Warner Bros. acquired The Wolper Organization, which produced ABC-TV's phenomenally successful presentation of *Roots.* Warner Communications, parent of Warner Bros., has continued to diversify its entertainment-related activities. One of its more recent acquisitions has been Atari Inc., the electronic games manufacturer, for $28 million.

Universal, the company which had thrived on television, was unable to duplicate its success in theatrical films. The studio's drain on MCA's other profitable operations ran into millions of dollars. Lew Wasserman, who had ruled the MCA empire from 1946 on, seemed unable to rescue Universal from the sea of red ink. Rumors began to circulate that perhaps Wasserman had outlived his usefulness to the company. Part of the problem apparently was that he had a tendency to involve himself too much in casting, script approval, promotion and other aspects of film-making where he lacked specific expertise. Such interference operated to inhibit the contributions of his subordinates, resulting in pictures that were critically and financially uninspiring. It is doubtful, however, that Jules Stein, MCA's aging founder, ever seriously contemplated withdrawing his support from Wasserman. All talk of Wasserman's imminent demise subsided when, at the March 31, 1969 board meeting, he was re-elected president for another 15-month term. The whole affair nevertheless seemed to spark a change in policy at MCA, allowing division heads much greater freedom in the control of their respective domains. Financial success came to the motion picture division when it invested $10 million in *Airport,* a 1970 release that ultimately earned seven times that amount. Universal also profited from the release of such diversified film fare as *High Plains Drifter, Day of the Jackal* and *Jesus Christ, Superstar.* Ned Tanen, who later became president of Universal Theatrical Pictures, was given the authority to do six feature films for about $1 million each. These relatively low-budget pictures were intended to turn a modest but almost sure profit. One huge hit that emerged unexpectedly from this project was George Lucas' *American Graffiti,* which to date has grossed some $47 million in domestic rentals. Several successful independent producers were recruited to make pictures for Universal, including the Mirisch Corporation, the Filmmakers Group (Robert Wise and Mark Robson), and the team of Richard Zanuck and David Brown. The Zanuck/Brown team have turned out a number of hits since their abrupt departure from Fox in 1970. For Universal they produced George Roy Hill's *The Sting,* the smash hit of 1974. They followed this success with *Jaws,* the 1975 Universal release based on Peter Benchley's best-selling novel about a marauding shark. This film, directed by Steven Spielberg, cost about $8 million to produce and had reported box-office receipts of $25.7 million for the first 13 days of showing around the world. It has since gone on to gross over $200 million.

In recent years, MCA's subsidiary, Universal Television, has expanded its already highly profitable television operation. Working in conjunction with ABC, Universal-TV produced a 12-part series based on Irwin Shaw's best-selling novel *Rich Man, Poor Man.* For NBC, Universal has produced television serializations of such popular novels as Taylor Caldwell's *Captains and the Kings* and Robert Ludhum's *The Rhinemann Exchange.* Universal is also developing a new outlet for its products by producing feature films expressly for syndication.

A poster from the smash box-office hit, *Jaws*. The real star of this film was a 24-foot mechanical great white shark, which the technical crew christened "Bruce." In actuality, Bruce was the collective name for three mechanical sharks: Two were one-sided for photographing from the right or left; and a third was all-round for underwater scenes. Some 500 feet of plastic tubing, 25 remote-controlled valves and 20 electric and pneumatic hoses were used to power the mechanical marvels. Each shark weighed 1½ tons and cost about $150,000 to construct.

COURTESY OF UNIVERSAL

The studio's six-hour television movie, *Testimony of Two Men,* based on the Taylor Caldwell novel, played on about 100 independent stations.

In addition to motion picture and television production, MCA's other income-producing enterprises include the Universal Studio Tour, which has become one of the nation's most profitable tourist attractions. Some three million visitors a year ride the attractively colored trams through the company's vast studio facilities. The stable of artists in MCA's profitable record division include Elton John, Neil Sedaka and Olivia Newton-John. MCA has also diversified its activities, acquiring such companies as Spencer Gifts, a national mail order and retail gift operation, and Columbia Savings and Loan of Colorado. In December 1975 MCA acquired G. P. Putnam's Sons, a leading publisher of hardcover and paperback books.

After 17 years as Universal's production head, Edward Muhl stepped down in 1969; he was replaced by an executive committee. In January 1973, Henry H. Martin succeeded Milton Rackmil as president of Universal. When Lew Wasserman moved upstairs to the chairmanship of MCA in 1973, he selected as his heir apparent Sidney Sheinberg, a Columbia Law School graduate who had been head of Universal Television. As MCA's president, Sheinberg makes a yearly salary of $250,000. Control of the company, however, still rests with founder Jules Stein and Chairman Lew Wasserman, who together own nearly 30 per cent of MCA's stock. Their hold on MCA was strengthened when, in August 1975, the company filed with the Securities and Exchange Commission an amendment to its certificate of incorporation requiring the approval of those owning 75 per cent of the MCA's stock before an outside takeover can be effected.

ON THE HORIZON

In yet another way, in the coming decade prospects for MCA and its shareholders look even more promising. The company, in conjunction with N. V. Philips' Gloeilampenfabrieken, has developed a video disc for home use, which will provide an even richer market for the abundant MCA film library. The small MCA-owned laboratory, run by Dr. Kent Broadbent, developed the video disc, while Philips holds key patents on the playback unit. The Philips-MCA system, called Disco-Vision, uses a laser (acronym for *l*ight *a*mplification by *s*timulated *e*mission of *r*adiation) beam to record and play back the program material. The technology for this system is quite complex, yet it has many technical advantages, including a freeze-frame control (a feature that is important for instructional purposes). The playback units will be manufactured and sold by Magnavox, which is almost wholly owned by a Philips' subsidiary. Magnavox will assemble the videoplayers at one of its Tennessee plants. MCA, of course, will provide the program material for the discs. To market the discs, MCA will use its ready-made record distribution network and the 200-plus retail stores in its Spencer Gifts chain. The playback units are expected to sell for about $500. An album of discs, containing a full-length movie, should sell for $10 or $15. MCA's large archive of old movies should yield enormous profits. If the company, for example, sold video-disc copies of a film like *All Quiet on the Western Front* or *Animal Crackers,* for $8 each, a sale of just 500,000 (there are 72 million television-owning homes) would bring in $4 million. Since the Screen Actors' Guild has waived all rights to pre-1948 features, the sale of old movies will return an especially high profit.

MCA, however, is not the only company that is attempting to tap this rich source of new income. RCA also has prospects for a disc system. Unlike Philips-MCA's laser system, RCA's disc unit makes use of a stylus and an electron beam for playback. The Philips-MCA disc spins at a rate of 1,800 revolutions per minute, or 30 times per second, while RCA's disc revolves more slowly, only 450 r.p.m. Both discs have an approximate playing time of 30 minutes. Since the RCA unit is simpler technically, it does not incorporate the desirable features of control that the MCA unit can offer. RCA, however, has the edge over Philips-MCA in marketing its playback unit; the RCA network of sales and service centers is superior to that of Magnavox. RCA, which has had several false starts with its disc system, has decided to hold up further development indefinitely. This may give Philips-MCA a sizeable advantage—under any circumstances, MCA's library of 11,000 films gives it an inestimable headstart over the competition. The crucial factors which will ultimately determine the victor in what may well become a multi-billion dollar business are: price, reliability and, above all, available programming.

Several giant corporations have attempted to develop

video-recorder and player systems, with which motion pictures and other materials could be viewed on home television sets. Many of these projects, however, failed to achieve reliability at a cost consumers could afford. CBS was compelled to write-off a $40 million loss in 1972 on its process called electronic video recording, or simply EVR. The following year, Cartridge Television, an affiliate of Avco Corporation, filed for bankruptcy after suffering a deficit of $50 million. Nearly every large electronics firm in the world is working on some sort of home video player system, including Germany's A.E.G. Telefunken, Decca, Ltd. of England and France's Thomson-CSF. In March of 1975, the TeleDec system, a joint effort of Telefunken and Decca, made its debut on the West German market. The TeleDec process uses a plastic video disc for playback on a special high-speed (1,800 revolutions per minute) record player.

Two Japanese electronics firms are in the forefront of the home video recorder industry. In the fall of 1975, Japan's Sony Corporation introduced its Betamax video cassette system on the American market as part of a $2,000-plus color television console unit. Within a short period, Sony was offering at about $1,300 a separate video recorder-playback unit, attachable to most television sets. Several companies, among them Zenith, Sears, Sanyo and Toshiba, are now selling Sony-manufactured machines under their own brand names in the United States. Sony has developed a three-hour cassette which, with the use of a changer, gives the machine operator up to six hours of continuous recording or playback time.

Sony's most formidable competitor is Japan-based Matsushita Electric, the world's largest manufacturer of television sets. Matsushita owns Quasar, controls Japan Victor Company (JVC) and also markets in the United States under the Panasonic brand name. RCA, Magnavox, Sylvania, MGA Mitsubishi Electric and Curtis Mathes are committed along with JVC, Quasar and Panasonic to selling Matsushita-manufactured home recorder units. In the fall of 1977, RCA alone earmarked some $4 million for an advertising and merchandising campaign to launch its $1,000 SelectaVision video cassette recorder and playback machine. The SelectaVision unit, which uses Matsushita's technology and RCA's design, is equipped to transcribe television programs on two-hour or four-hour tape cassettes. The battle for consumer acceptance between the Sony and Matsushita systems will have no quarter, since the two systems are incompatible, i.e. a cassette made for one unit cannot be played on the other.

Since the Sony and Matsushita systems can record as well as play back they have raised serious questions of copyright infringement. MCA is, understandably, fearful that widespread acceptance of these home recorder systems will result in premature decision by consumers, and resulting seizure of the market. Since the Sony and Matsushita units are costly, it is not likely that the consumer, having purchased one of them, will easily replace or complement it with additional expensive purchases. To forestall this happening, Universal, MCA's subsidiary, joined with Walt Disney Productions in a legal action aimed at prohibiting the sale of the Sony units (and by implication the rest of the video recording units on the market). The two companies charge that the taping of televised movies and other programs violates federal copyright laws. Victory is dubious in this suit; however, a delaying action may be achieved. An additional possibility is the promulgation of some vague code of rights relating to use of reproductions.

Another fertile field for the exploitation of movies is pay television. Despite numerous premature starts—and failures— pay television's ability to present multiple showings of attractively packaged, unedited, uninterrupted motion pictures is already a commercial reality. After several abortive over-the-air pay television attempts, cable TV has moved to the forefront. Cable TV had its inception as a solution to reception problems in rural areas. By running coaxial cable from a high, central-area antenna to each individual home, it was possible to bring in signals clearly where none were received before.

It was quickly realized that not only network and local television shows, but some additional 20 to 40 channels were available for subscriber use. This felicitous finding was promptly exploited by program suppliers and movie suppliers. This devolved into a form of pay television usually referred to as "pay-cable."

The leading company in the pay-cable field is Home Box Office (HBO), a wholly owned subsidiary of Time, Inc. Within the stark, white walls of its domain on the 15th floor of a Manhattan skyscraper, HBO makes decisions each day that may eventually cause a restructuring of the entertainment industry's pyramid of power, prestige and prosperity. HBO functions as an intermediary between program suppliers and cable TV systems, packaging and transmitting programs which the cable operator, in turn, sends out on one of his "origination" channels. The average pay-cable subscriber pays a monthly fee of about $8, in addition to his regular monthly bill for simply "being on the cable." (Viewers who pay the standard cable fee but do not subscribe to HBO cannot receive its programs.) HBO keeps about half of the $8-subscription fee. As a program financing scheme, pay cable may reasonably be viewed as having a greater potential than the conventional system of motion picture distribution and exhibition. If 10 per cent of America's 70 million television households subscribed to Home Box Office, the company would have an astonishing monthly gross income of $28 million. Even the major movie companies, long accustomed to substantial earnings, must find this figure impressive. A special feature, offered on a per-show fee basis, could recoup its production costs in a single showing.

At the center of pay-cable's nerve system is fortyish Gerald Manuel Levin, chairman of HBO's board of directors. In a business where brashness and self-assertion is almost de rigeur, Mr. Levin is quiet and unassuming. His quiet deportment, however, belies a shrewd sense of corporate finance and public taste. Under Levin's direction, HBO is attempting to enrich the television landscape with diversified entertainment presented in a format not generally possible on the standard channels because of commercial considerations.

The Federal Communications Commission, traditionally sensitive to the economic welfare of conventional broadcasters, had set forth rules to prevent pay television operators from purveying many motion pictures that are now available on "free television." The FCC rules, in essence, permitted pay television systems to show theatrical films that have been in general release in theatres for less than three years, or more than 10 years, providing that the over 10-year-old films have not been shown on conventional television in the pay television market for three years preceding the pay television presentation. HBO, along with several other companies, filed a brief with the U.S. Court of Appeals in Washington contending that the FCC's pay television rules were unconstitutionally restrictive in that they violated the First Amendment. HBO argued that the Commission's rules restrained pay cable's freedom to select programs, limited the freedom of program suppliers to seek access to new markets, and violated the public's freedom to make choices among alternative media.

HBO, like any business concern, has profit as the first imperative. Nevertheless, its legal arguments were difficult to deny. In March of 1977, the United States Court of Appeals for the District of Columbia ruled that the FCC's existing regulation of pay television was unconstitutional and improper. The following fall, the U.S. Supreme Court declined to review the appeals court ruling. While the refusal of the High Court could not be construed as sustaining the lower court findings as a matter of law and precedent, it did leave the appeals court decision intact for practical purposes. Thus, the way has been opened to competition between the pay cable interests and the conventional television networks and stations for the right to dip into the rich reservoir of old movies. Many features are, of course, still tied up in complex, long-term contracts with television stations that vary from market to market. Some television outlets, it will be recalled, received the rights to many of RKO's films in perpetuity. Pay-cable operations that program nationally are particularly hampered by extant television contracts.

The eventual impact of HBO on the motion picture industry is difficult to predict. The company's growth in recent years has been explosive. In January 1975, there were fewer than 60,000 HBO subscribers. Within three years, the number had catapulted to about 950,000 subscribers. HBO began satellite transmission to its network of cable systems in the fall of 1975. The use of RCA's synchronous orbiting domestic communications satellite, stationed 22,300 miles above the earth, permits enormous expansion without substantial investment in additional equipment or extra personnel. In addition to the satellite interconnection, HBO also transmits its programs via terrestrial microwave links; but the satellite relay is about one-half the price of microwave transmission.

Pay-cable appears to be emerging as a major force in the entertainment industry. Already one can sense some shape of things to come in the knowledge that a subsidiary of Warner Communications, for instance, is testing an ambitious two-way pay-cable system in Columbus, Ohio. This much-ballyhooed system, called "Qube," lets subscribers choose programs at different prices on 10 pay channels. In the final analysis, the prognosis for the nation's pay television systems depends on the consumer's willingness to pay for the service, but intensive research and program testing will be necessary to determine the type of programming that will attract new subscribers and hold them. Pay television, if unfettered, can potentially eliminate conventional means of motion picture distribution and exhibition.

There is an even more astonishing development in the assault against the older methods of motion picture distribution—fiber optics—which, in substituting for the current copper used in cable transmission may make possible for the individual subscriber a selection range of hundreds of programs and other services. This system uses flexible, hair-thin optical fibers to carry television and other electrical signals in the form of light pulses. A microscopic laser converts electrical signals into intense, concentrated beams of infrared light. The optical fiber transmits the laser light (in much the same manner that a copper wire transmits electricity) to its destination where it is reconverted into electrical energy.

Fiber-optics technology has many advantages over conventional cable. A single strand of optical fiber, for example, can carry up to 167 television channels. A bundle of six fibers, no thicker than a lamp cord, makes possible more than 1,000 channels. In addition, fiber is immune to electrical interference and can carry light pulses for several miles, even around curves and corners, without a booster. Although the cheapest fiber currently costs $1 a meter (just over three feet), developing technology will eventually bring the price down to a few cents a foot. And while the copper used in coaxial cable may soon be in short supply, the raw material used to make optical fiber is plentiful and cheap. (The fibers are made from highly purified silica, which in its most common form is sand.) Researchers at Bell Laboratories have developed a protective resin coating for the hair-thin optical fibers that make them stronger than stainless steel wires of the same diameter.

The rapidly developing technology of fiber optics will have a tremendous impact on all forms of communication media. Already there is operating in Japan, on an experimental basis, a two-way fiber optics cable system which provides such services as television programs on request, computer-assisted instruction, television shopping, and police and fire protection.

The outline of the future of the entertainment industry can be clearly discerned in the wings, ready to appear for its turn on the stage of corporate development and consumer change. The Big Five and Little Three who loomed so large in the 1930s—with the advent of sound—have metamorphosed completely. It has become evident that the key to change has been essentially neither technology nor artistry, but the control of distribution. In the coming years the melding of new technology with new distribution methods will produce further transformations. But for the present, a review of the motion picture industry at the closing of the decade of the 1970s finds most of the major studios now employing a two-pronged approach to motion picture investments—financing a combination of relatively low-budgeted features and a few high-risk, but potentially very profitable, expensively-produced pictures. There is a continuing trend, among the big companies at least, to make fewer and fewer films but with increasingly larger budgets. The boom-or-bust economy of film-making has been tempered somewhat through greater diversification. And the recent upsurge in movie attendance coupled with an expanding "television" market presages even greater profits in the next decade. The major movie companies have regained their economic equilibrium. This appears to be the case, at least, for the fewer but larger entities that now control a major part of the information and entertainment disseminated throughout the world. Concentration and consolidation of power has reached unparalleled levels. The big companies have even joined forces in many endeavors. Columbia and Warner Bros., for example, created a jointly owned enterprise in 1972, called Burbank Studios Inc., which contains all the studio facilities of both companies. Operating costs and profits are shared. Paramount and Universal have combined to distribute their films through one organization. Co-production of big-budgeted films is also becoming increasingly more common. As manuscript and production costs spiral upward, such co-operative ventures are likely to continue.

So one can see that, although the despotic moguls of old have either died off or have been deposed by conglomerates, financiers, lawyers and computers, the oligarchical character of the movie industry—and for that matter the entire information-entertainment field—remains intact. *Plus ça change, plus ça même chose.*

Appendix I

MOTION PICTURE PRODUCTION CODE

(*The Motion Picture Production Code was formally adopted by the Association of Motion Picture Producers, Inc., [California] and the Motion Picture Producers and Distributors of America, Inc., [New York] in March, 1930. [The name of the latter organization was changed, on December 14, 1945, to the Motion Picture Association of America.] The code as presented here contains all revisions and amendments through 1954.*)

PREAMBLE

Motion picture producers recognize the high trust and confidence which have been placed in them by the people of the world and which have made motion pictures a universal form of entertainment.

They recognize their responsibility to the public because of this trust and because entertainment and art are important influences in the life of a nation.

Hence though regarding motion pictures primarily as entertainment without any explicit purpose of teaching or propaganda, they know that the motion picture within its own field of entertainment may be directly responsible for spiritual or moral progress, for higher types of social life, and for much correct thinking.

During the rapid transition from silent to talking pictures they realized the necessity and the opportunity of subscribing to a Code to govern the production of talking pictures and of reacknowledging this responsibility.

On their part, they ask from the public and from public leaders a sympathetic understanding of their purposes and problems and a spirit of cooperation that will allow them the freedom and opportunity necessary to bring the motion picture to a still higher level of wholesome entertainment for all the people.

GENERAL PRINCIPLES

1. No picture shall be produced which will lower the moral standards of those who see it. Hence the sympathy of the audience shall never be thrown to the side of crime, wrongdoing, evil or sin.

2. Correct standards of life, subject only to the requirements of drama and entertainment, shall be presented.

3. Law, natural or human, shall not be ridiculed, nor shall sympathy be created for its violation.

PARTICULAR APPLICATIONS

I. Crimes against the law *

These shall never be presented in such a way as to throw sympathy with the crime as against law and justice or to inspire others with a desire for imitation.

1. *Murder*

    a) The technique of murder must be presented in a way that will not inspire imitation.

    b) Brutal killings are not to be presented in detail.

    c) Revenge in modern times shall not be justified.

2. *Methods of crime* should not be explicitly presented.

    a) Theft, robbery, safe-cracking, and dynamiting of trains, mines, buildings, etc., should not be detailed in method.

    b) Arson must be subject to the same safeguards.

    c) The use of firearms should be restricted to essentials.

    d) Methods of smuggling should not be presented.

3. *The illegal drug traffic* must not be portrayed in such a way as to stimulate curiosity concerning the use of, or traffic in, such drugs; nor shall scenes be approved which show the use of illegal drugs, or their effects, in detail (as amended September 11, 1946).

4. *The use of liquor* in American life, when not required by the plot or for proper characterization, will not be shown.

II. Sex

The sanctity of the institution of marriage and the home shall be upheld. Pictures shall not infer that low forms of sex relationship are the accepted or common thing.

1. *Adultery and illicit sex,* sometimes necessary plot material, must not be explicitly treated or justified, or presented attractively.

2. *Scenes of passion*

    a) These should not be introduced except where they are definitely essential to the plot.

    b) Excessive and lustful kissing, lustful embraces, suggestive postures and gestures are not to be shown.

    c) In general, passion should be treated in such manner as not to stimulate the lower and baser emotions.

3. *Seduction or rape*

    a) These should never be more than suggested, and then only when essential for the plot. They must never be shown by explicit method.

    b) They are never the proper subject for comedy.

4. *Sex perversion* or any inference of it is forbidden.

* See also Special Regulations on Crime on pages 279, 280 and 281.

5. *White slavery* shall not be treated.

6. *Abortion, sex hygiene, and venereal diseases* are not proper subjects for theatrical motion pictures.

7. Scenes of *actual childbirth,* in fact or in silhouette, are never to be presented.

8. *Children's sex organs* are never to be exposed.

III. Vulgarity

The treatment of low, disgusting, unpleasant, though not necessarily evil, subjects should be guided always by the dictates of good taste and a proper regard for the sensibilities of the audience.

IV. Obscenity

Obscenity in word, gesture, reference, song, joke, or by suggestion (even when likely to be understood only by part of the audience) is forbidden.

V. Profanity

Pointed profanity and every other profane or vulgar expression, however used, are forbidden.

No approval by the Production Code Administration shall be given to the use of words and phrases in motion pictures including, but not limited to, the following:

Bronx cheer (the sound); chippie; God, Lord, Jesus, Christ (unless used reverently); cripes; fairy (in a vulgar sense); finger (the); fire, cries of; Gawd; goose (in a vulgar sense); hot (applied to a woman); "in your hat"; Madam (relating to prostitution); nance; nuts (except when meaning crazy); pansy; razzberry (the sound); S.O.B.; son-of-a; tart; toilet gags; whore.

In the administration of Section V of the Production Code, the Production Code Administration may take cognizance of the fact that the following words and phrases are obviously offensive to the patrons of motion pictures in the United States and more particularly to the patrons of motion pictures in foreign countries:

Chink, Dago, Frog, Greaser, Hunkie, Kike, Nigger, Spig, Wop, Yid.

It should also be noted that the words "hell" and "damn," if used without moderation, will be considered offensive by many members of the audience. Their use, therefore, should be governed by the discretion and the prudent advice of the Code Administration.

VI. Costumes *

1. *Complete nudity* is never permitted. This includes nudity in fact or in silhouette, or any licentious notice thereof by other characters in the pictures.

2. *Undressing scenes* should be avoided, and never used save where essential to the plot.

3. *Indecent or undue exposure* is forbidden.

* See also Special Resolution on Costumes on page 281.

4. *Dancing costumes* intended to permit undue exposure or indecent movements in the dance are forbidden.

VII. Dances

1. Dances suggesting or representing sexual actions or indecent passion are forbidden.
2. Dances which emphasize indecent movements are to be regarded as obscene.

VIII. Religion

1. No film or episode may throw *ridicule* on any religious faith.
2. *Ministers of religion* in their character as ministers of religion should not be used as comic characters or as villains.
3. *Ceremonies* of any definite religion should be carefully and respectfully handled.

IX. Locations

The treatment of bedrooms must be governed by good taste and delicacy.

X. National feelings

1. *The use of the Flag* shall be consistently respectful.
2. *The history,* institutions, prominent people and citizenry of all nations shall be represented fairly.

XI. Titles

The following titles shall not be used:

1. Titles which are salacious, indecent, obscene, profane or vulgar.
2. Titles which suggest or are currently associated in the public mind with material, characters or occupations unsuitable for the screen.
3. Titles which are otherwise objectionable.

XII. Special subjects

The following subjects must be treated within the careful limits of good taste:

1. *Actual hangings* or *electrocutions* as legal punishments for crime.
2. *Third Degree* methods.
3. *Brutality* and possible gruesomeness.
4. The *sale of women,* or a woman selling her virtue.
5. *Surgical operations.*
6. *Miscegenation.*
7. *Liquor and drinking.*

SPECIAL REGULATIONS ON CRIME IN MOTION PICTURES

Resolved (December 20, 1938), that the Board of Directors of the Motion Picture Association of America, Incorporated, hereby ratifies, approves, and confirms the interpretations of the Production Code, the practices thereunder, and the resolutions indicating and confirming such interpretations heretofore adopted by the Association of Motion Picture Producers, Incorporated, all effectuating regulations relative to the treatment of crime in motion pictures, as follows:

1. Details of crime must never be shown and care should be exercised at all times in discussing such details.

2. Action suggestive of wholesale slaughter of human beings, either by criminals in conflict with police, or as between warring factions of criminals, or in public disorder of any kind, will not be allowed.

3. There must be no suggestion, at any time, of excessive brutality.

4. Because of the increase in the number of films in which murder is frequently committed, action showing the taking of human life, even in the mystery stories, is to be cut to the minimum. These frequent presentations of murder tend to lessen regard for the sacredness of life.

5. Suicide, as a solution of problems occurring in the development of screen drama, is to be discouraged as morally questionable and as bad theatre—unless absolutely necessary for the development of the plot. It should never be justified or glorified, or used to defeat the due processes of law.

6. There must be no display, at any time, of machine guns, submachine guns or other weapons generally classified as illegal weapons in the hands of gangsters, or other criminals, and there are to be no off-stage sounds of the repercussions of these guns.

7. There must be no new, unique or trick methods shown for concealing guns.

8. The flaunting of weapons by gangsters, or other criminals, will not be allowed.

9. All discussions and dialogue on the part of gangsters regarding guns should be cut to the minimum.

10. There must be no scenes, at any time, showing law-enforcing officers dying at the hands of criminals, unless such scenes are absolutely necessary to the development of the plot. This includes private detectives and guards for banks, motor trucks, etc.

11. With special reference to the crime of kidnapping—or illegal abduction—such stories are acceptable under the Code only when (a) the kidnapping or abduction is not the main theme of the story; (b) the person kidnapped is not a child; (c) there are no details of the crime of kidnapping; (d) no profit accrues to the abductors or kidnappers; and (e) where the kidnappers are punished.

    It is understood, and agreed, that the word kidnapping, as used in paragraph 11 of these Regulations, is intended to mean abduction, or illegal detention, in modern times, by criminals for ransom.

12. Pictures dealing with criminal activities, in which minors participate, or to which minors are related, shall not be approved if they incite demoralizing imitation on the part of youth.

13. No picture shall be approved dealing with the life of a notorious criminal of current or recent times which uses the name, nickname or alias of such notorious criminal in the film, nor shall a picture be approved if based upon the life of such a notorious criminal unless the character

shown in the film be punished for crimes shown in the film as committed by him.

SPECIAL RESOLUTION ON COSTUMES

On October 25, 1939, the Board of Directors of the Motion Picture Association of America, Inc., adopted the following resolution:

Resolved, that the provisions of Paragraphs 1, 3 and 4 of subdivision VI of the Production Code, in their application to costumes, nudity, indecent or undue exposure and dancing costumes, shall not be interpreted to exclude authentically photographed scenes photographed in a foreign land, of natives of such foreign land, showing native life, if such scenes are a necessary and integral part of a motion picture depicting exclusively such land and native life, provided that no such scenes shall be intrinsically objectionable nor made a part of any motion picture produced in any studio; and provided further that no emphasis shall be made in any scenes of the customs or garb of such natives or in the exploitation thereof.

SPECIAL REGULATIONS ON CRUELTY TO ANIMALS

On December 27, 1940, the Board of Directors of the Motion Picture Association of America, Inc., approved a resolution adopted by the Association of Motion Picture Producers, Inc., reaffirming previous resolutions of the California Association concerning brutality and possible gruesomeness, and apparent cruelty to animals:

Resolved, by the Board of Directors of the Association of Motion Picture Producers, Inc., that

1. Hereafter, in the production of motion pictures there shall be no use by the members of the Association of the contrivance or apparatus in connection with animals which is known as the "running W," nor shall any picture submitted to the Production Code Administration be approved if reasonable grounds exist for believing that use of any similar device by the producer of such picture resulted in apparent cruelty to animals; and

2. Hereafter, in the production of motion pictures by the members of the Association, such members shall, as to any picture involving the use of animals, invite on the lot during such shooting and consult with the authorized representative of the American Humane Association; and

3. Steps shall be taken immediately by the members of the Association and by the Production Code Administration *to require compliance with these resolutions,* which shall bear the same relationship to the sections of the Production Code quoted herein as the Association's Special Regulations re: Crime in Motion Pictures bear to the sections of the Production Code dealing therewith; and it is

Further resolved, that the resolutions of February 19, 1925, and all other resolutions of this Board establishing its policy to prevent all cruelty to animals in the production of motion pictures and reflecting its determination to prevent any such cruelty, be and the same hereby are in all respects reaffirmed.

REASONS SUPPORTING PREAMBLE OF CODE

1. Theatrical motion pictures, that is, pictures intended for the theatre as distinct from pictures intended for churches, schools, lecture halls, educational movements, social reform movements, etc., are primarily to be regarded as ENTERTAINMENT.

   Mankind has always recognized the importance of entertainment and its value in rebuilding the bodies and souls of human beings.

   But it has always recognized that entertainment can be of a character either HELPFUL or HARMFUL to the human race, and in consequence has clearly distinguished between:

   a) *Entertainment which tends to improve* the race, or at least to re-create and rebuild human beings exhausted with the realities of life; and

   b) Entertainment which tends to degrade human beings, or to lower their standards of life and living.

   Hence the MORAL IMPORTANCE of entertainment is something which has been universally recognized. It enters intimately into the lives of men and women and affects them closely; it occupies their minds and affections during leisure hours; and ultimately touches the whole of their lives. A man may be judged by his standard of entertainment as easily as by the standard of his work.

   So *correct entertainment raises* the whole standard of a nation.

   Wrong entertainment lowers the whole living conditions and moral ideals of a race.

   Note, for example, the healthy reactions to healthful sports, like baseball, golf; the unhealthy reactions to sports like cockfighting, bullfighting, bear baiting, etc.

   Note, too, the effect on ancient nations of gladiatorial combats, the obscene plays of Roman times, etc.

2. Motion pictures are very important as ART.

   Though a new art, possibly a combination art, it has the same object as the other arts, the presentation of human thought, emotion, and experience, in terms of an appeal to the soul through the senses.

   Here, as in entertainment,

   Art *enters intimately* into the lives of human beings.

   Art can be *morally good,* lifting men to higher levels. This has been done through good music, great painting, authentic fiction, poetry, drama. Art can be *morally evil* in its effects. This is the case clearly enough with unclean art, indecent books, suggestive drama. The effect on the lives of men and women is obvious.

Note: It has often been argued that art in itself is unmoral, neither good nor bad. This is perhaps true of the THING which is music, painting, poetry, etc. But the thing is the PRODUCT of some person's mind, and the intention of that mind was either good or bad morally when it produced the thing. Besides, the thing has its EFFECT upon those who come into contact with it. In both these ways, that is, as a product of a mind and as the cause of definite effects, it has a deep moral significance and an unmistakable moral quality.

Hence: The motion pictures, which are the most popular of modern arts for the masses, have their moral quality from the intention of the minds which produce them and from their effects on the moral lives and reactions of their audiences. This gives them a most important morality.

   1. They *reproduce* the morality of the men who use the pictures as a medium for the expression of their ideas and ideals.

   2. They *affect* the moral standards of those who, through the screen, take in these ideas and ideals.

In the case of the motion pictures, this effect may be particularly emphasized because no art has so quick and so widespread an appeal to the masses. It has become in an incredibly short period *the art of the multitudes.*

3. The motion picture, because of its importance as entertainment and because of the trust placed in it by the peoples of the world, has special MORAL OBLIGATIONS.

   A. Most arts appeal to the mature. This art appeals at once to every class, mature, immature, developed, undeveloped, law abiding, criminal. Music has its grades for different classes; so have literature and drama. This art of the motion picture, combining as it does the two fundamental appeals of looking at a *picture* and *listening to a story,* at once reaches every class of society.

   B. By reason of the mobility of a film and the ease of picture distribution, and because of the possibility of duplicating positives in large quantities, this art *reaches places* unpenetrated by other forms of art.

   C. Because of these two facts, it is difficult to produce films intended for only certain classes of people. The exhibitors' theatres are built for the masses, for the cultivated and the rude, the mature and the immature, the self-respecting and the criminal. Films, unlike books and music, can with difficulty be confined to certain selected groups.

   D. The latitude given to film material cannot, in consequence, be as wide as the latitude given to *book material.* In addition:

     a) A book describes; a film vividly presents. One presents on a cold page; the other by apparently living people.

     b) A book reaches the mind through words merely; a film reaches the eyes and ears through the reproduction of actual events.

     c) The reaction of a reader to a book depends largely on the keenness of the reader's imagination; the reaction to a film depends on the vividness of presentation.

Hence many things which might be described or suggested in a book could not possibly be presented in a film.

E. This is also true when comparing the film with the newspaper.

   a) Newspapers present by description, films by actual presentation.

   b) Newspapers are after the fact and present things as having taken place; the film gives the events in the process of enactment and with the apparent reality of life.

F. Everything possible in a *play* is not possible in a film:

   a) Because of the *larger audience of the film,* and its consequential mixed character. Psychologically, the larger the audience, the lower the moral mass resistance to suggestion.

   b) Because through light, enlargement of character, presentation, scenic emphasis, etc., the screen story is *brought closer* to the audience than the play.

   c) The enthusiasm for and interest in the film *actors* and *actresses,* developed beyond anything of the sort in history, makes the audience largely sympathetic toward the characters they portray and the stories in which they figure. Hence the audience is more ready to confuse actor and actress and the characters they portray, and it is most receptive of the emotions and ideals presented by their favorite stars.

G. *Small communities,* remote from sophistication and from the hardening process which often takes place in the ethical and moral standards of groups in larger cities, are easily and readily reached by any sort of film.

H. The grandeur of mass settings, large action, spectacular features, etc., affects and arouses more intensely the emotional side of the audience.

In general, the mobility, popularity, accessibility, emotional appeal, vividness, straight-forward presentation of fact in the film make for more intimate contact with a larger audience and for greater emotional appeal.

Hence the larger moral responsibilities of the motion pictures.

REASONS UNDERLYING THE GENERAL PRINCIPLES

I. No picture shall be produced which will lower the moral standards of those who see it. Hence the sympathy of the audience should never be thrown to the side of crime, wrong-doing, evil or sin.

   This is done:

    1. When *evil* is made to appear *attractive* or *alluring,* and good is made to appear *unattractive.*

    2. When the *sympathy* of the audience is thrown on the side of crime, wrong-doing, evil, sin. The same thing is true of a film that would throw sympathy against goodness, honor, innocence, purity or honesty.

Note: Sympathy with a person who sins is not the same as sympathy with the sin or crime of which he is guilty. We may feel sorry for the plight of the murderer or even understand the circumstances which led him to his crime. We may not feel sympathy with the wrong which he has done.

The *presentation of evil* is often essential for art or fiction or drama. This in itself is not wrong provided:

 a) That evil is *not presented alluringly.* Even if later in the film the evil is condemned or punished, it must not be allowed to appear so attractive that the audience's emotions are drawn to desire or approve so strongly that later the condemnation is forgotten and only the apparent joy of the sin remembered.

 b) That throughout, the audience feels sure that *evil is wrong* and *good is right.*

2. Correct standards of life, shall, as far as possible, be presented.

 A *wide knowledge of life and of living* is made possible through the film. When right standards are consistently presented, the motion picture exercises the most powerful influences. It builds character, develops right ideals, inculcates correct principles, and all this in attractive story form. If motion pictures consistently *hold up for admiration high types of characters* and present stories that will affect lives for the better, they can become the most powerful natural force for the improvement of mankind.

3. Law, natural or human, shall not be ridiculed, nor shall sympathy be created for its violation.

 By *natural law* is understood the law which is written in the hearts of all mankind, the great underlying principles of right and justice dictated by conscience.

 By *human law* is understood the law written by civilized nations.

 1. *The presentation of crimes* against the law is *often necessary* for the carrying out of the plot. But the presentation must not throw sympathy with the crime as against the law nor with the criminal as against those who punish him.

 2. *The courts of the land* should not be presented as unjust. This does not mean that a single court may not be represented as unjust, much less that a single court official must not be presented this way. But the court system of the country must not suffer as a result of this presentation.

REASONS UNDERLYING PARTICULAR APPLICATIONS

1. *Sin and evil* enter into the story of human beings and hence in themselves *are valid dramatic material.*

2. In the use of this material, it must be distinguished between *sins which repel* by their very nature, and *sins which often attract.*

 a) In the first class come murder, most theft, many legal crimes, lying, hypocrisy, cruelty, etc.

b) In the second class come sex sins, sins and crimes of apparent heroism, such as banditry, daring thefts, leadership in evil, organized crime, revenge, etc.

The first class needs less care in treatment, as sins and crimes of this class are naturally unattractive. The audience instinctively condemns all such and is repelled.

Hence the important objective must be to avoid the hardening of the audience, especially of those who are young and impressionable, to the thought and fact of crime. People can become accustomed even to murder, cruelty, brutality, and repellent crimes, if these are too frequently repeated. The second class needs great care in handling, as the response of human nature to their appeal is obvious. This is treated more fully below.

3. A careful distinction can be made between films intended for *general distribution,* and films intended for use in theatres restricted to a *limited audience.* Themes and plots quite appropriate for the latter would be altogether out of place and dangerous in the former.

Note: The practice of using a general theatre and limiting its patronage during the showing of a certain film to "Adults Only" is not completely satisfactory and is only partially effective.

However, maturer minds may easily understand and accept without harm subject matter in plots which do younger people positive harm.

Hence: If there should be created a special type of theatre, catering exclusively to an adult audience, for plays of this character (plays with problem themes, difficult discussions and maturer treatment) it would seem to afford an outlet, which does not now exist, for pictures unsuitable for general distribution but permissible for exhibitions to a restricted audience.

I. Crimes against the law

The *treatment of crimes* against the law must not:

1. *Teach methods* of crime.
2. *Inspire potential criminals* with a desire for imitation.
3. *Make criminals seem heroic* and justified.

Revenge in modern times shall not be justified. In lands and ages of less developed civilization and moral principles, revenge may sometimes be presented. This would be the case especially in places where no law exists to cover the crime because of which revenge is committed. Because of its evil consequences, *the drug traffic* should not be presented in any form. The existence of the trade should not be brought to the attention of audiences.

II. Sex

Out of regard for the sanctity of marriage and the home, the *triangle,* that is, the love of a third party for one already married, needs careful handling. The treatment should not throw sympathy against marriage as an institution.

Scenes of passion must be treated with an honest acknowledgment of human nature and its normal reactions. Many scenes cannot be presented without arousing dangerous emotions on the part of the immature, the young or the *criminal classes.*

Even within the limits of *pure love,* certain facts have been universally regarded by lawmakers as outside the limits of safe presentation.

In the case of *impure love,* the love which society has always regarded as wrong and which has been banned by divine law, the following are important:

1. Impure love must not be presented as *attractive and beautiful.*
2. It must *not* be the subject of *comedy or farce,* or treated as material *for laughter.*
3. It must *not* be presented in such a way as *to arouse passion* or morbid curiosity on the part of the audience.
4. It must *not* be made to seem *right* and *permissible.*
5. In general, it must *not* be *detailed* in method and manner.

III. Vulgarity; IV. Obscenity; V. Profanity

Hardly need further explanation than is contained in the Code.

VI. Costumes

General principles:

1. *The effect of nudity or semi-nudity* upon the normal man or woman, and much more upon the young and upon immature persons, has been honestly recognized by all lawmakers and moralists.
2. Hence the fact that the nude or semi-nude body may be *beautiful* does not make its use in the films moral. For, in addition to its beauty, the effect of the nude or semi-nude body on the normal individual must be taken into consideration.
3. Nudity or semi-nudity used simply to put a *"punch"* into a picture comes under the head of immoral actions. It is immoral in its effect on the average audience.
4. Nudity can never be permitted as being *necessary for the plot.* Semi-nudity must not result in undue or indecent exposures.
5. *Transparent* or *translucent materials* and silhouette are frequently more suggestive than actual exposure.

VII. Dances

Dancing in general is recognized as an *art* and as a *beautiful* form of expressing human emotions.

But dances which suggest or represent sexual actions, whether performed solo or with two or more; dances intended to excite the emotional reaction of an audience; dances with movement of the breasts, excessive body movements while the feet are stationary, violate decency and are wrong.

VIII. Religion

The reason why ministers of religion may not be comic characters or villains is simply because the attitude taken toward them may easily become the attitude taken toward religion in general. Religion is lowered in the minds of the audience because of the lowering of the audience's respect for a minister.

IX. Locations

Certain places are so closely and thoroughly associated with sexual life or with sexual sin that their use must be carefully limited.

X. National feelings

The just rights, history, and feelings of any nation are entitled to most careful consideration and respectful treatment.

XI. Titles

As the title of a picture is the brand on that particular type of goods, it must conform to the ethical practices of all such honest business.

XII. Special subjects

Such subjects are occasionally necessary for the plot. Their treatment must never offend good taste nor injure the sensibilities of an audience. The use of liquor should never be excessively presented. In scenes from American life, the necessities of plot and proper characterization alone justify its use. And in this case, it should be shown with moderation.

RESOLUTION FOR UNIFORM INTERPRETATION
as amended
June 13, 1934.

1. When requested by production managers, the Motion Picture Association of America, Incorporated, shall secure any facts, information or suggestions concerning the probable reception of stories or the manner in which in its opinion they may best be treated.

2. Each production manager shall submit in confidence a copy of each or any script to the Production Code Administration of the Motion Picture Association of America, Incorporated (and of the Association of Motion Picture Producers, Inc., California). The Production Code Administration will give the production manager for his guidance such confidential advice and suggestions as experience, research, and information indicate, designating wherein in its judgment the script departs from the provisions of the Code, or wherein from experience or knowledge it is believed that exception will be taken to the story or treatment.

3. Each production manager of a company belonging to the Motion Picture Association of America, Incorporated, and any producer proposing

to distribute and/or distributing his picture through the facilities of any member of the Motion Picture Association of America, Incorporated, shall submit to such Production Code Administration every picture he produces before the negative goes to the laboratory for printing. Said Production Code Administration, having seen the picture, shall inform the production manager in writing whether in its opinion the picture conforms or does not conform to the Code, stating specifically wherein either by theme, treatment or incident, the picture violates the provisions of the Code. In such latter event, the picture shall not be released until the changes indicated by the Production Code Administration have been made; provided, however, that the production manager may appeal from such opinion of said Production Code Administration, so indicated in writing, to the Board of Directors of the Motion Picture Association of America, Incorporated, whose finding shall be final, and such production manager and company shall be governed accordingly.

Appendix II

AN ADVERTISING CODE FOR MOTION PICTURES

(*The Advertising Code was adopted by the Board of Directors of the Motion Picture Producers and Distributors of America, Inc. [now the Motion Picture Association of America, Inc.] June 10, 1930. It was amended and reaffirmed by the Board of Directors of the Motion Picture Association of America, Inc., July 30, 1947, and further amended December 3, 1947.*)

PREAMBLE

The purpose of the Advertising Code is to apply to motion picture advertising, publicity and exploitation, within their range, the high principles which the Production Code applies to the content of motion pictures.

The provisions of the Advertising Code shall apply to pressbooks, newspaper, magazine and trade paper advertising, publicity material, trailers, posters, lobby displays and all other outdoor displays, novelty distribution, radio copy and every form of motion picture exploitation.

We urge all motion picture producers, distributors and exhibitors, and their advertising agents, whether affiliated with the undersigned or not, to adhere to these principles; and, for ourselves, we pledge compliance with these principles without reservation.

THE CODE

1. We subscribe to a code of ethics based upon truth, honesty and integrity. All motion picture advertising shall
   a) Conform to fact.
   b) Scrupulously avoid all misrepresentation.
2. Good taste shall be the guiding rule of motion picture advertising.
3. Illustrations and text in advertising shall faithfully represent the pictures themselves.
4. No false or misleading statements shall be used directly, or implied by type arrangements or by distorted quotations.
5. No text or illustration shall ridicule or tend to ridicule any race, religion or religious faith; no illustration of a character in clerical garb shall be shown in any but a respectful manner.
6. The history, institutions and nationals of all countries shall be represented with fairness.
7. Profanity and vulgarity shall be avoided.
8. Pictorial and copy treatment of officers of the law shall not be of such a nature as to undermine their authority.
9. Specific details of crime, inciting imitation, shall not be used.
10. Motion picture advertisers shall be guided by the provision of the Production Code that the use of liquor in American life shall be restricted to the necessities of characterization and plot.
11. Nudity with meretricious purpose and salacious postures shall not be used; and clothed figures shall not be represented in such manner as to be offensive or contrary to good taste or morals.
12. Court actions relating to censoring of pictures, or other censorship disputes, are not to be capitalized in advertising or publicity.
13. Titles of source materials or occupations or names of characters on which motion pictures may be based, should not be exploited in advertising or upon the screen if such title or names are in conflict with the provisions of the Production Code affecting titles.

A Selective
Bibliography

BOOKS

Archer, Gleason. *Big Business and Radio.* New York: The American Historical Company, Inc., 1939.

Balio, Tino (ed.) *The American Film Industry.* Madison, Wisconsin: The University of Wisconsin Press, 1976.

_____. *United Artists: The Company Built by the Stars.* Madison Wisconsin: The University of Wisconsin Press, 1975.

Barnouw, Erik. *Tube of Plenty: The Evolution of American Television.* New York: Oxford University Press, 1975.

Behlmer, Rudy (ed.) *Memo from David O. Selznick.* New York: The Viking Press, 1972.

Bergman, Andrew. *We're in the Money: Depression America and its Films.* New York: Harper Colophon Books, 1972.

Brosman, John. *Movie Magic: The Story of Special Effects in the Cinema.* New York: New American Library, 1976.

Brownlow, Kevin. *The Parade's Gone By.* New York: Alfred A. Knopf, 1968.

Capra, Frank. *The Name Above the Title.* New York: Macmillan Company, 1971.

Carmen, Ira H. *Movies, Censorship and the Law.* Ann Arbor: University of Michigan Press, 1968.

Cogley, John. *Report on Blacklisting I: Movies.* Fund for the Republic, 1956.

Conant, Michael. *Antitrust in the Motion Picture Industry.* Berkeley: University of California Press, 1960.

Crowther, Bosley. *The Lion's Share: The Story of an Entertainment Empire.* New York: E. P. Dutton, 1957.

_____. *Hollywood Rajah: The Life and Times of Louis B. Mayer.* New York: Holt, Rinehart and Winston, 1960.

Curti, Carlo. *Skouras: King of Fox Studios.* Los Angeles, California: Holloway House Publishing Company, 1967.

Dale, Edgar. *The Content of Motion Pictures.* New York: Macmillan Company, 1933.

Danielian, N. R. *AT&T: The Story of Industrial Conquest.* New York: The Vanguard Press, 1939.

Dowdy, Andrew. *The Films of the Fifties: the American State of Mind.* New York: William Morrow and Company, 1973.

Drinkwater, John. *The Life and Adventures of Carl Laemmle.* New York: G. P. Putnam's Sons, 1931.

Facey, Paul W. *The Legion of Decency: A Sociological Analysis of the Emergence and Development of a Pressure Group.* New York: Arno Press, 1974.

Farber, Stephen. *The Movie Rating Game.* Washington, D.C.: Public Affairs Press, 1972.

Fielding, Raymond. *The American Newsreel, 1911–1967.* Norman: University of Oklahoma Press, 1973.

_____. *A Technological History of Motion Pictures and Television.* Berkeley: University of California Press, 1967.

Forman, Henry James. *Our Movie Made Children.* New York: Macmillan Company, 1933.

French, Philip. *The Movie Moguls: An Informal History of the Hollywood Tycoons.* Chicago: Henry Regnery, Company, 1971.

Geduld, Harry. *The Birth of the Talkies: From Edison to Jolson.* Bloomington, Indiana: Indiana University Press, 1975.

Gerber, Albert. *Bashful Billionaire.* New York: Dell Publishing Company, Inc., 1967.

Goodman, Ezra. *The Fifty-Year Decline and Fall of Hollywood.* New York: Simon and Schuster, 1961.

Gordon, George N. *The Communications Revolution: A History of Mass Media in the United States.* New York: Hastings House, 1977.

Guild, Leo. *Zanuck: Hollywood's Last Tycoon.* Los Angeles, California: Holloway House Publishing Company, 1970.

Guiles, Fred L. *Hanging on in Paradise.* New York: McGraw-Hill, 1975.

_____. *Marion Davies: A Biography.* New York: Bantam Books, 1973.

Gussow, Mel. *Don't Say Yes Until I Finish Talking: A Biography Of Darryl F. Zanuck.* New York: Pocket Books, 1972.

Hampton, Benjamin. *History of the American Film Industry: from its beginning to 1931.* New York: Dover Publications, Inc., 1970.

Henderson, R. M. *D. W. Griffith: The Years at Biograph.* New York: Farrar, Straus and Giroux, 1970.

Hendricks, Gordon. *Beginnings of the Biograph*. New York: Beginnings of the American Film, 1964.

_____. *The Edison Motion Picture Myth*. Berkeley: University of California Press, 1961.

_____. *The Kinetoscope*. New York: Beginnings of the American Film, 1966.

Higham, Charles. *Warner Brothers*. New York: Charles Scribner's Sons, 1975.

_____. *Cecil B. DeMille*. New York: Charles Scribner's Sons, 1973.

_____. *Hollywood at Sunset*. New York: Saturday Review Press, 1972.

Higham, Charles, and Joel Greenberg. *Hollywood in the Forties*. New York: A. S. Barnes and Company, 1968.

Huettig, Mae D. *Economic Control of the Motion Picture Industry*. Philadelphia: University of Pennsylvania Press, 1944: reprint ed., New York: Jerome S. Ozer, 1971.

Huff, Theodore. *Charles Chaplin: A Biography*. New York: Pyramid Books, 1964.

Hunnings, Neville March. *Film Censors and the Law*. London: George Allen and Unwin, 1967.

Inglis, Ruth. *Freedom of the Movies*. Chicago: University of Chicago Press, 1947.

Jacobs, Lewis. *The Rise of the American Film*. New York: Teacher's College Press, 1969.

Jobes, Gertrude. *Motion Picture Empire*. Hamden, Connecticut: Archon Books, 1966.

Josephson, Matthew. *Edison: A Biography*. New York: McGraw-Hill, 1959.

Jowett, Garth. *Film: The Democratic Art*. Boston: Little, Brown, and Company, 1976.

Karpf, Stephen. *The Gangster Film: Emergence, Variation and Decay of a Genre, 1930–1940*. New York: Arno Press, 1973.

Keats, John. *Howard Hughes*. New York: Pyramid Books, 1970.

Kennedy, Joseph P., ed. *The Story of the Films*. Chicago: A. W. Shaw Company, 1927; reprint ed., New York: Jerome S. Ozer, 1971.

Klingender, F. D., and Stuart Legg. *Money Behind the Screen*. London: Lawrence and Wishart, 1937.

Knight, Arthur. *The Liveliest Art*. New York: Macmillan Company, 1957.

Koenig, Allen. *Broadcasting and Bargaining: Labor Relations in Radio and Television*. Madison, Wisconsin: The University of Wisconsin Press, 1970.

Koskoff, David. *Joseph P. Kennedy: A Life and Times*. Englewood Cliffs, N.J.: Prentice-Hall, Inc., 1974.

Kutz, Myer. *Rockefeller Power: America's Chosen Family*. New York: Simon and Schuster, 1974.

294   ○   A Selective Bibliography

Lawson, John Howard. *Film in the Battle of Ideas.* New York: Masses and Mainstream, 1953.

Lewis, Howard T. *The Motion Picture Industry.* New York: D. Van Nostrand Company, 1933.

Limbacher, James L. *Four Faces of the Film.* New York: Brussel and Brussel, 1968.

Lyons, Eugene. *David Sarnoff.* New York: Harper and Row, 1966.

MacCann, Richard Dyer. *Hollywood in Transition.* Boston: Houghton Mifflin Company, 1962.

MacGowan, Kenneth. *Behind the Screen.* New York: Dell Publishing Company, 1965.

Madsen, Axel, *The New Hollywood.* New York: Thomas Y. Crowell Company, 1975.

Manwell, Roger. *Films and the Second World War.* New York: Dell Publishing Company, Inc., 1976.

Mast, Gerald. *A Short History of the Movies.* Indianapolis: Bobbs-Merrill Company, Inc., 1976.

Marx, Arthur. *Goldwyn: A Biography of the Man Behind the Myth.* New York: Ballantine Books, 1976.

Marx, Samuel. *Mayer and Thalberg: The Make-Believe Saints.* New York: Random House, 1975.

Mayer, Arthur. *Merely Colossal.* New York: Simon and Schuster, 1953.

Mayer, Michael F. *The Film Industries.* New York: Hastings House, 1978.

McCarthy, Todd and Charles Flynn (ed.) *Kings of the Bs.* New York: E. P. Dutton and Company, Inc., 1975.

McClelland, Doug. *The Unkindest Cuts: The Scissors and the Cinema.* New York: A. S. Barnes and Company, 1972.

McClure, Arthur F., (ed.) *The Movies: An American Idiom.* Rutherford: Farleigh Dickinson University Press, 1971.

Miller, Don. *"B" Movies.* New York: Curtis Books, 1973.

Miller, Merle. *The Judges and the Judged.* Garden City: Doubleday and Company, 1952.

Moley, Raymond. *Are We Movie Made?* New York: Macy-Masius, 1938.

_____. *The Hays Office.* New York: Bobbs-Merrill Company, 1945; reprint ed., New York: Jerome S. Ozer, 1971.

Nizer, Louis. *New Courts of Industry: Self-Regulation Under the Motion Picture Code.* New York: Longacre Press, 1935; reprint ed., New York: Jerome S. Ozer, 1971.

North, Joseph H. *The Early Development of the Motion Picture, 1887–1909.* New York: Arno Press, 1973.

Nye, Russell B. *The Unembarrassed Muse: The Popular Arts in America.* New York: The Dial Press, 1970.

Pfranger, Julius. *The Motion Picture from Magic Lantern to Sound Film.* Great Britain: Balley Brothers and Swinfen, Ltd., 1974.

Powdermaker, Hortense. *Hollywood: the Dream Factory.* Boston: Little, Brown and Company, 1950.

Ramsaye, Terry. *A Million and One Nights.* New York: Simon and Schuster, 1926.

Randall, Richard S. *Censorship of the Movies.* Madison: University of Wisconsin Press, 1968.

Report of the Commission on Obscenity and Pornography. New York: Bantam Books, 1970.

Rhode, Eric. *A History of the Cinema from its Origins to 1970.* New York: Hill and Wang, 1976.

Robinson, David. *Hollywood in the Twenties.* New York: Paperback Library, 1970.

Rochester, Anna. *Rulers of America: A Study of Finance Capital.* New York: International Publishers, 1936.

Rosen, Marjorie. *Popcorn Venus.* New York: Coward, McCann and Geoghegan, 1973.

Ross, Murray. *Stars and Strikes: Unionism of Hollywood.* New York: Columbia University Press, 1941.

Rosten, Leo C. *Hollywood: The Movie Colony and the Movie Makers.* New York: Harcourt, Brace and Company, 1941.

Sands, Pierre N. *A Historical Study of the Academy of Motion Picture Arts and Sciences (1927–1947).* New York: Arno Press, 1973.

Schickel, Richard. *The Disney Version.* New York: Avon Books, 1968.

_____. *Movies: The History of an Art and an Institution.* New York: Basic Books, 1964.

_____. *The Stars.* New York. Bonanza Books, 1962.

_____. *His Picture in the Papers.* New York: Charterhouse, 1973.

Schumach, Murray. *The Face on the Cutting Room Floor.* New York: William Morrow and Company, 1964.

Seligman, Ben B. *The Potentates: Business and Businessmen in American History.* New York: Dial Press, 1971.

Sinclair, Upton. *Upton Sinclair Presents William Fox.* Los Angeles: Upton Sinclair Publishing Company, 1933.

Sklar, Robert. *Movie-Made America.* New York: Random House, 1975.

Stanley, Robert H. and Charles S. Steinberg. *The Media Environment.* New York: Hastings House, Publishers, 1976.

Swanberg, W. A. *Citizen Hearst.* New York: Charles Scribner's Sons, 1961.

Thomas, Bob. *Thalberg: Life and Legend.* New York: Bantam Books, 1970.

_____. *Walt Disney: An American Original.* New York: Simon and Schuster, 1976.

_____. *King Cohn: The Life and Times of Harry Cohn.* New York: G. P. Putnam's Sons, 1967.

_____. *Selznick.* New York: Pocket Books, 1972.

Toeplitz, Jerzy. *Hollywood and After: The Changing Face of Movies In America.* Chicago: Henry Regnery, Company, 1974.

Thorp, Margaret. *America at the Movies.* New Haven: Yale University Press, 1939.

Turan, Kenneth, and Stephen F. Zito. *Sinema.* New York: Praeger Publishers, 1974.

Vaughn, Robert. *Only Victims.* New York: G. P. Putnam's Sons, 1972.

Vizzard, Jack. *See No Evil.* New York: Simon and Schuster, 1970.

Whalen, Richard. *The Founding Father: The Story of Joseph P. Kennedy.* New York: The New American Library, Inc., 1966.

Zierold, Norman. *The Moguls.* New York: Coward-McCann, Inc., 1969.

PERIODICALS

"A Vigorous Broom." *Publishers Weekly,* vol. 126 (July 21, 1934), pp. 196–197.

Alpert, Hollis. "View From the 28th Floor." *Saturday Review,* December 24, 1966, pp. 17–19.

Angly, Edward. "Producers Cleansing Films, But Will Reform Last?" *Literary Digest,* vol. 118 (July 21, 1934), p. 7+.

Ayer, Douglas, Roy E. Bates, and Peter J. Herman. "Self-Censorship in the Movie Industry: An Historical Perspective on Law and Social Change," no. 3. *Wisconsin Law Review* (1970), pp. 791–838.

"Baby Doll." *Commonweal,* vol. 65 (Jan. 11, 1957), pp. 371–372.

Barrett, Wilton A. "The Work of the National Board of Review." *Annals of the American Academy of Political and Social Science,* Nov., 1926, pp. 175–186.

Barrows, Edward. "Motion Pictures: Success Through Self-Regulation." *Review of Reviews,* vol. 85 (March, 1932), pp. 32–35.

Batman, Richard Dale. "The Founding of the Hollywood Motion Picture Industry." *Journal of the West,* vol. 10 (October, 1971), pp. 609–23.

Beach, E. R. "Double Features in Motion-Picture Exhibition." *Harvard Business Review,* vol. 10 (July, 1932), pp. 505–15.

Bennett, Ralph Culver. "Merger Movement in the Motion Picture Industry." *Annals of the American Academy of Political and Social Science,* Jan., 1930, pp. 89–94.

Berchtold, William E. "The Hollywood Purge." *North American Review,* vol. 238 (December, 1934), pp. 503–512.

Bergman, Mark. "Hollywood in the Forties Revisited." *Velvet Light Trap*, no. 5 (Summer, 1972), pp. 2–5.

Berman, Sam. "The Hays Office." *Fortune*, vol. 18 (Dec., 1938), pp. 68–72.

"Big Business Story—the Hollywood Comeback." *U.S. News and World Report*, August 28, 1972, pp. 38–41.

"Bioff Show." *Newsweek*, vol. 18 (November 10, 1941), pp. 52+.

Bloom, Murray T. "What Two Lawyers are Doing in Hollywood." *Harper's*, vol. 216 (February, 1958), pp. 42–49.

" 'Body and Soul' Is (Here) Put Together." *Fortune*, vol. 4 (August, 1931), pp. 26–34.

Borneman, Ernest. "United States vs. Hollywood: The Case History of an Anti-Trust Suit." *Sight and Sound*, March, 1951, pp. 448–450.

————. "Rebellion in Hollywood: A Case Study in Motion Picture Finance." *Harper's*, vol. 193 (October, 1946), pp. 337–43.

Broun, Heywood. "Boys in the Higher Brackets." *Nation*, vol. 144 (May 15, 1937), p. 565.

Brown, Stanley. "That Old Villian TV Comes to the Rescue and . . . Hollywood Rides Again." *Fortune*, vol. 74 (November, 1966), p. 18+.

"Business Abroad—Battle of the Screen." *Fortune*, vol. 33 (March, 1946), p. 200+.

"Caging the Lion." *Newsweek*, vol. 50 (October 28, 1957), pp. 82–84.

Campbell, Russell. "Warner Brothers in the Thirties." *Velvet Light Trap*, no. 1 (June, 1971), pp. 2–4.

Capra, Frank. "Breaking Hollywood's Pattern of Sameness." *New York Times Magazine*, May 5, 1946, p. 18+.

Carlson, Oliver. "The Communist Record in Hollywood." *American Mercury*, vol. 66 (February, 1948), pp. 135–143.

Cassady, Ralph, Jr., "Impact of the Paramount Decision on Motion Picture Distribution and Price Making." *Southern California Law Review*, vol. 31 (February, 1958), pp. 150–80.

————. "Monopoly in Motion Picture Production and Distribution: 1908–1915." *Southern California Law Review*, vol. 32 (Summer, 1959), pp. 325–390.

"Censorship of Motion Pictures." *Yale Law Review Journal*, vol. 48 (November, 1939), pp. 87–113.

Chaplin, John. "Hollywood Goes Closed Shop." *Nation*, vol. 142 (February 19, 1936), pp. 225–226.

"Cinerama—the Broad Picture." *Fortune*, vol. 47 (January, 1953), pp. 92–93.

"Color and Sound on Film." *Fortune*, vol. 2 (November, 1930), pp. 33–35+.

Coughlan, Robert. "O'Neil's Money Machine." *Life*, vol. 39 (December 5, 1955), pp. 186–190+.

Crowther, Bosley. "The Movies Follow the Flag." *New York Times Magazine*, August 13, 1944, p. 18.

_____. "The Strange Case of 'The Miracle.' " *Atlantic*, vol. 187 (April, 1951), pp. 35–39.

Cuskelly, Richard. "The Cinemobile Revolution." *Los Angeles Herald-Examiner* (May 10, 1970), p. F-3.

Davis, John. "RKO: A Studio Chronology." *Velvet Light Trap*, no. 10 (Fall, 1973), pp. 6–12.

Dawson, Anthony A. P. "Hollywood's Labor Troubles." *Industrial and Labor Relations Review*, vol. 1 (July, 1948), pp. 638–647.

_____. "Motion Picture Economics." *Hollywood Quarterly*, vol. 3 (1948), pp. 217–240.

"Deanna Durbin." *Fortune*, vol. 20 (October, 1939), p. 66+.

Delehantz, Theodore. "The Disney Studio at War." *Theatre Arts*, vol. 27 (January, 1943), pp. 31–39.

"Derring-Doers of Movie Business." *Fortune*, vol. 57 (May, 1958), pp. 137–141.

Disney, Walt. "Mickey as Professor." *Public Opinion Quarterly* (1945), pp. 119–125.

Donavon, William and Breck P. McAllister. "Consent Decrees in the Enforcement of Federal Anti-Trust Laws: The Moving Picture Industry." *Harvard Law Review*, vol. 46 (April, 1933), pp. 929–931.

Dugan, James. "Goldwyn's Hairshirt." *New Masses*, vol. 27 (May 17, 1938), pp. 27–28.

Eastman, Fred. "Now Watch Mr. Hays!" *Christian Century*, vol. 51 (September 19, 1934), pp. 1172–1173.

"Effects of Technological Changes upon Employment in the Amusement Industry." *Monthly Labor Review*, vol. 32 (August 1931), pp. 261–267.

Ephron, Nora. "Women." *Esquire*, vol. 89 (February, 1973), p. 14+.

Ernst, Morris. "Supercolossal: The Movies." *Atlantic Monthly*, vol. 166 (July, 1940), pp. 17–28.

"ERPI's Fadeout: Bell System to Retreat From Theatre Equipment Field." *Business Week*, September 11, 1937, pp. 57–58.

"Explosion on the Movie Lot." *Business Week*, August 17, 1957, pp. 43–47+.

"Fade Out for Blockbuster Films?" *Business Week*, October 20, 1962, pp. 172–174.

Fadiman, William. "Hollywood: Shivering in the Sun." *New Republic*, vol. 162 (June 27, 1970), pp. 17–19.

"Film Censorship: An Administrative Analysis." *Columbia Law Review*, vol. 39 (December, 1939), pp. 1383–1405.

Fleming, Karl. "Who is Ted Ashely? Just the King of Hollywood, Baby." *New York* (June 24, 1974), pp. 30–35.

"Fox Loses." *Business Week*, March 9, 1935, pp. 10–11.

Frakes, Margaret. "Why the Movie Investigation?" *Christian Century*, vol. 58 (September 24, 1941), pp. 1172–1174.

"French Line." *Commonweal*, vol. 60 (Augut 6, 1954), p. 428.

Furnas, J. C. "False Fronts in Hollywood." *Virginia Quarterly Review*, vol. 8 (July, 1932), pp. 337–349.

Gardner, John. "Saint Walt: The Greatest Artist the World Has Ever Known, Except for, Possibly, Apollonius of Rhodes." *New York*, November 12, 1973, pp. 64–71.

Greenwald, William I. "The Impact of Sound Upon the Film Industry: A Case Study in Innovation." *Exploration in Entrepreneural History*, vol. 4 (May, 1952), pp. 178–192.

Gussow, Mel. "The Last Movie Tycoon." *New York*, February 1, 1971, pp. 27–41.

Hamill, Katherine. "The Supercolossal—Well, Pretty Good—World of Joe Levine." *Fortune*, vol. 69 (March, 1964), p. 130+.

Harmetz, Aljean. "The Dime-Store Way to Make Movies—and Money." *New York Times Magazine*, August 4, 1974, pp. 12+.

Hawkins, Richard C. "Perspective on 3-D." *Quarterly of Film, Radio and Television*, vol. 7 (1952), pp. 325–334.

Hellmuth, William F., Jr. "The Motion Picture Industry." In *The Structure of American Industry*, edited by Walter Adams, pp. 360–402. New York: Macmillan Company, 1967.

Hollister, P. "Walt Disney: Genius at Work." *Atlantic Monthly*, vol. 166 (December, 1940), pp. 689–701.

"Hollywood: Fewer Stars, More Profits." *U.S. News and World Report*, January 18, 1971, pp. 48–50.

"Hollywood in New York." *New York Times Magazine*, December 22, 1946, p. 44.

"Hollywood in Uniform." *Fortune*, vol. 25 (April, 1942), pp. 92–95.

"Hollywood's Magic Mountain." *Fortune*, vol. 31 (February, 1945), pp. 152–156.

"Hollywood's Newest Studio." *Look*, vol. 2 (September 30, 1947), pp. 90–91.

"Hollywood's New Leader." *Business Week*. January 17, 1967, p. 80+.

"Hollywood Wins a Truce." *Commonweal*, vol. 20 (July 20, 1934), pp. 295–296.

Houseman, John. "Hollywood Faces the Fifties, Part I: The Lost Enthusiasm." *Harper's*, vol. 200 (April, 1950), pp. 50–59.

"Howard Hughes and Self-Regulation in the Motion Picture Industry: The Court's Decisions in the case of 'The Outlaw.' " Motion Picture Association of America, pp. 1–48.

Hughes, Emmet J. "M.G.M.: War Among the Lion Tamers." *Fortune,* vol. 56 (August, 1957), pp. 98–103.

Hullinger, Edwain Ware. "Fumigating the Movies." *North American Review,* vol. 223 (May, 1932), pp. 445–449.

Ingles, Ruth. "Need for Voluntary Self-Regulation." *Annals of the American Academy of Political and Social Science,* November, 1947, pp. 153–159.

Isaacs, Hermine Rich. "Presenting the Warner Brothers." *Theatre Arts,* vol. 28 (February, 1944), pp. 99–108.

————. "Fact is Stranger than Fiction." *Theatre Arts,* vol. 25 (December, 1941), pp. 881–883.

"Is There Any Future in Hollywood?" *Economist,* February 28, 1970, pp. 52–53.

Jacobs, Lewis. "World War II and the American Film." In *The Movies: An American Idiom,* edited by Arthur F. McClure, pp. 153–157. Rutherford: Farleigh Dickinson University Press, 1971.

Jones, Dorothy. "The Hollywood War Film: 1942–1944." *Hollywood Quarterly,* vol. 1 (October, 1945), pp. 1–19.

————. "Hollywood Goes to War." *Nation,* vol. 160 (January 27, 1945), pp. 93–95.

Joseph, Robert. "Re: Unions in Hollywood." *Films (US),* vol. 1 (Summer 1940), pp. 34–50.

Kael, Pauline. "Raising Kane." In *The Citizen Kane Book,* by Pauline Kael, Herman J. Mankiewicz and Orson Welles, pp. 1–124. New York: Bantam Books, 1974.

————. "Are Movies Going to Pieces?" *Atlantic Monthly,* vol. 214 (December, 1964), pp. 61–66.

————. "On the Future of the Movies." *New Yorker* (August 5, 1974), pp. 43–58.

Kasendorf, Martin. "How Now, Dick Darling?" *New York Times Magazine,* September 10, 1972, p. 54+.

Kent, George. "The New Crisis in the Motion Picture Industry." *Current History,* vol. 33 (March, 1931), pp. 887–889.

Knight, Arthur. "Ring Around 'The Moon is Blue.'" *Saturday Review,* vol. 36 (June 27, 1953), pp. 33–36.

————. "The United Artists Story." *Saturday Review,* vol. 40 (December 21, 1957), pp. 12–13.

Kohler, A. "Some Aspects of Conditions of Employment in the Film Industry." *International Labor Review,* vol. 23 (June 1931), pp. 773–804.

Larson, Cedric. "The Domestic Motion Picture Work of the Office of War Information." *Hollywood Quarterly,* vol. 3 (1948), pp. 434–443.

"Last Days of Babylon?" *Forbes,* vol. 104 (November 1, 1969), pp. 65–66+.

"Little Gems from Jason Joy." *Christian Century,* vol. 49 (August 10, 1932), p. 973.

Lincoln, Freeman. "The Comeback of the Movies." *Fortune,* vol. 51 (February, 1955), pp. 127–31+.

"Loew's Inc., the World's Most Profitable Trust." *Fortune,* vol. 20 (August, 1939), pp. 24–31+.

MacCann, Richard Dyer. "Hollywood Faces the World." *Yale Review,* vol. 51 (June 1963), pp. 593–608.

MacGowan, Kenneth. "The Screen's New Look—Wider and Deeper." *Film Quarterly,* vol. 11 (1956), pp. 109–130.

Mayer, Arthur. "The Origins of United Artists." *Films in Review,* vol. 10 (August–September, 1959), pp. 390–399.

_____. "Growing Pains of Shrinking Industry." *Saturday Review,* vol. 44 (February 25, 1961), pp. 21–23+.

Mayer, Martin. "Elliot Gould as 'the Entrepreneur.' " *Fortune,* vol. 82 (October, 1970), p. 109+.

McCormick, J. Byron. "Some Legal Problems of the Motion Picture Industry." *American Bar Association Journal,* vol. 17 (May, 1931), pp. 316–332.

McDonald, J. "Now the Bankers Come to Disney." *Fortune,* vol. 73 (May, 1966), pp. 138–141).

McWilliams, Carey. "Racketeers and Movie Magnates." *New Republic,* vol. 105 (October 27, 1941), pp. 533–535.

"Men Behind Kung-Fooey." *Time,* June 11, 1973, p. 46.

Merritt, Russell. "RKO Radio: The Little Studio that Couldn't," in *The Marque Theatre,* ed. by Hayward Allen, pp. 7–25. Madison, Wisconsin: Privately Printed, 1973.

"Metro-Goldwyn-Mayer." *Fortune,* vol. 6 (December, 1932), pp. 51–58+.

"MGM's Own Drama: The Great Proxy War." *Business Week,* March 4, 1967, pp. 126–128.

Michener, Charles. "The New Hollywood." *Newweek,* November 25, 1974, pp. 71–73.

"Milliken Lining Up Protestants to Aid Films." *Christian Century,* vol. 49 (October 26, 1932), p. 1292.

"More Trouble in Paradise." *Fortune,* November 1946, p. 154+.

"Movies and Radio Join Varied Brood of Blue Eagle." *Newsweek,* vol. 2 (December 9, 1933), p. 34.

"Movies: End of an Era?" *Fortune,* vol. 39 (April, 1949), pp. 99–102+.

"Movies Get New Moguls: Conglomerates Wooing Hollywood." *Business Week,* February 8, 1969, pp. 29–30.

"Movie-Struck: Hollywood Walkout over Union Jurisdiction Ties Up Studios," *Business Week,* March 17, 1945, p. 106+.

Muir, F. "All Right Gentlemen, Do We Get The Money?" *Saturday Evening Post,* vol. 212 (January 27, 1940), pp. 9–11+.

Nizer, Louis. "Proxy Battle: The Struggle Over Loew's." In *My Life in Court,* by Louis Nizer, pp. 491–607. New York: Pyramid Books, 1963.

North, Christopher. "MGM's First 30 Years." *Films in Review,* vol. 5 (May, 1954), pp. 216–220.

Nugent, Frank. "That Million Dollar Mouse." *New York Times Magazine,* September 21, 1947, p. 22+.

Nye, Gerald P. "War Propaganda: Our Madness Increases as Our Emergency Shrinks." *Vital Speeches,* no. 7 (September 15, 1941), pp. 720–723.

Orton, William. "Hollywood Has Nothing to Learn." *Atlantic,* vol. 147 (June 1931), pp. 681–689.

"Paramount: Oscar for Profits." *Fortune,* vol. 35 (June, 1947), pp. 88–95+.

"Paramount Pictures Inc." *Fortune,* vol. 15 (March, 1937), pp. 86–96.

Parsons, L. O. "Hollywood and Censorship." *Cosmopolitan,* vol. 136 (April, 1954), p. 8.

"Play Safe But be Suggestive." *New Republic,* vol. 115 (December 30, 1946), pp. 907–909.

Poster, William. "Hollywood Caters to the Middle Class: An Appraisal of MGM." *American Mercury,* vol. 73 (August, 1951), pp. 82–91.

"Propaganda or History?" *Nation,* vol. 153 (September 20, 1941), pp. 241–242.

Quigley, Martin J. "The Motion-Picture Production Code." *America,* vol. 94 (March 10, 1956), pp. 630–632.

"Radio Corporation of America." *Fortune,* February, 1930, pp. 82–84+.

"Record at Stake." *Business Week,* September 8, 1945, p. 106+.

Redman, B. R. "Pictures and Censorship." *Saturday Review of Literature,* vol. 19 (December 31, 1938), pp. 3–4.

"Reformers Look Back on First Year and Find It Good." *Newsweek,* vol. 6 (August 17, 1935), pp. 16–17.

Rembar, Charles. "Obscenity—Forget It." *Atlantic,* May, 1977, pp. 37–41.

Ringstad, Robert C. "The Great Transition in Motion Picture Industry." *Magazine of Wall Street,* vol. 103 (October 25, 1958), pp. 76–78+.

"RKO: It's Only Money." *Fortune,* vol. 47 (May, 1953), pp. 122–127+.

Ross, Murray. "Labor Relations in Hollywood." *Annals of the American Academy of Political and Social Science,* vol. 254 (November, 1947), pp. 58–64.

———. "C.I.O. Loses Hollywood." *Nation,* vol. 149 (October 7, 1939), pp. 374–377.

Rukeyser, William. "Gulf & Western's Rambunctious Conservatism." *Fortune,* March, 1968, p. 122+.

Schumach, Murray. "The Censor as Movie Director." *New York Times Magazine,* February 12, 1961, pp. 15+.

Schuyten, Peter. "How MCA Rediscovered Movieland's Golden Lode." *Fortune,* November, 1976, p. 122+.

Seiler, Conrad. "Hollywood Rebellion." *New Republic,* vol. 113 (November 5, 1945), pp. 597–599.

Shaw, Bernard. "Saint Joan Banned: Film Censorship in the United States." *London Mercury,* vol. 34 (October, 1936), pp. 490–496.

Sheehan, R. "Cliff-hanger at M.G.M." *Fortune,* vol. 56 (October, 1957), pp. 134–135+.

Shurlock, Geoffrey. "The Motion Picture Production Code." *Annals of the American Academy of Political and Social Science,* vol. 254 (November, 1947), pp. 140–146.

Straight, Michael. "The Anti-Semitic Conspiracy." *New Republic,* vol. 105 (September 22, 1941), pp. 362–363.

Swenson, Joel. "The Entrepreneur's Role in Introducing the Sound Motion Picture." *Political Science Quarterly,* vol. 63 (September, 1948), pp. 404–423.

"The Big Bad Wolf." *Fortune,* vol. 10 (November, 1934), pp. 88–95.

"The Case of William Fox." *Fortune,* vol. 1 (May, 1930), pp. 48–49+.

"The Cash-Rich Movie Companies." *Business Week,* May 16, 1977, pp. 114–124.

"The Men Who Revived Paramount Go to Work on RKO." *Newsweek,* vol. 6 (November 16, 1935), p. 30+.

"The Universal Appeal." *Life,* vol. 34 (June 15, 1953), pp. 104–106+.

Thompson, Edward. "There's No Show Business Like MCA's Business." *Fortune,* vol. 62 (June, 1960), p. 114+.

Tobias, Andrew. "The Apprenticeship of Frank Yablans." *New York,* September 23, 1974, pp. 43–57.

_____. "The Hidden Fight that Finally Made MCA the Greatest." *New West,* April 26, 1976, pp. 89–104.

"Trouble in Paradise." *Time,* vol. 45 (January 29, 1945), pp. 38–39.

"Twentieth Century-Fox." *Fortune,* vol. 12 (December, 1935), pp. 85–93.

"United Artists: Final Shooting Script." *Fortune,* vol. 22 (December, 1940), pp. 95–102+.

"Vast Interests Now Have a Voice in the Talkies." *Business Week,* September 17, 1930, pp. 22–23.

Wanger, Walter. "The O.W.I. and Motion Pictures." *Public Opinion Quarterly,* vol. 7 (Spring, 1943), pp. 100–107.

"Walt Disney: Great Teacher." *Fortune,* vol. 25 (August, 1942), pp. 91+.

"War Hits Hollywood." *Business Week,* February 3, 1940, pp. 49–50.

"Warner Brothers Pictures, Inc." *Fortune,* vol. 16 (December, 1937), pp. 110–113+.

Weinberger, Julius. "Economic Aspects of Recreation." *Harvard Business Review,* vol. 15 (Summer, 1937), pp. 448–463.

Welles, Chris. "Starting Next Week: The End of the Last Tycoon and Coming Attractions in the Fox Proxy Fight." *New York,* May 17, 1971, p. 43+.

"What? Color in the Movies Again." *Fortune,* vol. 10 (October, 1934), p. 92+.

"What's Playing at the Grove? *Fortune,* vol. 38 (August, 1948), pp. 94–99.

Whelan, Russell. "The Legion of Decency." *American Mercury,* vol. 60 (June, 1945), pp. 655–663.

"Who Bought United Artists?" *Business Week,* August 12, 1950, pp. 78–79.

Young, Kimball. "Review of the Payne Fund Studies." *American Journal of Sociology,* September, 1935, pp. 250–255.

Ziesse, Francis E. "America's Highest Paid Labor Body." *American Federationist,* vol. 37 (May, 1930), pp. 570–576.

UNPUBLISHED MATERIAL

Barrett, Rex. "Organization of the Motion Picture Industry." Ph.D. dissertation, University of Missouri, 1934.

Bohn, Thomas. "An Historical and Descriptive Analysis of the 'Why We Fight' Series." Ph.D. dissertation, University of Wisconsin, 1968.

Burke, William. "The Presentation of the American Negro in Hollywood Films, 1946–1961: Analysis of a Selected Sample of Feature Films." Ph.D. dissertation, Northwestern University, 1965.

Carmen, Ira. "State and Local Motion Picture Censorship and Constitutional Liberties with Special Emphasis on the Communal Acceptance of Supreme Court Decision-Making." Ph.D. dissertation, University of Michigan, 1964.

Gartley, Linda Jo. "The American Film Industry in Transition: 1946–1956." Ph.D. dissertation, University of Michigan, 1972.

Giglio, Ernest David. "The Decade of the Miracle, 1952–1962: A Study in the Censorship of the American Motion Picture." D.SS. dissertation, Syracuse University, 1964.

Gomery, J. Douglas. "The Coming of Sound to the American Cinema: A History of the Transformation of an Industry." Ph.D. dissertation, University of Wisconsin, 1975.

Greenwald, William. "The Motion Picture Industry: An Economic Study of the History and Practices of a Business." Ph.D. dissertation, New York University, 1950.

Jess, Paul. "Antitrust Law: A New Approach to Access to the Media." Ph.D. dissertation, University of Minnesota, 1972.

Jowett, Garth. "Media Power and Social Control: The Motion Picture in America, 1894–1936." Ph.D. dissertation, University of Pennsylvania, 1972.

Linden, Kathryn B. "The Film Censorship Struggle in the United States from 1926 to 1957, and the Social Values Involved." Ph.D. dissertation, New York University, 1972.

Paine, Jeffrey. "The Simplification of American Life: Hollywood Films of the 1930's." Ph.D. dissertation, Princeton University, 1971.

Perry, Donald L. "An Analysis of the Financial Plans of the Motion Picture Industry for the Period 1929 to 1962." Ph.D. dissertation, University of Illinois, 1966.

Phelan, John M., S.J. "The National Catholic Office for Motion Pictures: An Investigation of the Policy and Practice of Film Classification." Ph.D. dissertation, New York University, 1968.

Pryluck, Calvin. "Sources of Meaning in Motion Pictures and Television." Ph.D. dissertation, University of Iowa, 1973.

Sargent, John A. "Self-Regulation: The Motion Picture Production Code, 1930–1961." Ph.D. dissertation, University of Michigan, 1963.

Schnapper, Amy. "The Distribution of Theatrical Feature Films to Television." Ph.D. dissertation, University of Wisconsin, 1975.

Shain, Russell. "An Analysis of Motion Pictures About War Released by the American Film Industry, 1939–1970." Ph.D. dissertation, University of Illinois, 1972.

Suber, Howard. "The Anti-Communist Blacklist in the Hollywood Motion Picture Industry." Ph.D. dissertation, University of California, Los Angeles, 1968.

GOVERNMENT DOCUMENTS

Bertrand, Daniel, Duane Evans and Edna Blanchard. United States Temporary National Economic Committee Investigation of Concentration of Economic Power, 76th Congress. *The Motion Picture Industry; A Pattern of Control.* Washington: U.S.G.P.O., 1941.

Bertrand, Daniel. *Work Materials No. 34—The Motion Picture Industry, 1936.* Washington: Publication of the National Recovery Administration, Division of Review.

U.S. Congress. House. Committee on Patents, *Hearings on H.R. 4523: Pooling of Patents.* 74th Congress 1st Session, 1935.

U.S. Congress. House. Un-American Activities Committee. *Hearings, Communist Infiltration of Motion Picture Industry.* 80th Congress, 1st Session, 1947.

U.S. Congress. House. Un-American Activities Committee. *Hearings, Communist Infiltration of Hollywood Motion Picture Industry.* 82nd Congress, 1st Session, 1951, 2nd Session, 1952.

U.S. Federal Communications Commission. *Telephone Investigation.* Washington: U.S.G.P.O., 1935–1938, 43 nos. in 3 v.

U.S. Congress, Senate Subcommittee of the Committee on Interstate Commerce. *Propaganda in Motion Pictures.* 77th Congress, 1st Session, 1941. Washington: U.S.G.P.O., 1942.

U.S. SUPREME COURT CASES

Mutual Film Corp. v. Ohio, 236 U.S. 230 (1915)

Gitlow v. New York, 268 U.S. 652 (1925).

Paramount Publix Corporation v. American Tri-Ergon Corporation, 294 U.S. 454 (1935)

General Talking Pictures v. Western Electric Company et al., 305 U.S. 675 (1939)

United States v. Paramount Pictures et al., 334 U.S. 131 (1948)

Joseph Burstyn, Inc. v. Wilson, 343 U.S. 495 (1952)

Roth v. U.S., 354 U.S. 476 (1957)

Times Film Corp. v. Chicago, 365 U.S. 43 (1961)

Jacobellis v. Ohio, 378 U.S. 184 (1964)

Freedman v. Maryland, 380 U.S. 51 (1965)

Memoirs v. Massachusetts, 383 U.S. 413 (1966)

Ginsberg v. New York, 390 U.S. 629 (1968)

Interstate Circuit, Inc. v. Dallas, 390 U.S. 676 (1968)

Miller v. California, 413 U.S. 15 (1973)

Paris Adult Theatre I v. Slaton, 413 U.S. 49 (1973)

U.S. v. Orito, 413 U.S. 139 (1973)

Kaplan v. California, 413 U.S. 115 (1973)

United States v. Twelve 200-Foot Reels of Super 8 mm Film, 413 U.S. 123 (1973)

Jenkins v. Georgia, 418 U.S. 153 (1974)

LOWER COURT DECISIONS

Electrical Research Products, Inc. v. Vitaphone Corporation, 171 A. 738 (1934).

General Talking Pictures Corporation, et al. v. American Telephone and Telegraph Company, et al., 18 F. Supp. 650 (1937).

Koplar (Scharaf et al., Interveners) v. Warner Brothers Pictures, Inc., et al., 19 F. Supp. 173 (1937).

Republic Pictures Inc., v. Rogers, 213 F. (2d) 662 (1954).

Autry v. Republic Pictures Inc., 213 F. (2d) 667 (1954).

Index